WITHDRAWN

European Textile Printers
in the Eighteenth Century

European Textile Printers in the Eighteenth Century

A Study of Peel and Oberkampf

S. D. Chapman
University of Nottingham

and

S. Chassagne
Université de Haute-Bretagne, Rennes

Heinemann Educational Books
The Pasold Fund

Heinemann Educational Books Ltd
22 Bedford Square, London WC1B 3HH
LONDON   EDINBURGH   MELBOURNE   AUCKLAND
HONG KONG   SINGAPORE   KUALA LUMPUR   NEW DELHI
IBADAN   NAIROBI   JOHANNESBURG
EXETER (NH)   KINGSTON   PORT OF SPAIN

© Stanley Chapman and Serge Chassagne, 1981
First published 1981

To Jacques Whitfield
With thanks

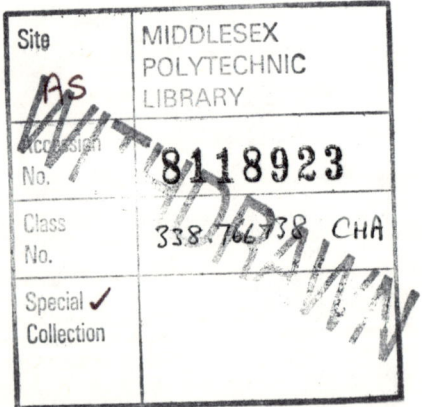

Filmset in Great Britain by
Northumberland Press Ltd, Gateshead, Tyne and Wear
Printed by Richard Clay (The Chaucer Press) Ltd, Bungay, Suffolk

Contents

List of Plates	vii
List of Figures	vii
List of Tables	viii
Preface	xi
Note on Currency	xiii
Note on Sources	xiii

PART I. Introduction: The Role of Calico Printing in the Eighteenth-Century European Economy — 1

PART II. The Peels of Lancashire — 23

1. The Origins of Calico Printing in Lancashire — 25
2. The Peels: Origins and Technical Innovations — 34
3. The Expansion of the Peel Industrial Empire under Robert ('Parsley') Peel — 45
4. The Structure of Sir Robert Peel's Enterprises — 54
5. Capital, Managers and Partners — 70
6. Domestic and Overseas Markets — 78
7. Labour and Industrial Relations — 94

PART III. Oberkampf of Jouy — 101

8. French Textile Printing and Fashion before 1759 — 103

9	The Making of an Entrepreneur	111
10	The Jouy Works, 1760–1815	125
11	Markets and Sources of Supply, 1760–1805	147
12	The Extension to Spinning and Weaving, 1805–20	162
13	Labour Recruitment and Relations	171

PART IV. Conclusion — 183

Appendices to Conclusion — 216
Notes and References — 220
Index of Subjects — 247
Index of People and Places — 250

List of Plates

1 The first Sir Robert Peel, from a portrait by Sir Thomas Lawrence (Earl Peel's collection)   55
2 Summerseat cotton spinning mills, from an old print in Manchester Public Library   64
3 Frontispiece of C. O'Brien's *The... Callico Printer's Assistant* (1790), depicting typical print patterns used in eighteenth-century Britain   80
4 A page from the Church Peels' Pattern Book, in Bolton Museum   83
5 Christoff–Philipp Oberkampf, from a contemporary print   112
6 The Jouy works, taken from a painting by J. B. Huet, c. 1806   141
7 Jouy floral design, with the celebrated inscription of the *Manufacture Royale*   193
8 One of J. B. Huet's famous designs, *Les Travaux de la Manufacture* (1783), showing the sequence of processes in calico printing   206

List of Figures

1 Structure of Livesey, Hargreaves & Co., 1780–8   30
2 Dispersion of the Peels' printworks, cotton mills and putting-out agents in Lancashire, c. 1805   63
3 Plan of Fazeley (Tamworth) as developed by the Peels, 1790–c. 1805   66
4 The Peel family pedigree   68
5 Simplified pedigree of the Oberkampf family   114
6 The main building at the Jouy works, 1793   127
7 Plan of the Jouy works under the Empire   128
8 Location of Jouy's customers, 1790–2   152
9 Distribution of unsold Jouy fabrics, 1815   155

List of Tables

1	Distribution of calico printers in Western Europe in 1760–1762 and 1784–7	8
2	The cotton printing industry in Central Europe, 1790–1800	11
3	The workforce and division of labour at some continental printing plants	15
4	Valuation of property of William Wilson of Ainsworth, 1774	27
5	Distribution of principal creditors of Livesey, Hargreaves & Co., 1788	29
6	Principal owners of warp spinning mills, 1788	38
7	Size of the mule spinning industry at principal centres, 1788 and 1811	41
8	Size of the ten largest mule spinning firms in the British cotton industry, 1811	42
9	Valuation of Peel, Yates & Co.'s Church works, 1787	46
10	Valuation of Peel, Yates & Co.'s cotton mills at Burton-on-Trent, 1795	48
11	Valuation of Peel, Ainsworth & Co.'s property, 1 May 1795	51
12	Valuation of the Peels' industrial property in the Blackburn District, 1787–1811	53
13	British output of printed textiles, 1784	58
14	Valuation of Peel, Yates & Co.'s works in the Bury area, 1795	59
15	Amount of goods sent by Peel, Yates & Co. To North America, 1797–1800	86
16	British consumption of printed textiles, 1797, analysed by price ranges	90
17	British consumption of home and foreign produced printed muslins and calicoes, 1790–1800	91
18	The development of the supply of fabrics by Ittier & Reboul of Montpellier, 1751–61	109
19	Assets of some French textile printing firms, 1767–89	109
20	Comparative structure of the assets of several calico printing businesses contemporary to the Jouy works	135
21	Evolution of capital recorded in the Jouy factory accounts, 1770–1814	137
22	Structure of Oberkampf's costs of production, 1765–92	139
23	Drawings of the Oberkampf family partners from the Company, 1793–1810	144
24	Jouy's output and sales, 1771–1817	145

List of Tables   ix

25	Oberkampf's markets, 1790–1800: regional distribution of 'good' debtors	149
26	The results of 'internationalisation' of Oberkampf's supplies, 1769–78	157
27	Sources of cloth in Oberkampf's stock, 1783–92	158
28	The 'take-off' of the French cotton industry, c. 1760–1805	165
29	Origin of French raw cotton imports during the Empire, 1800–09	165
30	Size of the French cotton industry (spinning and weaving sectors), 1811	166
31	Factories and dispersed workshops in a rival enterprise: Richard-Lenoir in 1810	169
32	Occupational distribution of the Jouy workforce, 1791–1836	173
33	The concentration of workers in some leading cotton works in France, Alsace, Switzerland and the Low Countries, 1765–1806	175
34	Geographical origins of workers in several French calico printing centres and in Cortaillod	178
35	Duration of employment of male workers in several calico printing centres	178
36	The productivity of some leading European calico printing works in the eighteenth century	213

Preface

Peel and Oberkampf were the most successful and most celebrated textile manufacturers of their respective countries, England and France, in the eighteenth century. The study of their achievements is not only a study of the policies and techniques of successful industrial and commercial enterprise at the time but also reveals much of the process and scale of industrialisation in Western Europe. Textile printing was a highly-developed factory industry in several European countries and cotton prints were a principal commodity of international commerce a generation or two before the better known Arkwright system appeared. It deserves much fuller treatment than has so far been given to it by economic and social historians, at any rate in Britain.

It would have been a relatively easy matter for each of us to have written a biography for publication in our own countries, and indeed a study of Oberkampf's career is to appear in France, but we believe such a conventional approach can be narrow and limiting.[1] The growth of the textile industries in the period can only be properly appreciated in the wider context of European development, while the comparison of one leading entrepreneur with another brings out the significance of each. Comparative studies bring their own problems, of course, but we have sought to minimise these by offering an opening survey of developments in textile printing across Europe and a concluding section in which we link our men with other eminent textile printers of the age, especially Schuele of Augsburg and Leitenberg of Bohemia.

It is conventional at the commencement of books of this kind to mention the division of labour between the two authors. Dr Chap-

[1] S. Chassagne, *Oberkampf: Un entrepreneur capitaliste au Siècle des Lumières* (Aubier Montaigne, Paris, 1980).

man has been responsible primarily for the Introduction and Conclusion as well as the section on the Peels, while M Chassagne has researched and written the work on Oberkampf. However, throughout our five-year partnership we have fed each other with references and read each other's drafts, so that the first and last sections owe a great deal to research in the Archives Nationales and the Archives Départementales. Regular meetings in England and France have kept us in close contact and growing friendship through the period of the research, and the whole work is based on continuous exchange of ideas and information. Most of the section on Oberkampf was originally written in French and then translated by Dr Katrina Honeyman during the period that she was a research assistant at Nottingham University, but it has gone through several revisions since then.

In the course of the development of our research and publication programme we have incurred debts to friends, colleagues, librarians, archivists, publishers and academic trusts. Space does not allow us to detail all the support we have enjoyed, but we must pay tribute to three individuals whose interest has been of the greatest value to our partnership in this book. The original idea for this volume was pressed on us by the enthusiasm of Dr Jacques Whitfield, whose research on J. H. von Schuele, extending over many years, has given him a unique vision of the European dimensions of the eighteenth-century industry. He has generously placed some of the fruits of his life-long interest at our disposal and given detailed guidance in the composition of our Conclusion. We are also glad to acknowledge the regular encouragement and support of Professor Louis Bergeron of the École des Hautes Études, Paris, and Mr K. G. Ponting, the Director of the Pasold Research Foundation. The Pasold Fund has provided the necessary funds for the publication of this work and we should like to express our grateful thanks to the governors. Earlier versions of the Introduction and Conclusion to this work were presented as papers to Conferences at Eleutherian Mills (Wilmington, Delaware, USA) in December 1977 and at Wolfenbuttel (West Germany) in October 1978, and we acknowledge with thanks the warm hospitality and helpful suggestions offered by our American and German colleagues at these meetings.

S.D.C
S.C.
Autumn 1979

Note on Currency

The basic unit of currency under the *ancien régime* was the *livre*, which was divided into 20 *sous*, each of 12 *deniers*. The reforms of the Revolution replaced the *livre* with the *franc* but the two were practically identical in value. The exchange rate of the British and French currencies fluctuated during this period but for the sake of consistency we have assumed £1 = 24 *livres* (*l.*) or *francs* (*f.*).

Note on Sources

As a substantial part of the framework of the first two parts of this book rests on the evidence of insurance inventories, still a relatively novel source for eighteenth-century historical research, readers may appreciate some illustrations of the typical contents of the larger industrial valuations. The size and location of the various collections of insurance registers are detailed in H. A. L. Cockerell and Edwin Green, *The British Insurance Business 1547–1970. An Introduction and Guide to Historical Records in the United Kingdom* (1976). The authors explain that 'insured property was valued at replacement value rather than historic cost or current value' (p. 30). A list of inventories for early London calico printing works may be found in S. D. Chapman 'The Textile Factory before Arkwright', *BHR*, XLVIII (1974), while some indication of the extent and richness of this material for another industrial region may be gathered from the same author's *Devon Cloth Industry in the Eighteenth Century: Sun Fire Office Inventories of Merchants' and Manufacturers' Property, 1726–1770* (Devon & Cornwall Record Society, 1978).

PART ONE

Introduction

Introduction: the Role of Calico Printing in the Eighteenth-Century European Economy

Calico printing is not just another industry that has been passed over or lightly treated by economic historians. It is true that it has received little attention from British and German scholars, but this is not its essential claim to deeper research. The industry is known to have been organised in factories in a number of centres of European commerce for two or three generations before the better-known advent of the factory system in cotton spinning. It evidently played a leading role in the industrialisation of Europe and its precise contribution needs to be explored.

It is well-known that the rapid growth of the cotton industry in the later decades of the eighteenth century constituted one of the 'leading sectors' of the industrial revolution in Britain. The basic statistics, which show the dramatic rise in imports of the raw material, have often been quoted, but they tell us nothing about the nature of consumer demand.[1] Producers were manufacturing not just millions more yards of plain cotton fabrics but an increasing variety of fashion goods, the most popular of which were printed cottons and fustians (cotton and linen mixtures). The intimate connection between the growth of some of the early leaders of the cotton industry and the printing sector of the rising industry can readily be illustrated from the case histories of pace-making English firms like Livesey, Hargreaves & Co., Arkwright, Strutt, Oldknow and Peel, each of which combined factory spinning with weaving and printing activities.[2] Another way of illustrating the importance of printing is to list the wide variety of cotton fabrics that were printed in the late eighteenth century – jeanets, ribbed fabrics, sattinets, thicksetts, velveretts, dimities, muslinets, quiltings, and others besides – but probably this will impress only the textile specialist.[3] The most effective way of demonstrating the massive contribution of printing to the rise of cotton is simply to recognise the proportion of imported cottons absorbed by the printers. Estimates are not easy to come by but some figures produced by the spokesman of the London mercers in 1792 appear to be authentic. He estimated that 'little short' of a million pieces of white cotton cloth were being produced in Britain at that time, of which 600,000 – at least 60 per cent – were sent to the printers. Consumers' interest in cottons embellished with fashionable designs clearly played a major role in the fast-growing popularity of the new fabric.[4]

The French experience of industrialisation was, of course, different from the British, particularly in the earlier stages (or proto-industrialisation phase). French historians have argued that the early stages of industrialisation in their country focused on *quality* rather than on cheap mass-production, and they like to exhibit calico printing as the most striking example of this development. French labour was relatively expensive compared with that of the neighbouring states of Switzerland and Germany, and France lacked some of the advantages which brought early mechanisation to the 'new frontier' regions of industrial Britain. The problem was later exacerbated by British export of cheap yarns to Germany and eastern Europe. The French *indienneurs* were able to buy fine Indian calicoes and muslins in London, Amsterdam, Paris, Lorient and other international markets, and then used their skills to transform them into quality prints.[5] Later in this chapter we shall see that the contrast with Britain and some other European countries can be overdrawn, for calico printing workshops became a feature of the economies of numerous European states in the middle decades of the eighteenth century. However, the substantial point remains that these workshops (or proto-factories, as we shall call them) represent a highly significant transitional stage in the evolution from dispersed domestic industry to the fully-evolved factory system, and that numbers of leading calico printers were associated with the introduction of mechanised spinning and weaving, i.e. with inaugurating the factory system. In France as in Britain the *grandes dynasties d'hommes d'affaires* often originated in calico printing; names like Oberkampf, Koechlin or Dolfuss recall wealth and celebrity that began in a modest way in this industry.

Calico printing also played a leading role in the evolution of European commerce through the eighteenth century. It became the most important commodity handled by those international families who conducted such a large part of Continental trade. Lüthy has shown how the dispersed Huguenot merchant dynasties, with branches of their families settled in one or more Swiss cities, in Frankfurt or Hamburg, in Amsterdam or London, became merchant bankers, financing the European trade in imported oriental textiles.[6] Indeed, it has been suggested that their original desertion from France may have been prompted as much by the royal edict of October 1686 prohibiting calico printing as by the persecution of the Huguenots which followed the revocation of the Edict of Nantes in October 1685.[7] In the last years of the *ancien régime* several of these houses returned to Paris from their Swiss bases, not only to subscribe to royal loans, but to take advantage of the revocation in 1759 of the ban on textile printing. All of these houses, Lévy-Leboyer writes, 'supported manufacturing to a greater or lesser degree, recruiting capital for the marketing of fabrics, buying calicoes and other oriental goods on commission, contributing to the settlement of bills of exchange on provincial and foreign places, opening credits in case of need...'[8] The most recent work on the French international banking houses by Louis Bergeron describes late eighteenth-century colonial trade and the international trade in calicoes and *indiennes* as 'les deux grandes affaires du temps.'[9]

The phenomenon of the international merchant house not only continued into the nineteenth century but actually grew in importance. But it was now dominated by German families, especially German Jews from Hamburg and Frankfurt, and then, from the 1840s to the 1860s, by Greeks. Huguenot families like the Passavants, Dufays and Gontards made their way to London and Manchester,[10] but they were soon overtaken by the Rothschild cousinhood and their rivals from Hamburg, Berlin and Leipzig.[11] This group quickly came to dominate the textile trade with the Continent much as the Huguenot families of the previous generation had done. The important point to emphasise here is that Rothschild and the early German international trading houses were at first primarily involved in the trade in printed textiles, and if their later celebrity came from other activities such as government loans contracts it was on the basis of fortunes first made *au circuit de l'indienne*.[12] In other words, the calico printing trade played a leading role in the evolution of European commerce, a development that paralleled the contribution of the calico printing industry to the evolution of the factory system.

Why was this new industry and trade so important? The simple answer lies in the enormous impact that oriental design, technique and manufacturing methods had on European fashion from the late seventeenth century to the early nineteenth century. The introduction of light, gaily-patterned Indian cottons created a sensation that lasted a century, a consumer craze that overrode the opposition of governments, vested interests (the existing wool and silk industries) and, above all, the centuries-old vernacular traditions in dress. Moreover, home produced prints offered a relatively cheap and effective substitute for tapestries, exotic silks and expensive imported chintzes, and different varieties were as popular for furnishings as dress materials. Local and regional variations in dress, even where supported by the *Kleiderordnung* (state regulations on the appropriate dress for different social classes), were submerged as the new passion spread from western to eastern Europe and percolated down the social hierarchy.[13] For the first time in European history consumer taste was nearly uniform, and this large and growing demand for the new fashions was supported by the emergence of the Atlantic economy as colonial demand from the American and West Indian settlements grew steadily. Such an homogeneous market, unprecedented in size, wealth and extent, stimulated the emergence of manufacturing and trading organisations on a uniquely grand scale, not least because the leadership was from the first held by two or three premier trading countries.

At first, all the new printed cottons were imported, but in order to stimulate and protect supply the East India trading companies were soon to be found organising their own 'factories' (or compounds) to assemble and direct the Indian artisans.[14] It was a short step from this to the foundation of factories at the main importing ports of London, Amsterdam and Marseilles. The earliest reference to a calico printing works occurs in a contract signed in Marseilles in 1648. By a striking coincidence the first clear mention of a calico printing industry both in London and Amsterdam occurs in the same year, 1676. William Sherwin, a London calico printer, took out a patent at this time, while the Dutch notarial archives contain a contract formed between three *Katoendruckers*. In the early 1680s the same source refers to several *sitsendruckers* (chintz printers), and one of the best-known Huguenot families connected with the industry, the Deneufvilles, made its first appearance.[15] The Amsterdam marriage registers show that the Dutch printers attracted skilled labour from numerous towns in the Low Countries and Germany, so it is not surprising that the industry took early root in Hamburg and Bremen.[16]

From these centres of trade calico printing soon found its way to other parts of Europe. Before the end of the seventeenth century Huguenots had carried the industry to Berlin, Bremen, Frankfurt, Neuchâtel (1688), Lausanne (1698) and Geneva (1691).[17] Skilled artisans trained in Amsterdam workshops found it profitable to set up their own businesses – the Neuhofer brothers at Augsburg in 1680, Samuel Ryhiner at Basle in 1717, and Jan De Broen in Stockholm in 1722. The dispersion continued: in 1737 the industry was established in Barcelona, in 1750 in Copenhagen and by 1753 in Antwerp.[18]

In the second half of the eighteenth century autocratic regimes of central and eastern Europe contrived to attract calico printing to their countries. The earliest printworks in Vienna (1724), at Erlangen in Franconia (1744) and in Munich (1747) were set up under the patronage of the local rulers, while in 1753 Maria Theresa granted the first monopoly for printing in the Austrian Netherlands. The English firm of Chamberlain & Cuzzins were attracted to St Petersburg by the offer of a 10-year monopoly from 1753, a loan of 30,000 roubles, and 300 factory serfs. The factory became a school for Russian craftsmen, some of whom may have moved to Moscow. J. H. Schuele, the most successful printer in the Habsburg Empire in the third quarter of the century, suffered from the persistent opposition of the Augsburg weavers' guild, but Emperor Joseph II granted him an Imperial *privilegium* in 1772. The Emperor's personal interest found a parallel in the enterprise of some of his nobility; the earliest calico printing factories in Bohemia were founded by Count Kinsky in 1763 and Count Bolza in 1764. When the Habsburgs started drawing schools to promote the aesthetic trades, the Emperor decreed his intention that they should teach the art of printing on cottons and linens. However, the most numerous successes seem to have been achieved by the enterprise of migrating artisans and small tradesmen. Schuele learned his expertise from a sequence of visits to Hamburg between 1755 and 1762, while his successor as leader of the industry in the Habsburg Empire, J. J. Leitenberg of Levin (Bohemia), spent eight years away from home working in Swiss and German centres (1750–8). The calico printing industry of Saxony started when a Nuremburg entrepreneur called Neumeister moved to Plauen in 1754. In Moscow the growth of calico printing – there were at least 10 factories by 1776 – was largely the work of serf-entrepreneurs, while the earliest printing factories in Prague (1766–87) were founded by local residents of German, Czech, Polish and Jewish origin. Some of this growth must have been at the expense of the western centres of Amsterdam, Antwerp and Hamburg, whose output declined in this period.[19]

In 1776 printed cottons became the most important fashion goods at the Leipzig fair, the centre of trade of central Europe. Jewish

Table 1 Distribution of calico printers in Western Europe in 1760–2 and 1784–7

Country	1760–2 No. of firms	1785 No. of firms	1785 Production (pieces)	1785 Production (million metres)
France				
Region				
Normandy	1	40	152,000	
Paris and its region	6	13	130,000	
Anjou, Touraine	6	3	12,000	
Lyons	2	14	25,000	
Dauphiné	1	4	10,000	
Nantes	7	8	112,000	
Orléans, Bourges	1	2	44,000	
Aix-en-Provence	3	6	55,800	
Marseilles	2	?	nd	
Bordeaux and Agen	1	5	24,000	
Montpellier, Languedoc	2	2	20,000	
Troyes, Champagne	1	4	19,000	
Alsace	5	7	156,000	
Others (dispersed)	5	6	nd	
Total	**42+**	**115+**	**800,000+**	**16.0**
Switzerland and Mulhouse				
Region				
Geneva	7	12	nd	nd
Neuchâtel	9	10	160,000	3.2
Basle	2+	6	nd	nd
Mulhouse	15	21	146,000	3.0
Total	**33+**	**49**		
Great Britain	(1760)	(1784–7)		
Region				
Manchester	1	45		
Blackburn	1	12		
London	20+	13		
Dublin	5+	14		
Glasgow	1+	27		
Total	**28+**	**111**	13.5 million yds (1784–7)	12.4 (1784–7)
Spain				
Region	(1760)	(1775)	(1775)	
Barcelona	c. 18	27	90,000	c. 1.8

Introduction 9

dealers carried the prints into Poland, Russia and the Danubian principalities, so maintaining a continuously growing market for the manufacturers.[20] Government prohibition of calico printing in France (1686), Britain (1720) and Prussia (1721) restrained the rapid growth of the industry in those countries but by no means stopped it. Ways were found of evading the law by printing on linens or cotton-linen mixtures in Britain, or migration to privileged locations such as Marseilles in France, and a volume of clandestine printing was maintained in various places throughout France. The main consequence of the French prohibition was to encourage the migration of the industry to frontier districts of Switzerland (Neuchâtel, Geneva, Basle and Berne) and to non-Prussian parts of Germany, but when the prohibition was withdrawn many of the migrants returned.

Some scholars have attempted to measure the importance of calico printing by counting the number of plants in various places at benchmark dates, but the results have not been very systematic. Lévy-Leboyer has assembled figures for France, Switzerland and Britain, but comparisons are impossible because he omits London and Dublin, and found no data for Glasgow and little for Manchester. In Table 1 we have tried to make good these omissions for the eighteenth-century part of his table. Obviously these figures tell us little about the size of individual firms but they do illustrate two developments which are of great significance for our story. The lifting

SOURCES: France: 1760 data assembled by S. Chassagne from diverse sources, notably AN: F12/1404–1408, and AD, Paris; 1785 data in AN: F12/1404A.
    Switzerland and Mulhouse: data summarised in M. Lévy-Leboyer, *Les banques* p. 51; Mulhouse figures from AN: F12/1564.
    Great Britain: W. Bailey, *Western and Midland Directory* (various edns., 1781–4); A. K. Longfield, 'History of the Irish Linen and Cotton Printing Industry in the Eighteenth Century', *Journal Royal Soc. Antiquaries Ireland*, LXVII (1937), pp. 51–6, Jones's *Glasgow Directory* (1787), cited in F. Irwin, 'Scottish Eighteenth Century Chintz and its Design', *Burlington Magazine*, Sep.–Oct. 1965, p. 456; for early data on Lancashire, see Chapter 1.
    The towns listed represent the regions at whose centre they stood, e.g. the London list includes works at Waltham Abbey (Essex), Merton (Surrey), Crayford (Kent) and Fordingbridge (Hants.).
    Spain: J. Carrera Pujal, *Historia Politica y Economica di Catalona* (Barcelona, 1943–7), IV, p. 135, notes 15 printing works with royal privileges in 1756 and 22 in 1768, plus two at Manresa and one at Mataro. Biblioteca Central di Barcelona. Archivio di la Junto di Comercio: leg. 53, p. 286, records 27 printing works in 1775 and 92 in 1796 in Barcelona and district.

of the French ban on calico printing in 1759 was the signal for the migration of Swiss printers into France with the aim of moving closer to the consumer – Paris and Versailles for luxury fabrics, Nantes and the ports for exporting. In 1769 some Nantes traders asked the royal government for permission to import Dutch calicoes 'to be painted or dyed for the slave trade'. They explained that 'By this means France will pay no more tribute to Dutch industry and a ready market will be found for indigo from Carolina'. Old-established manufacturing centres like Lyons and Ghent seized the opportunity to extend their industry. About 120 calico printing workshops of all sizes are known to have existed in France in the period 1750–75 and of these at least 35, nearly one-third, were set up by Protestant entrepreneurs or with the help of Protestant technicians, most of them foreign-born. The other important development was the migration of the British industry from London into the provinces. It reached Dublin in 1720, Edinburgh in 1723, Glasgow in 1742, Preston and Manchester in the early 1750s, Carlisle in 1761 and Belfast in 1766, but of course Lancashire emerged as the major centre. In this case the industry appears to have been moving away from the centre of fashion, but such an interpretation of this elementary data is too naïve. The luxury end of the industry remained in the metropolis while the production of more popular prints shifted to the centre of mass-production. (These themes are further explored in research on Oberkampf and the Peels later in this book.[21])

Ruth Schillinger has assembled some useful material for central Europe, although unfortunately it is difficult to be sure of the reliability of some of her sources (Table 2). (For instance, the standard work on Saxony, Rudolf Forberger's *Die Manufaktur in Sachsen Vom ende des 16. bis zum Anfang des 19. Jahrhunderts* (Berlin, 1958), chronicles the foundation of 36 firms from 1754 to 1802, but Frau Schillinger records 56, possibly because the two writers define the region in different ways). However, the data at least gives some notion of the spread of the industry across central Europe in the second half of the eighteenth century.

Data on the number and size of firms tell us little of the economic causes of the relative importance of the different centres, and for this purpose we must turn briefly to the development of the technology of calico printing. Book printing with type and engraved copper plates was already a well-developed art in the seventeenth century, and historians of the industry have revealed that a sequence of early printers tried to adapt their expertise to

Table 2 The cotton printing industry in Central Europe, 1790–1800

Location	Total number of manufacturing units	Total number of people employed	Average employment of each manufacturing unit
Alsace and Lorraine	37	7,000	189
Augsburg	9	3,200	356
Austria	18	1,300	72
Bohemia-Moravia	31	2,100	67
Franconia	7	700	100
Hamburg	21	3,200	153
Prussia	14	700	50
Saxony	56	3,800	68
Silesia	8	100	13
Switzerland	59	4,300	73
Vorarlberg	3	100	34

SOURCE: Ruth Schillinger, *Die Wirtschaftliche Entwicklung des Stoffdrucks* (Cologne, 1964), maps on pp. 20–21. The author's sources are given on pp. 117–18 of her book.

printing on fabrics. New techniques in calico printing invariably followed on those in book printing after an interval of years or decades. As early as 1400 an Italian called Cennini published a description of block printing on linen, while a further and more precise account appeared in Nuremburg towards the end of the fifteenth century. Printed wallpapers, which in the eighteenth century were often manufactured by calico printers, were introduced in France by 1586. Copper plate printing on fabrics was first attempted in Amiens in 1660, while in 1688 we hear of Indian bleached cottons being imported into London and into Ghent specially for such experiments. By this time fine delicate prints were already being made on silk, but the problem was that these printed fabrics could not be washed without losing the pattern. At the end of the seventeenth century book printers were already familiar with the idea of roller printing to judge from an engraving published in Nuremburg in 1699. We shall see that a form of this machine was the pinnacle of mechanical invention in textile printing towards the end of the eighteenth century. There were two kinds of innovation in the industry which we may loosely call chemical and mechanical. The chemical developments came first and were directly or indirectly the outcome of trade with the Orient. They are fairly well chronicled in the nineteenth-century manuals and, more recently, in the work of historians of fashion and design, and especially research centred on museum collections. The new technology consisted in fixing the design in the fabric, i.e. making fast prints.

Essentially, there were three developments:

1. The adaptation of Indian mordants (i.e. chemicals applied to cloth to retain the colouring power of madder after washing), developed in the last quarter of the seventeenth century. It was easy to copy the Indian mordants, alum and iron acetate (produced in India by dissolving rusty iron in stale rice water, and in Europe by dissolving old iron in stale beer or wine). The more difficult problem was to find suitable thickeners (starch, flour, gums) to thicken the mordant to prevent it spreading beyond the printed areas. Madder and one or both mordants in varying strengths produced various shades of red, lilac and black. Every printer had his own 'recipes' but the results were often disappointing and led to a search for better mordants. Lead acetate, possibly discovered in Britain before 1754, proved to be the ideal mordant for madder, while nitrate of iron (*c.* 1765) produced much better blacks. After 1775 quercitron bark was imported from North America and united with the mordants to produce a range of yellows. In this way the textile printer's palette was steadily extended.

2. Printing with indigo (i.e. in various shades of blue) was a development of the 1730s and 1740s. Dyeing with indigo was formerly prohibited in England, France and Saxony because it was thought to be a poisonous drug. In India the Hindus would not dye in blue because the colour meant shame to them and they practically restricted themselves to madder reds. The European printers' problem was that indigo was insoluble, and the Indians never solved the problem of printing in blue. European persistence achieved success in several directions. The simplest solution was called 'resist dyeing'. The printer waxed the parts of a fabric that were desired to remain white then immersed the whole cloth in an indigo vat. When the dyed cloth was dry the wax could be dissolved away to leave a blue and white patterned fabric. Surviving examples in museums show that the technique could achieve pleasing results for large-patterned furnishing fabrics. A later development consisted in 'pencilling' the indigo on to the fabric. The indigo was ground to a fine powder and made into a paste by mixing with ferrous sulphate or (later) orpiment. Girls

were then able to pencil it on to the patterns traced on the cloth.

3. Printing with large engraved copper plates was developed soon after the mid eighteenth century. Here again the secret of success lay in the correct thickening of the mordants. The best thickener was soon found to be gum senegal, imported from the west coast of Africa. The introduction of copper plate printing advanced the textile printer's art in two most important respects: it made it possible to obtain any degree of fineness, and it enlarged the maximum convenient size of repeat from less than a foot square (30 mm × 30 mm) to over a yard square (one square metre).[22] With the copper plate calico printing became a superior art form in its own right, supported by some of the most celebrated designers and engravers of the age. The great collections of printed fabrics at the Victoria & Albert Museum (London), the Smithsonian Museum (Washington), the Musée de l'Impression sur Étoffes de Mulhouse, and other centres, are built around the finest eighteenth-century copper plate prints.

The earliest development, the adaptation of Indian techniques, was achieved about the same period in London and Amsterdam with both competing for leadership. The Dutch produced prints in two or three shades of red which were called *surates rouges et violets* and *pattenas rouges et noires* and which had a vast international sale. They were imitated by printers in Hamburg, Bremen and Switzerland and soon came to be known as *indiennes ordinaires*. However, if we can believe Ryhiner of Basle, the earliest commentator on the subject, the English took an early lead in the quality of their prints:

> It was reserved for the English to attempt an imitation of the best Indian work in prints, and to arrive at a degree of perfection no-one would have thought possible. Everyone knows that the industriousness and plodding patience of these people in overcoming every kind of difficulty exceeds all imagination ... They have, moreover, the advantages of making their finest prints on linen, which renders them more durable.[23]

This last sentence is important because it is the earliest clear reference to the contribution of British fustians, increasing quantities of which were produced around Blackburn in Lancashire and in the Glasgow–Paisley area of Scotland. According to Holker, reporting to the French government about 1750, the Lancashire output of calicoes was 'so large that scarcely a week goes by without a thousand rolls being sold and sent to London unbleached'. The figure discloses that the northern suppliers were providing very nearly 40 per cent of the London printers' needs at the time.[24] Some German linens were imported through Holland, but most of the remaining 60 per cent would be supplied by cottons brought to London by the East India Company. Cottons were less durable but the colours could be applied more perfectly. The Swiss took an early lead in producing the finest cottons, and the cantons of Berne, Zurich, Appenzell and Toggenbourg were the leading European producers until the 1790s.[25]

From the earliest years calico printing was an industry distinguished by large manufacturing units and investments. We must content ourselves with a few examples here. A petition of London printers drawn up in 1719 claims one factory employing 205 men and boys, a second 121 and a third 49.[26] A list of Dutch printers made 10 years later contains four firms with more than 100 workers and seven further ones with more than 60.[27] When the industry was dispersed this characteristic did not disappear. The six or eight factories in Geneva in 1765 each had more than 100 workers.[28] Probably they were similar to the one analysed by Ryhiner at Basle in the following year which had a workforce of 96 and an investment of 20,000 florins (about £2,000).[29] In Dublin, Samuel Grant, an Englishman who took the industry there in 1720, had an investment of £5,000 and employed 108 people 40 years later. The first Spanish printing works, established by Esteban Canals at Barcelona before 1738, is said to have employed about 300 workers, while the biggest of the Antwerp works had 576 workers at its peak in 1769.[30] At the same time numerous small works continued in all centres throughout the eighteenth century. Probably that of the Ryhiners at Basle was fairly typical of those run by entrepreneurs with only modest ambitions. It consisted of a small wooden house containing three or four printing tables and a bleach field, the total capacity amounting to only 6,000 f. (£240). All goods were sold without difficulty in Lorraine and Italy. A later generation of the founding family explained:

> The demand for these goods [prints] grew very large ... and if at this time and for thirty years afterwards [1716–46] the business had been pushed, great fortunes might have been made. But our predecessors were satisfied with moderate advantages, did not care to trade on borrowed capital, and were very cautious in giving credit, satisfying themselves with modest rather than brilliant fortunes. The buyers waited upon them, they had the choice of

their customers and stated the credit they would allow, they fixed their own prices, and it is fair to say that the trade was the best of the period.[31]

Although research has been concerned largely with some of the most thrusting entrepreneurs of the eighteenth century, it is important to understand at the outset that they were not typical. Most calico printers of the age were evidently more like the Ryhiners than Schuele, Oberkampf, the Peels or other 'big names' of the age. The large scale of the vanguard firms may be recognised as part of an endeavour to cut costs of materials, tools and, above all, labour. Productivity was increased by pressing the advantages of division of labour. In the second half of the eighteenth century most larger concerns employed a dozen or so different occupations, and one of them recognised as many as 24 varied skills. Wage costs were also saved by the extensive employment of juveniles and women, training boys as *tireurs* ('tear-boys', or assistants to the printers) and

Table 3 The work force and division of labour at some continental printing plants

Plant and location	Year	Pay-roll	No. of specialised functions	Boys	Females
Wetter, Orange	1764	530	16	85	196
De Wisser, Antwerp	1769	576	24		136+
De Waldner, Alsace	1772	293	12	40	150
Baron, Sallé & Cie, Beauvais	1778	809	9	65	350
Dollfus & Cie, Thann, Alsace	1788	724	24	100	400

SOURCES: H. Chobaut, 'L'industrie des Indiennes à Avignon et à Orange 1677–1884', *Mém. de l'Acad. de Vaucluse*, 1938.
A. K. J. Thijs, 'Aspecten van de opkomst der textieldrukkerij als grootbedrijf Ec Antwerpen in de 18.e.', *Bijdragen en Mededelingen Betreffende de Geschiedenis der Nederlanden*, LXXXVI (1971).
E. Albrecht-Mathey, *The Fabrics of Mulhouse and Alsace, 1750–1800* (Leigh-on-Sea, 1968), p. 15.
J. M. Schmitt, *Aux origines de la révolution industrielle en Alsace . . .* (unpublished thesis, University of Strasbourg, 1979), p. 692.
Beauvais: AN: F12/676.

young females as *pinceauteuses* ('pencillers', or hand painters on the fabrics). It is possible to illustrate this development for a few well-known Continental works, and the details are set out in Table 3. It is worth noticing that the Derby silk mill and the larger Arkwright mills, which have received so much attention in British texts, employed only about 300 people, mostly unskilled women and children, a smaller number than the labour force concentrated in the biggest calico printing concerns on the Continent.

The second and third innovations outlined above were products of English and Irish ingenuity according to Peter Floud, the leading writer on the technology of the eighteenth-century printing industry. The famous 'china blue' prints, whose colours and designs are still familiar in the ceramic ware of the period, created an exciting new fashion, an attractive alternative to the reds, violets, purples and browns of the *indiennes ordinaires*. Their success probably helped to increase the prosperity and hence the scale of the industry in London. At any rate, the indigo printworks of Stevens & Parker were by far the largest manufacturing concern insured by the Sun Fire Office in the five years 1751–5:

	Premises (£)	'Utensils, stock and goods' (£)
Pencilling shop	200	400
Warehouse separate	200	3,000
Printing shop and stove	200	1,500
Copperhouse [indigo printing] and offices	200	500
Calender room, printing shop, grinding shop and printers' workroom		3,000
Storehouse stock		100
Total	£800	£8,500

As a basis for comparison, the earliest of the English cotton spinning mills, built by Wyatt & Paul, was insured in 1755 for £1,000, while a typical woollen manufacturer had an insured capital of between £300 and £500.[32]

In France, too, there is evidence of investment in proto-factory enterprise on an impressive scale before the Arkwright system crossed the Channel. The earliest inventories available date from 1768, but we must limit ourselves to one example only here. Jacques

Introduction 17

Baron's works at Essonnes, near Corbeil, was later bought by Oberkampf for his younger brother Frédéric. It was already a considerable concern:

	l.	£
A calender shop	6,000	250
A 'mill' for printing with copper [plates]	600	25
Five engraved copper plates	1,000	42
22 tables for printing [with wooden blocks]	300	13
Six tables for pencilling	18	1
Boilers, tuns	1,850	77
Fixed capital	19,899	829
347 wooden blocks (ready for use)	694	29
214 wooden blocks (not yet engraved)	188	8
715 designs	4,500	188
'Drugs' (i.e. dyestuffs)	26,182	1,091
White cloths (ready for printing)	50,574	2,107
Finished goods (in store)	57,143	2,381
Working capital	139,281	5,803

Dupasquier, the largest of the Neuchâtel calico printers, had a capital of 60,000 *l*. (about £2,500) and a working capital of nearly £3,000 in 1775.[33] Unfortunately the English sources do not reveal the working capital apart from stock, but there can be no doubt that, as in France, it was several times larger than the fixed capital. Dupasquier's stocks were probably smaller than was usual for his size because he worked on commission.

The contrast between the printing proto-factories with their capitalist entrepreneurs, advanced technology, high labour productivity and continuously expanding markets, and the small masters producing traditional textiles for stable markets inevitably generated local tensions. Periodically jealousy erupted into violent opposition to the new order, first in London and later in Augsburg, Nantes, Orange, Mulhouse and other towns. For the moment it is sufficient to recognise that the contrast between the calico printing proto-factories and more traditional methods of production was not a mutation found only in a few unrepresentative locations; it was a widespread feature of European industrial growth in the eighteenth century.

The inventor of copper plate printing was said to be Francis Nixon of the Drumcondra printworks, Dublin. In the years 1755–7 he sold the technique to George Amyand, a wealthy London East India merchant who had started a printworks near Merton in Surrey, England. The secret was soon out. Peter Floud notes that a print by Robert Jones of Old Ford (East London) dated 1761 'already demonstrates such a mastery of the new technique that we must conclude that Jones had already discovered Nixon's secret several years earlier'. Schuele took the technique to Augsburg in 1766 and Oberkampf to Jouy in 1770. A London artisan called Parsons carried the secret to France under the patronage of the French government. The process reached Sèvres in 1763, Corbeil in 1766, Orange in 1774, Colmar and Neuchâtel in 1780 and Bourgoin and Mulhouse in 1782. As Floud explains, it 'quickly led to the development of an entirely new type of printed fabric, decorated with elegant pictorial designs with figures, landscapes and architecture, often incorporating mythological, romantic, theatrical or commemorative scenes of a type completely beyond the scope of the humbler wood block printer'. In 1760 the English were generally pre-eminent in this field, but Schuele's prints were said to be finished even better and Oberkampf was shortly to win distinction in this kind of production.[34]

Ryhiner thought that the British lead in eighteenth-century technology was due to the printers' ingenuity and devotion to business, but there are some other explanations. During the century they overtook the Dutch as the premier trading nation and, in particular, won the best connections with India. The outcome can be illustrated from a petition of 1766 from a new Nantes calico printer: 'The cotton goods made in France on which I try to do most of my printing, cannot compare with those of India which serve the Dutch and English, and which are our masters in this respect, the Dutch for the common people and the English for more refined taste ...'[35] Moreover, it has been calculated that the British Isles and the American Colonies represented the largest free trade area, in terms of population, in the eighteenth century, and average *per capita* income was the highest. This is particularly important in considering a product for which there was potentially a mass consumption market.[36] Finally, it is relevant to note that for much of the eighteenth century English fashions (which meant London fashions) led European taste, at any rate in men's clothing; even France was not immune from 'Anglomania'. The London printers stood at one of the two centres of the world of fashion.[37]

There is a little evidence to suggest that copper plate printing encouraged the further growth in minimum scale of calico printing firms. Campbell's *London Tradesman* (1747) considers the work of the calico printer, but only with reference to wood block printing and wax printing. (He does not mention either indigo pencilling, which was new when he wrote, or copper plate work, which was not yet invented.) He recorded that it was possible to start in business as a master printer with a capital of between £200 and £2,000.[38] This seems consistent with the data for 1719 mentioned earlier and with Ryhiner's starting capital (1716) of 6,000 ƒ. However, a printer who was trying to introduce copper plate work into Lancashire and sought to emphasise the modest nature of his financial requirements calculated a minimum of £896, which did not include any property.[39] Moreover, as Ryhiner pointed out, the demand for more expensive prints was less regular and the turnover likely to be less, so more working capital was required.[40]

Oriental printed fabrics were labour-intensive and inexpensive so European producers still feared competition from them until after the middle of the eighteenth century. Consequently, attempts were soon being made to find cheaper alternatives to the Indian handicraft techniques, and this is the origin of the mechanical innovations referred to above. Unfortunately this aspect of the technology of the industry has scarcely been noticed by earlier researchers and was seldom heeded by contemporary writers, so we have only modest evidence with which to support our thesis. However, it seems to us that there were four important developments, all of which appeared in the second half of the eighteenth century. Once again it is most convenient to summarise them before considering some of their economic implications:

1. *Picotage*, or the use of printing blocks made of pins (or studs) tapped into wooden blocks to form patterns, made its appearance around the middle of the eighteenth century and may have anticipated the development of copper plate work. Copper plate engraving was a slow and expensive process because the work was confined to a few highly-skilled and highly-paid engravers. Pin work could be done by girls and consequently was quick and cheap, so it was easy to respond to sudden shifts of fashion. Examples of fabrics in museums produced by this technique show that it was highly effective. The heads of the 'pins' were often in the shape of simple patterns (lines, crescents, stars, etc.) to make the assembly of the block design quicker and more authentic.[41]

2. The employment of mechanical power (horse gins, water wheels and, later, steam engines) to work pumps to expedite the process of making 'iron liquor', for grinding indigo, for polishing copper plates, and for operating calenders, washing stocks, and squeezers, was common in London in the second half of the eighteenth century. Oberkampf's letters show that the Swiss printers were using gins by 1764, and we should expect this simple idea to have been widely used. A London printer was using a steam engine as early as 1760. The increase of labour productivity must have been considerable.[42]

3. The employment of a copper plate printing machine is first recorded in 1760 in the factory of a large London firm, Asterleys of Wandsworth. The machine was sketched and described in some detail by John Rennie, the famous Scots engineer, at a Carlisle printworks in 1782. It was a manually operated machine that conveyed the cloth from a roll, pressed it on to the flat copper plate and spread the colour ready for the next repeat of the design. Two French inventories of 1768, one for the Essonnes factory, the other for the Sèvres factory, mention a 'mill for printing with copper plates', and three 'mechanical frames for printing with copper plates', and almost certainly refer to the same machine. The former was, as we have already noted, valued at £30, which seems about right for the apparatus shown in Rennie's drawing. The machine is presumably the same as Schuele's *Rollwerk* which he carried from London to Augsburg in 1772; Oberkampf tried to secure one in the following year.[43]

4. Thomas Bell's celebrated invention of roller printing (1785) appears to have been a development of this early printing machine. As is well-known, it was first used at Livesey, Hargreaves' works near Preston, and on their bankruptcy (1788) it was quickly taken over by the Peels. For the moment we need only quote Baines' striking remark that printing with engraved copper rollers was *the* 'grand improvement in the art' of textile printing and that the invention bore 'nearly the same relation in point of despatch to block printing by hand as throstle or mule spinning bears to spinning by the one thread wheel.' The triumph of Lancashire came when the two lines of technical evolution were united under the direction of some of the great textile entrepreneurs of the eighteenth century.[44]

The increase in productivity and its consequences are recorded in the archives of the British East India Co. The Directors estimated in 1793 that the Indian producers had to employ 15 operatives for every one employed in the British industry. Spinning by mules was reckoned to be 50 times more productive than the traditional Indian technique. Consequently 'Every shop [in Britain] offers British muslins for sale, equal in appearance and of more elegant patterns than those of India for one-fourth or perhaps more than one-third less in price'.[45] The prints that were produced for popular consumption were probably closer to the selection of simple designs offered by Charles O'Brien, the London designer who wrote *The Calico Printer's Assistant* in 1790 (see Plate 3), than those usually exhibited in museums.[46] Nevertheless the achievement was an impressive one.

PART TWO

The Peels of Lancashire

Chapter 1

The Origins of Calico Printing in Lancashire

The calico printing industry did not arrive in Lancashire until about the middle of the eighteenth century, a late date considering that the region was the principal domestic supplier of the basic material to the London printers and that the industry was established in Dublin in about 1715 and in Edinburgh in 1723.[1] The earliest reference to calico printing in the north-west appears to be one made in the *London Magazine* in 1750. An article on Manchester notes: 'Here has been for long a manufacture of fustians called Manchester cottons, much improved of late by dyeing, printing, etc. . . .' Unfortunately no names are given and the enterprise was probably very small. Moreover, if Holker's report to the French government can be trusted, the Manchester and Blackburn calico dealers continued to rely on London's traditional skills in bleaching as well as colouring materials despite the growing pressure on land along the banks of the Lea and Wandle.[2] The most remarkable feature of the Lancashire industry in the mid eighteenth century was the concentration of a large trade – as much as 1,000 rolls a week – in the hands of a small number of merchant houses. An advertisement in the *Manchester Mercury* in 1774 lists seven leading firms in the trade, and Abram's well-documented *History of Blackburn* confirms that there were few others of any consequence at the time.[3] Most of the leading Lancashire calico printers of the first generation were drawn from the ranks of the Blackburn 'chapmen' or *verlegers* in 'Blackburn Grays', including the Claytons, the Liveseys and the Peels.[4]

All the sources record that the first Lancashire calico printer was Edward Clayton of Bamber Bridge, near Preston. Edward Baines' well-known *History of the Cotton Manufacture* (1835), which is commonly quoted in this connection, says that Clayton and his sons 'began the business on a small scale as early as the year 1764',[5] but the local sources show that they started a decade or so before this. Edward Clayton is mentioned as a calico printer in Walton-le-Dale parish register in 1753, and in 1759 he was advertising for sale a 'great variety of the newest and most fashionable patterns' in the columns of the *Manchester Mercury*.[6] A usually reliable account adds that Claytons' works were 'first supplied with men from London'.[7] In 1765 one of Edward Clayton's sons moved to Bolton to open a printworks but a summary of his stock indicates that techniques were still elementary. All his prints were in two colours in purples, reds and blacks, which would be created with madder and the iron mordant.[8] The next printworks in the north of England is said to have been established at Chadkirk, near Stockport, apparently by a Blackburn dealer in 1755.[9] In the early 1760s several printworks were opened in Manchester. William Wilson's at Ainsworth was probably the most successful, and his achievement indicates the rapid progress of the Lancashire industry in the 1770s. His insurance inventory of 1774 shows how he adapted a large country house for manufacturing, a development that was a familiar practice in the environs of London (Table 4). William Wilson was evidently in the vanguard of the fashion trade, for when he died in 1783 his printing blocks were said to 'consist of several hundred different garment patterns ... of the newest taste; likewise many valuable blocks of light chints patterns, well calculated for furniture or the foreign trade ... [and] now in great demand'. He had a warehouse in London as well as the Manchester one included in his inventory, a sure sign of success in the metropolitan market. His factory assets show that he was largely concerned in the labour-intensive pencilled indigo work and madder prints. The absence of any reference to copper plates in the sale of his property confirms that he did not graduate to the most elegant branch of the manufacture.[10] In the late 1770s and early 1780s the number of printworks in the Manchester and Blackburn areas began to multiply.[11]

Considering that the London calico printing business was concentrated in so few hands the bankruptcy rate was quite extraordinary. In the 30 years 1752–82, 36 London printers ended in the bankruptcy court. A large proportion of them were small firms that failed to find a place in the thin trade directories of the period but a few came of well-known houses like the Haverkuums, one of the Dutch firms that pioneered the business at the end of the seventeenth century, and the Wares and Munns, whose prints are still known to collectors.[12] O'Brien's pioneer work, *The Callico Printer's Assistant* (1790), blames the large number of failures on men rashly

Table 4 Valuation of property of William Wilson of Ainsworth (near Middleton, Manchester), Dyer, Printer and Merchant, 1774

Item	Buildings (£)	Utensils, stock etc. (£)
House called Ainsworth Hall	1,000	500[1]
House, barn, cowhouse, two stables, carpenters' shop, granaries and printing room	500	1,500
Warehouse called *The Garden House*, two stables, chaisehouse and cowhouse	60	200
Two stoves, two drug chambers, one pencilling room, one cutting room, room over and one print room	200	350
Black, blue, and light colour dyehouses, three colour shops and scouring house, dressing rooms, dye stuff chamber and cutting shop	300	1,500
New light coloured dye house and dressing rooms	60	500
Warehouse called *The Farmhouse*	200	5,000
New blue dye house and room over	60	500
Large printing house and stove rooms	200	1,000
Dyehouse and Storerooms adjoining	10	500
Buckhouse and scouring house	30	800
Millhouse and rooms over at the Brook	100	730[2]
Total at Ainsworth	**2,720**	**13,080**
Warehouse in King St, Manchester	—	1,700[3]
House and shop in Deansgate, Manchester	—	300
Warehouse of Mandwell & Kettle, King St, Manchester	—	2,000
Total	**2,720**	**17,080**
Policy total		**19,800**

SOURCE: Sun OS: 241/358485, 20 Sep. 1775; see also, *ibid.*: 230/339419, 28 Apr. 1774, for a similar policy.

NOTES: [1] Household goods, £500.
[2] 'including mills'.
[3] Including household goods, £200.

entering the industry without 'mechanical, chemical and philosophical knowledge', and the historical records can offer examples of such basic ignorance. The high bankruptcy rate might also be connected with the volatile nature of a fashion trade, for later evidence shows that choosing a successful design was something of a hit-and-miss affair. In the late 1770s and early 1780s there are clear signs that the London industry was under financial strain.

Several large and important calico printing works were sold up and in some cases disbanded at auction. They included a large works at Crayford (probably the Wares') with 1,500 blocks and 200 copper plates, Robert Jones's famous works at Old Ford, and Thomas Nash's old-established factory at Lambeth.[13] The immediate cause of the crisis was the chain of mercantile failures that followed the American War of Independence, but it seems that the colonists' dishonoured debts accelerated forces that were already at work. Despite the celebrity of his prints, two of Jones's successors at Old Ford failed to make the works pay while the next generation of Nash moved to Manchester.[14] Another sign of the rise of the Lancashire industry was the migration of Walker & Singleton's huge oil-of-vitriol works from Battersea to Manchester in 1783.[15]

It was inevitable that Lancashire printers should multiply as soon as London's technology was learned, for building and production costs were cheaper in the north of England. The London rivers were congested with industrial developments while the north offered an abundance of cheap sites for water power. By 1780 the only important restriction on growth was shortage of capital. Two earlier migrations of technology from the metropolis – the Italian silk reeling mill and the Dutch tape loom – had been accompanied by entrepreneurs and capital and it was inevitable that, sooner or later, textile printing would find direct support from London.[16] The earliest important connection with London merchants was built up by the Livesey family. As early as 1751 Robert Livesey claimed that he and his brothers employed 600 looms and 3,000 people in the Blackburn area and that eight-ninths of the fustians he sold in Manchester went to the printers, presumably in London.[17] In 1776 they added printing to their established calico dealing activities and two years later brought Smith, Anstie and Hall into partnership.[18] Josephus Smith was a London merchant and banker and John Anstie a Devizes (Wiltshire) clothier with an interest in the dyeing end of the trade.[19] Hall was probably one of the firm's local managers. There can be no doubt that these partners helped the firm draw capital and credit from London and the south of England while the metropolitan connection eased the flow of local credit. When the firm became involved in protracted bankruptcy proceedings in 1788 the wide dispersion of its creditors was revealed to public view. There is no comprehensive list available in the London sources but debts of over £90,000 to Allen & Co., Manchester bankers, and of £64,000 to Gibson & Johnson, London bankers, were proved.[20] A fuller list was specified to the Scottish bankruptcy court (Table 5).

Table 5 Distribution of principal creditors of Livesey, Hargreaves & Co., 1788

Location	Merchants Nos.	Total debt (£)	Bankers Nos.	Total debt (£)	Others Nos.	Total debt (£)	Totals Nos.	Debt (£)
London	9	17,351	3	3,272	8	12,077	20	32,700
Blackburn	7	39,527	0		0		7	39,527
Other places*	3	11,023	3	29,636	0		6	40,659
Total	**19**	**67,901**	**6**	**32,908**	**8**	**12,077**	**33**	**112,886**
Per cent		60.15		29.15		10.70		100

SOURCE: Scottish Record Office: RH15/747. Details kindly supplied by Prof. John Butt of Strathclyde University.
*Manchester, Liverpool, Wigan, Preston, Bristol and Salisbury.

Livesey, Hargreaves & Co.'s tangled financial affairs might constitute a study in their own right but there is no need to enter into further details. The important point to indicate here is the unprecedented scale of the partners' manufacturing operations, far surpassing rivals in Lancashire and London. They had factories at Mosney and Bannister Hall, near Preston, bleaching grounds at Hoghton Tower, near Blackburn, a coal pit at Standish (Wigan), and a house, offices, warehouse and factory in Manchester. At the time of the bankruptcy an Arkwright-type cotton mill and workers' tenements had recently been built near Clitheroe. There was also a London warehouse. The firm had leased some 960 acres, with rentals amounting to £2,870 per year.[21] In the course of their trade Livesey & Co. established country banks at Blackburn, Mosney and Preston and printed a large note issue, employing a full-time agent to press local tradesmen to accept them at their face value if possible or at a discount.[22] One account says that they employed all the population in and about Preston, another that they were the 'means of giving bread to near 20,000 persons'.[23] The last figure evidently includes dependents and domestic weavers for a calculation of 1784 suggests about 900 workers.[24]

The organisation of so large a concern is a matter of interest in its own right. Livesey, Hargreaves & Co. was formed of a chain of partnerships on a scale that was novel if not unique in Lancashire (Fig. 1). Its essential feature was a direct line of communication between Blackburn, Manchester and London, enabling the partners to draw freely on metropolitan capital by discounting bills there. The partnership was broken up at the firm's bankruptcy in 1788 but its features were copied by other Blackburn trading families, notably the Peels, Howarths and Smalleys.

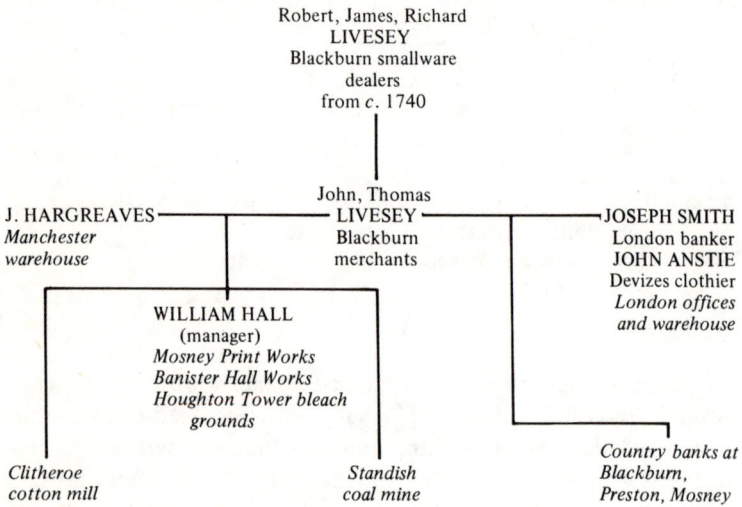

Fig. 1 Structure of Livesey, Hargreaves & Co., 1780–8 (SOURCES: PRO: BI/83, 156–9 (Livesey); BI/92, 107–11 (Smith); BI/93, 223–4 (Anstie); BI/91, 9–10 (partnership dates); BI/81, 105–6 (Hall). *MM*, 13 Jan. 1789 (property)

Although Livesey, Hargreaves & Co. were, as Baines remarked, 'celebrated for the extent of their concerns', they were still on the threshold of their greatest technical achievement in 1788. As explained in the Introduction, the most important eighteenth-century development in calico printing from the viewpoint of productivity was cylinder printing, i.e. printing with engraved copper cylinders rather than plates. The invention, by a Scot called Thomas Bell, was first successfully applied at Livesey, Hargreaves & Co.'s Mosney works in 1785.[25] The implications for the security of employment of the block printers were not missed. Although the printers' union had scarcely emerged, an anonymous group of workmen wrote to the Mosney management early in 1786 expressing their determination to suppress the new machines:

> Mrs. Levasy, Hargravs and Co. Mind this is to give you timely Notice that if you don't give over working your Macheens for Printing by which means the trade for the Gurneymen will be ruined there is twelve of us that have sworn to burn down your Premises both at Mosney and Manchester. So help us God and therr is another [factory] in Market Street Lane shall come down by God, so no more from Pore injured Workmen.

The other factory referred to was that of Charles Taylor, who received an even more uncompromising letter:

> You must immediately give over any more Mashan Work for we are determined there shall be no more of them made use of in the trade and it will be madness for you to contend with the [workmen in the] trade as we are combined by Oath to fix prices ... we are determined to destroy all Sorts of Masheens for Printing in the Kingdom for there is more Hands than is work ...[26]

No other firms were threatened so it seems evident that at this time only Liveseys and Taylor had the new technique. Ignoring all threats Liveseys raced ahead with the exploitation of Bell's invention. At the time of their bankruptcy in the summer of 1788 they had 6–700 cylinders cut or pinned, i.e. studded with designs. A militant printers' union was further antagonised by the employment of women dilutees and numerous apprentices.[27]

O'Brien's contentious book on calico printing describes Livesey, Hargreaves & Co.'s later prints as 'execrable', but it is difficult to be sure whether this refers to the imperfections of a new technology or was simply a prejudice consequent on the jealousy of the London printers of their upstart northern rivals. A further explanation is offered by the anonymous author of *Facts and Observations in the Calico Printing Business*, a pamphlet that appeared in 1807. This polemic was written by a Lancashire manufacturer or, at any rate, by one who saw the conflict from the northern capitalists' side. He blamed Livesey, Hargreaves & Co.'s downfall on the poor standard of work induced by a printers' trade union which had its origin in a group of journeymen recruited by the firm in London in about 1783. In view of the Peels' later struggles with the printers' union, it is useful to quote this interpretation of the development at some length:

So soon as these *gentlemen journeymen* (for they had more the appearance of gentlemen than workmen) got down into the Country, they assumed (as coming from London) a great degree of consequence, and making great professions of skill and ingenuity in the business, the acting partners at Messrs. Livesey & Co.'s works, who knew little of the nature of the business, were easily duped by them and gave them most extravagant wages, and as these journeymen had so long complained of the Country people doing their work [for] low [wages] ... their great object was to keep them as high in the Country as in London ...; but this was not the worst, so ill disposed were these journeymen to the Country masters that they executed their work in a very imperfect manner and would often tell the overlooker, when he complained of bad work, that it was good enough for the Country.... Though this house had hurt itself by speculations, yet this was the principal cause of its ruin; for though the execution of their work cost such enormous sums of ready money [for inflated wages] yet it was so imperfectly done they were constantly pushing the markets with quantities of spoiled work which they often sold for less than the price of the cloth and amount of the duty. This soon brought the house into an embarrassed situation.[28]

It was in this deteriorating financial climate, our anonymous author claims, that Livesey, Hargreaves attempted to cut the cost of labour by turning to the roller printing machine. A three months' strike in 1786 only served to increase the firm's desperation. Although this account is evidently partial, the details fit in with those supplied by O'Brien and the local sources and with the general context of developments. They persuade us that union militancy played a critical role in the rapid adoption of machinery and a lesser one in the innovator's early fall. Fortunately it is possible to find more objective evidence of the quality of the firm's output – the bankruptcy commissioners' inventory of stock at Liveseys' London warehouse. The list summarises some 1,600 pieces, which was only 6.5 per cent of the partners' total stock of printed and bleached pieces at the time of bankruptcy, but this is probably a representative sample of the kind of work they were doing. The total value of the prints at London was only £2,800 (1s. 4d. a yard), an average that clearly places Livesey, Hargreaves & Co.'s stock in the cheapest category of goods. The descriptions confirm this. Most of the patterns were stripes, stormonts (fine spots), checks, mosaics, vandykes (a zig-zag, or angular design) and porcupines (evidently a bristle effect).[29]

The Origins of Calico Printing in Lancashire

The months following the collapse of Livesey, Hargreaves & Co. was a period of great difficulty for the numerous entrepreneurs in the cotton industry who had extended credit to them or to their bankers. The Company's bank notes had been freely circulated in all the manufacturing country in and about Preston and men of all trades and callings had them in their possession. Arkwright lost £32,000, his son £9,000, Strutts nearly £6,000, and further substantial sums were lost by other cotton merchants.[30] Watsons, the leading Preston cotton spinners, were compelled to dismiss 'great numbers of workers, who were begging to work at half pay'.[31] Nevertheless the long term effect was beneficial because calico printing was relieved of the dominant firm. Lord Derby's steward probably expressed the mood of those who were sufficiently clear of the crisis to see the longer perspective:

> We continue in very great distress amongst the cotton manufacturers and likely to continue for some time, but ... monopoly of any trade is bad to the community at large and this added to the unbounded credit given to Mr. Livesey with his ambitious and overbearing spirit has been the ruin of himself and many others and done injury to the public and trade in general but once this is got over and the present stocks of manufactured goods sold off, I hope everything will come round again and the business divided into many hands.[32]

In the event Wareing's optimism was quite justified for, by the end of 1788, nearly all of these printers had been absorbed by other firms, and before long skilled men were being offered premiums of 5, 10 and 15 guineas to work for new employers.[33] In the pages that follow it will be seen that the various branches of the house of Peel assumed some of Livesey, Hargreaves' more worthy business policies and connections and slipped into the role of leader of the English calico printing trade. In this way Livesey, Hargreaves' experiences and achievements were not altogether lost to the industry.

Chapter 2

The Peels: Origins and Technical Innovations

The origins of the Peel family in the Blackburn district were quite modest, but the insistence on a yeoman farming background in the hagiography is misleading.[1] A mid seventeenth-century Robert Peele rose to wealth as a woollen manufacturer selling cloth stamped with patterns cut into elm blocks. The next generation failed to display comparable business acumen but the family interest in the textile industry was maintained. At the time Robert ('Parsley') Peel inherited the farm at Peel Fold which complemented his family's industrial pursuits it was said to be worth £100 a year rental, so that when he mortgaged it a few years later to raise capital for his calico printing partnership with Howarth and Yates, it might have realised something like £2,000, no mean start for any manufacturer in the period.[2] Nearly all of the Blackburn calico printers, cotton spinners, flax spinners and merchants whose earlier occupations can be traced, were drawn from the same stratum of local society – the 'chapmen' or dealers in the linen and cotton cloth known as 'Blackburn Greys'. 'Parsley' Peel and his partners Edmund and John Howarth were certainly active in this trade by 1760.[3] In the later decades of the eighteenth century Blackburn became the great mart for these goods and the chief source from which the printers of Lancashire as well as those of London and Glasgow were supplied. This trade was at first conducted by Blackburn merchant houses like those of the Sudells and Fieldens, who rose from the ranks of the chapmen a generation before Peel, but it was their middlemen suppliers – the Claytons, Liveseys, Peels, Howarths and others – who gradually developed the technique of manufacture in workshops which, from very small beginnings, rapidly advanced in size and efficiency.[4]

There are various recorded traditions of the origins of the Peel family's interest in cotton printing. One that was current at Bury early in the last century sounds authentic to the extent that it links the Peels with the Claytons, the firm who are known to have introduced the metropolitan techniques into Lancashire. According to this account the high profits that could be earned in calico printing were demonstrated to the Peels when they sent a length of cloth that had been spoiled in the weaving to Claytons to be printed as 'handkerchieves', i.e. the fashionable printed squares that women wore round their shoulders.[5] Business history is full of developments that begin with the exploitation of chance connections and the story is by no means to be discounted, but at best it only explains the incentive to enter the new industry.

A more convincing account of the origin of the Peels' interest in cotton printing comes from a collection of family traditions penned by Jane Howarth:

> Mr. Jonathon Howarth, a very intelligent and enterprising character with extended views of commerce which he had probably acquired during a residence of several years in London, returned home [to Blackburn] with a persevering desire to establish the printing of calicoes in Lancashire. In furtherance of this scheme he claimed the assistance of his brother-in-law, Mr. [Robert] Peel, and also of Mr. William Yates of Blackburn, about 1764. Their earliest experiments were upon handkerchiefs and shawls of the simplest patterns.... The firm was [called] Howarth, Peel and Yates, Mr. Howarth having two shares in the concern, his partners each one.

The writer fairly adds that Peel 'was peculiarly fortunate in his early associations....'[6]

Other family traditions suggest that Howarth derived his knowledge from a London printer of Dutch extraction called Voortman. When the Dutchman returned to Holland the partners started their experiments at Peel's farm 'with printing blocks bought from Voortman', while 'a woman of the family imitated with a clothing iron the sheen given by rolling'. The essential technique that Howarth learned from Voortman was the employment of iron acetate, the mordant with which the linen or cotton and linen cloth was treated before printing in black or brown colours with madder dyes. The use of mordants had been familiar to the London textile printers for almost a century but, incredible though it may seem, the idea was still a novelty in Lancashire.[7] New industrial methods spread very slowly in the seventeenth and much of the eighteenth century, particularly between one country or region and another.

The insurance records add a little more detail to this account. The first reference appears in 1757 when Edmund Howarth senior and junior were in business with Giles and Jonathon Howarth as dealers in checks in Blackburn. The business was run at two houses occupied by the partners where the insured stock amounted to £300.[8] In 1760 the partnership split up when the older Haworth died or retired and Edmund junior and Jonathan became partners with Robert Peel as Blackburn 'chapmen' (*verlegers*). Howarths & Peel occupied two warehouses in the town and a bleach croft, and their business appears to have been growing, but at the formation of this first partnership there is no evidence of printing.[9] It seems that they did not begin to print calicoes until 1764, when Yates, the publican of the Black Bull Inn, was brought into the partnership. The family legend that Yates learned the secret of textile printing from a travelling excise man seems to represent the origin of Yates' financial interest in the new venture rather than the source of the partners' technical expertise. It seems that Yates, like many other innkeepers of the period, was adding warehousing to his other activities, and so became involved in textiles.[10]

All the indications suggest that Peel's business was conducted on a very small scale up to this time. In the early years of the business Peel was recalled as 'a tall robust man, whose ordinary garb included a woollen apron, a calf-skin waistcoat, and wooden-soled clogs....'[11] He used to collect his Blackburn Greys and Checks with a horse and cart which rumbled up and down the country lanes of the Pennine district about his farm while one of his sons, the future Sir Robert, took milk for sale at Blackburn.[12] The smallness of the first factory at Brookside can be seen on the Oswaldtwistle enclosure map of 1774.[13] Peel's farm provided some of the necessary natural resources – tenter grounds for bleaching and cow dung for bringing out the colours after printing. Yates, at the Black Bull Inn, no doubt contributed the stale beer and rusty iron hoops out of which the 'iron liquor' mordant was made. The only public sign of Peel's outstanding talent as an entrepreneur in calico printing at this period was the commercial success of the parsley leaf design that he is said to have scratched out on a pewter plate and which earned him his trade nickname, 'Parsley' Peel.

Peel's earliest distinctions in the development of textile technology were won at the spinning rather than printing stage, a development understandable in the light of his activities as an organiser of the domestic production of fabrics in the Blackburn area. Peel had close connections with the three best-known inventors of new carding and spinning techniques, and in each case it is possible to trace the connection between invention and innovation in some detail.

James Hargreaves's daughter Mary, who was an eyewitness of the events of these years, maintained that her father was employed by 'Messrs. Howarth and Peel' in 1764 when he contrived his spinning jenny. Under pressure from Peel, who had detected an improvement in quantity and quality from Hargreaves's household at a time when he had dispensed with several spinners, the inventor gave way and disclosed his invention to Peel and a small group of Blackburn calico dealers. Peel then insisted on making the invention public while at the same time offering Hargreaves and his sons employment at his new printworks at Brookside. Within a year Hargreaves had 20 jennies installed in a converted barn, while he worked as a bookkeeper to Peel and his sons became apprentices. It was only the destruction of these jennies in the riots of 1768 that induced Hargreaves to accept an offer from Rawson, Heath & Watson, the Nottingham hosiers, to leave Lancashire.[14] It is surely more than a coincidence that the jenny made its debut in the same year that 'Parsley' Peel and his partners launched out into calico printing. The increased demand for calicoes must have brought the pressure on the spinners to crisis point.

The relationship with Arkwright, who took out two patents for his inventions and defended them with all the legal resources he could command, was less immediate. In later years Robert Peel II conceded his family's and the cotton industry's debt to Arkwright: 'Sir Richard Arkwright ... originated the buildings; we all looked up to him and imitated his mode of building', he acknowledged.[15] The basic truth of the admission is evident from examination of the physical dimensions of the early cotton mills that were all built to a basic pattern, now appropriately referred to as the Arkwright-prototype mill. The buildings were invariably simple functional blocks some 70 ft × 30 ft, intended for 1,000 spindles and a 10 hp water wheel, or twice the long dimension, spindlage, and power.[16] In the following sections it will be seen that the various branches of the Peel family eventually owned about 14 mills, several on this model. However, it must also be pointed out that in an indirect way 'Parsley' Peel and his partners contributed to the establishment of the Arkwright concerns. Our knowledge of Arkwright's most creative years is still obscure but it is quite clear that by 1774 (and probably earlier) his firm was already heavily involved in the textile printing trade as well as the spinning of yarns for white calicoes. Contrary to popular assumption Arkwright's most active partner, Jedediah Strutt, made little attempt to develop the Belper hosiery industry to absorb the yarns spun in the mills there but instead built a large printing works next to his mill at Milford. It seems that Arkwright and Strutt were much more interested in exploiting the possibilities of the calico printing industry that were being opened up by the Peels and their neighbours than they were in supplying the midland hosiers. In other words it was textile printing that provided the primary stimulus for Arkwright's enterprise. No wonder the Peels became so implacably opposed to Arkwright's patents and political manoeuvring![17]

It would be interesting to know if the Peels made any original contribution to the evolution of the Arkwright-type mills. John Holker, the Lancashire-born Jacobite who returned to his native country as an industrial spy in the service of the French government, certainly thought so. In 1783 he reported that a sample of thread from the Peels' Radcliffe Bridge mill was 'very strong, more clean and less fluffy than that from any spinning mill that I have seen', and concluded 'I consider this cotton mill as uniquely suitable for making the handkerchiefs and other fabrics of the type that come from India and that we have not been able to copy exactly until now....' The secret of this new degree of achievement lay not only in a modification of Arkwright's rollers but also in preparing and carding the cotton, Holker believed.[18] At the first census of the cotton spinning industry in 1788 the Peels were already third equal in size in the industry (Table 6).

Robert Peel II insisted that his father 'possessed in an eminent degree a mechanical genius', and there is evidence to support his

Table 6 Principal owners of warp-spinning (Arkwright-type) mills, 1788

Owner	No. of mills
Arkwright, Richard & partners (Cromford, Wirksworth, Bakewell, Rocester, Nottingham)	8
Robinson, Bulwell and Linby (Notts.)	5
Peel family, Burton (2 mills), Radcliffe and Hinds (Bury)	4
Douglas, Atherton & Co. (Manchester and Holywell, Flint)	4
Thackery & partners (Manchester and Cark-in-Cartmell)	2

SOURCE: Baker Library, Harvard University (USA): Ms.E.46. Patrick Colquhoun, 'An Account Shewing the Different Cotton Mills erected in Great Britain ...' 1788.

claim. The older Peel sought Hargreaves' assistance in 1762 in constructing a carding engine 'consisting of two or three cylinders' from which the cotton was stripped by two women using hand cards.[19] Peel's experiments appear to have reached a climax in his 1779 patent for carding, roving and spinning machinery, but the specification is not sufficiently clear to understand his techniques.[20] However, there can be no doubt that Peel devoted some years to producing the finest possible fabrics for calico printing and we have Holker's independent testimony that he and his partners were ultimately very successful. This achievement must have contributed much to their success as calico printers.

The Peels maintained their expertise as spinners by building up their own team of talented artisans, conducting experiments and building their own machinery. Locksmiths and copper founders were recruited to make the principal components and clockmakers to make the iron gear wheels. More experienced specialists worked on machine assembly.[21] James Thompson, one of Peels' managers, wrote an interesting account of the specialised machinery that was employed in textile machine building, no doubt with the Peels' works in mind:

> The tools and implements employed in constructing the different machines are very curious, for as there are such immense numbers of each part of every machine to be made it becomes, in the same manner as with the clockmaker, worth the machine maker's trouble to construct complicated tools and engines to expedite the manufacture of the parts [such as] cutting engines for forming the teeth of the numerous wheels....' Thompson also explained that 'such works as Messrs. Strutts at Belper, Mr. Arkwright at Cromford in Derbyshire, Messrs. Phillips & Lees at Manchester, Mr. Peele's and many others are schools for mechanics in almost every department of the science.... [of textile machine building].[22]

With no more than these fragments of evidence it is easy to recognise the Peels as members of the vanguard of technical innovation accelerated by Arkwright's achievements.

The Arkwright-type cotton mills were carefully planned to house a sequence of semi-automatic machines, arranged in series so that the raw material, admitted at the top of the building, flowed from one process to the next. The system required a large unskilled labour force supported by an élite of loyal overseers, maintenance men and book-keepers. The large unskilled section of the labour force consisted of women and juveniles. About 250 were employed in the larger Arkwright-prototype mill favoured by the Peels.[23]

The main problem was the organisation of the unskilled labour and here again Arkwright's example was paramount. Once more, according to Thompson, Arkwright introduced into every department of the cotton manufacture 'a system of industry, order and cleanliness, till then unknown in any manufactory where great numbers were employed together, but which he so effectually accomplished that his example may be regarded as the origin of almost all similar improvement'.[24] The ways in which the Peels tried to respond to this example will be examined below.

The yarn spun on Arkwright's principles had its limitations. Most of it was spun in the coarser counts (technically 16 to 20 hanks to the pound, expressed 16s–20s) and Arkwright found he could not spin finer than 60s. Moreover, the yarn was not suitable for weft (the cross-threads in the web) so hand spinning was never completely ousted. The important invention in fine spinning was Crompton's mule, a machine that the inventor used to spin 80s and which soon reached 300s. Crompton's discovery was immediately the subject of excited speculation in the small town of Bolton and the inventor, who, like Hargreaves, lacked entrepeneurial sense, gave way to pressure from a circle of manufacturers and disclosed his secret in return for a subscription. Peel, Yates & Co. of Bury were one of the larger firms who subscribed a guinea, and it is said that when Robert Peel II called at Hall-in-the-Wood to see the new machine and pay his due, he brought with him several of his mechanics, who devoured the details and carried them away to the Peels' workshops. Peel called on Crompton on two subsequent occasions to offer him a partnership but he foolishly declined, partly 'from a somewhat morbid desire for independence that clung to him through life, partly from a jealous suspicion of persons in superior social position ... but most of all from a feeling of personal dislike to the future baronet which he entertained all his life, arising (as we have been informed) from some disagreement on the occasion of Mr. Peel's first inspection of the mule'.[25]

Whatever Crompton's personal feelings about the way he was treated by the leading firms in the industry fine cotton spinning was certainly not dominated by the leaders of the industry in the early years of the invention. Petitions sent to the Board of Trade in 1788 protesting against imports of the East India Company show a large number of small firms among which is to be found Crompton's own signature (Table 7). At this period mule spinning was manually

Table 7 Size of the mule spinning industry at principal centres, 1788 and 1811

Centre	1788 Petitions		1811 Census	
	Firms	Spindles ('000s)	Firms	Spindles ('000s)
Manchester	43	nd	66	1,028
Stockport	39	nd	70	288
Ashton	78	nd	18	109
Bolton	63	nd	42	340
Total	223	155	196	1,764

SOURCES: PRO:BT 6/140, 1788 Petitions.
Bolton Civic Mus., Irving Bequest: 1811 Census returns.

NOTES: PRO:BT6/140, fo. 40, 25 Feb. 1788, claims 1,553 'spinning jennies' in the regional industry, which obviously refers to mules because it speaks of the 'jenny spinning of cotton into fine weft yarn chiefly for muslins ...' H. Catling, *The Spinning Mule* (Newton Abbot, 1970), pp. 42–3, implies that mules would average about 100 spindles each in 1788.

operated and too highly skilled to be concentrated in factories. The motive of the Peels and other firms in releasing Crompton's secret was to forestall an expensive patent monopoly of the type established by Arkwright. By 1788 fine spinning was so important a feature of calico printing that the traditional fabric suppliers were calling themselves 'calico and muslin manufacturers', while the printers grouped themselves as 'calico printers and muslin manufacturers'.[26] As we shall see in later chapters the Peels began to run down their manufacturing interests from about 1805. Even so, they were still among the leaders of the mule spinning sector at the first census of 1811 (Table 8).

The manufacture of muslins was introduced by Thomas Ainsworth at Bolton about the time that Crompton disclosed his invention, and shortly afterwards by Samuel Oldknow at Anderton and then Stockport.[27] Up to this time the Swiss towns of Zurich, Wadenswil, Horgen, Stafa and St Gall had practically the European monopoly. The Lancashire initiative was so successful that by 1788 Britain was producing 500,000 pieces, much of it for the printers. Ainsworth came of a Bolton family of whitsters (bleachers), and at the time of his new initiative was only 21 or 22 years old and in need of partners with capital and experience. The Peels promptly suggested

Table 8 The size of the ten largest mule spinning firms in the British cotton industry, 1811

Firm	No. of spindles	Approximate value (£)
Samuel Horrocks, Preston (8 mills)	107,136	80,350
McConnel & Kennedy, Manchester (2 mills)	85,000	63,750
A. & G. Murray, Manchester (1 mill)	84,300	63,225
Peter Marsland, Stockport (3 mills)	78,522	58,890
Robinson, Manchester (1 mill)	48,300	36,225
Peels, Bolton and Blackburn (6 mills)	39,640	29,730
Thomas Ainsworth, Warrington (1 mill)	38,000	28,500
James Kennedy, Manchester (2 mills)	39,548	29,660
David Holt & Co., Manchester (? 3 mills)	37,688	28,270
Henry Houldsworth, Manchester (2 mills)	35,632	26,725

SOURCE: Bolton Civic Mus., Irving Bequest: Samuel Crompton's Survey of Mule Spinning.

NOTES: The calculations in the second column refer to value of investments in buildings, power and machinery, and are based on a value of 17s. 6d. per spindle suggested by G. A. Lee: see G. J. French, *Life and Times of Samuel Crompton* (1860), pp. 274, 279.

Marsland, Peels, Holt and Houldsworth also had considerable investments in throstle spinning, the latter at Anderston (Glasgow).

The Peel mills were more dispersed than those of their rivals, Houldsworth excepted.

a partnership, and their offer was not spurned. Peel, Ainsworth & Co. was the leading firm of Bolton fine spinners and muslin manufacturers until the partnership was dissolved in 1801. Thomas Ainsworth's two brothers, Peter and Richard, succeeded their father in the bleaching business and about 1790 were among the first to introduce the new technique of bleaching by chlorine.[28] By a fortunate coincidence the Peels were once again close to the innovating entrepreneurs in the newly-developing sectors of the cotton industry.

Alongside the introduction of mass-produced cotton yarns the Peels attempted to perfect techniques of producing cheaper cotton prints with semi-skilled labour. The block printers at the London works were a highly paid group of artisans, partly because the occupation was traditionally seasonal and united to that of the more highly-skilled block cutting (or engraving), and partly because the men appear to have established a strong union which worked for restriction of apprenticeship.[29] Josephus Smith of Livesey, Hargreaves & Co. recruited a number of London workmen for the firm's

The Peels: Origins and Technical Innovations 43

Mosney factory, but the 'gentlemen' printers brought independent and insolent attitudes with them and proved to be an expensive asset to maintain. Most of the Lancashire printers, and particularly the Peels, increased their output by training up their own apprentices. The apprentices could undertake the 'plain and easy work', in which Lancashire came to specialise, leaving the fine and multi-coloured chintz work to the London specialists. Nevertheless the Peels soon made 'a considerable progress in the business which the Londoners beheld with an envious eye'.[30]

During the later 1770s the Peels were labouring to achieve the London standard in the quality of their printing. The details of their progress are unfortunately lost but there can be no doubt of their success. By 1783 they had attained the standard of the leading metropolitan firms, as attested by the journal of Samuel Rowland Fisher, a Philadelphia merchant who was travelling in England at this time:

> T. Johnston took me to the warehouse of Hayworth [Howarth], Peel, Yates, & Tipping, [a firm] very large in the printing Calicoes & Cottons of British manufacture. Very large quantities are made in the Neighbourhood of Bolton & Blackburn, their prints are done at Bury & they appear to me to be the best manufacture, well printed and the cheapest I have ever seen. They have and will command all the trade which used to be carried on near London.

The American sources leave no doubt that the Manchester warehouses were supplying copper plate prints from at least 1768, and that the Peels and their partners were among the leaders of this impressive capture of the London trade.[31]

The Peels began to experiment with the techniques of roller printing soon after the bankruptcy of Livesey, Hargreaves & Co. in the summer of 1788. The earliest discovery, made by one of their mechanics called Christopher Roberts, was the use of wooden rollers studded with pins in various simple patterns.[32] The main problem in roller printing was that of supplying an even flow of colour to the roller, but this was solved by Burch, another of the Peels' workmen, who devised a short, woollen endless-blanket which fed the colour evenly to the printing cylinder.[33] Engraved copper cylinders quickly followed wooden rollers but the older techniques of pencilling and block and copper plate printing survived for the better quality work. For some years the principal advantage of roller printing was in the fast production of monochrome prints. According to the Peels' Church manager, James Thompson, writing in 1808,

'With a well constructed cylinder press, and proper arrangements for accelerating the work, one man and a boy will print 200 pieces of 28 yards each in the same time that a flat press man will print twelve pieces or a block printer eight; that is, in one day'. The details can be elaborated as follows:

Daily output of an operative calico printer, 1808

	Pieces	Output (yards)
Block printer	8	224
Copper press printer	12	336
Copper cylinder printer	200	5,600

SOURCE: Abraham Rees, 'Copper Plate Calico Printing', *Cyclopaedia* (Mar. 1808).

Thompson went on to explain that the cylinder machines 'are constructed to work one, two, and even three colours, but are generally confined to one; the difficulty and delay in adjusting the several cylinders to each other when more than one colour is worked counteracting, in great measure, the chief advantage [economy of time and labour] of the machine'.[34] However, as Dingler explained, the taste of the ordinary consumer was satisfied with a good print of one or two colours rather than a *pot-pourri* of colours, and the new machine was 10 times as profitable as the more traditional technique. It was found easier to print with two colours by combining wooden rollers, whose surface was decorated with patterns traced in pins and copper wire, with the engraved copper rollers. This idea, called the union or mule printing machine, was contrived about 1805 by James Burton while he was engineer at the Peels' Church works.[35] Copper plate printing survived, though with diminishing importance, until after the middle of the nineteenth century.[36]

This brief survey of the Peels' technical interests leads to the impressive conclusion that they managed to maintain the closest possible contact with the rapid advance of textile technology for at least 50 years. Their ideal was to form partnerships with outstanding inventors and although this seldom succeeded they managed to obtain more advantage from these innovations than most of their British competitors. In the pages that follow it will be seen that the maximum exploitation of their interest was only inhibited by aspirations beyond technical achievement and profit maximisation.

Chapter 3

The Expansion of the Peel Industrial Empire under Robert ('Parsley') Peel

The Act of Parliament that required the warp of printed 'cottons' to be made of linen yarn was repealed in 1774, and the pioneers of calico printing in Lancashire saw the way clear for rapid expansion. Howarth, Peel & Yates dissolved their partnership 'to enable the principals to form more extensive concerns'.[1] 'Parsley' Peel built his own works at Church, a country site on the River Hindburn, near Blackburn. Three of his sons who had reached manhood – William, Jonathan and Lawrence – were taken into partnership, while young Robert, the most promising member of his family, moved to Bury to join his uncle Jonathan Howarth and William Yates in a new concern. The fifth son, Joseph, was still of school age at this time, but in 1789, when he was 23 or 24, he was made the principal partner in his father's Cheapside (London) warehouse, no doubt after a suitable apprenticeship in the City.[2]

The size and early growth of Peel, Yates & Co.'s works at Church can be traced in the Sun Fire Office policy of 1787 (Table 9). The original development is probably represented by the first three items in the policy: a small printing shop (for block and madder work), a pencilling shop (for 'China blue' work) and a 'bowkhouse' for cleaning the calicoes. The growing prosperity of the concern brought two further print shops, one about as big as the first – (which would be about the size of an eight-roomed house) – the other as much as three times the size. The three workshops were all built on different sites about the town and a calender house was built on a fourth. The total fixed capital investment, including a new development at Burnley, a rising centre of calico weaving 11 miles east of Blackburn, was only a little more than William Wilson's Ainsworth works had been a dozen years' earlier.[3]

Table 9 Valuation of Peel, Yates & Co.'s Church works, 1787

Item	Fixed assets (£)	'Utensils, stock and goods' (£)
Old printing shop	200	2,000
Long pencilling shop	150	500
Old bowkhouse and room	200	2,400
Great printing shop on Glebe Sands	600	1,400
New stove house on said Sands	50	250
Warehouse and room adjacent	100	1,500
New printing shop on Church Bank Estate	200	500
New pencilling shop on said estate	600	2,000
Calender house on Lord Petre's estate	60	550
Total at Church	**2,160**	**11,000**
New pencilling shop and warehouse at Burnley	400	1,000
Cotton factory at James Topper's estate, Burnley	600	300
Total at Burnley	**1,000**	**1,300**
Policy total		**15,460**

SOURCE: Sun OS: 347/535221, 25 Sep. 1787.

The Church printworks grew rapidly in its first five years and in 1779 Peel had opened a 'manufacturing warehouse' at Altham, six miles from Blackburn, to card and spin yarn for the domestic calico weavers and to receive the completed fabrics. The shortage of yarn that Hargreaves had suffered 10 years earlier had now become a shortage of woven cloth. But the destruction of the machinery at Altham in the riots of 1779 induced Peel to divert his capital to Burton-on-Trent and to Bolton, leaving Bury as the centre for calico printing.[4] The works at Church were not closed down but plans for expansion in the country districts of north-east Lancashire were left to the second generation, in the 1790s. This is a theme to which we shall return.

The Howarths separated from the Peels in 1781 and built their own works at Stakes Hall, Mill Hill, to the south-west of Blackburn. The partners were 'Parsley' Peel's nephews, Edmund and John Howarth and, later, Josephus Smith, a former partner in Livesey, Hargreaves & Co.[5] The firm reached its meridian about 1794 when its assets in Blackburn, Manchester and London were valued at £28,650, placing it amongst the leading dozen firms in the cotton industry at the time, though much inferior in size to the Peels. The Mill Hill printworks were valued at £9,615 and the adjacent cotton mill at £4,045. There were large warehouses in Cannon Street, Manchester (£5,600) and 129 Cheapside, London (£6,500), as well as smaller ones in Blackburn and Manchester. Two surviving corn mills on the site and a variety of small property made up the rest of the insurance valuation.[6] In 1795 the Howarths' business assets were suddenly reduced to £17,200, mainly by a fall in the value of their stock in London and Manchester, and in 1799 they became bankrupt.[7] The reasons for this disaster are not on record, but the close family connections between the Peels and the Howarths suggest that the former were not unaffected.

There were good economic reasons for choosing Burton-on-Trent as a site for the development of cotton mills. The growing town stood at the head of the Trent Navigation and its proximity to the Trent and Mersey Canal, recently completed, gave it a good position on the main route between Nottingham and Manchester, which were the two principal centres of the cotton industry at the time. An energetic group of merchants that included Joseph Wilkes, cheese factor and banker, and Sampson Lloyd, the Birmingham owner of Burton foundry, had taken control of the Trent Navigation in 1762 and embarked on a policy of expansion. In 1766 they had secured a lease of the site of the old-town fulling mill so as to repair the sluices and regulate the flow of water into the Navigation, and it was this site that they sub-leased to Peel in 1780. Burton's once famous manufacture of heavy woollen cloth had virtually disappeared by the middle of the eighteenth century, but fragmentary records show that Peel developed a trading relationship with brewers like Wilson and Dickinson, while his dependence on the Lloyds may be inferred from the fact that, unlike other cotton spinners in peripheral situations, he did not find it necessary to build extensive workshops for machine building near his mills.[8]

The value of the Burton site can be assessed by comparison with the remote sites chosen by other Manchester-based cotton spinners in the late 1770s and 1780s - Joseph Thackeray at Cark-in-Cartmel on the edge of the Lake District, Salvin Brothers at Durham, William Douglas and Peter Atherton at Hollywell and Greenfield (North Wales), John Haigh at Marsden, high in the Pennines in the upper Colne Valley, and Gideon Bickerdike in Perthshire, to mention but a few.[9] Those who found sites nearer to Manchester or Nottingham were frequently frustrated by inadequate supplies of water for power. Peel had the ample sources of the Trent at his disposal and landlords - the owner and lessees of the Trent Navigation - who were anxious, in their own interest, to encourage the growth of local trade.

Peel was established in Burton by March 1780 and in the same year his first cotton mill, the Weir Mill, was opened. Arkwright's patent was still in force at the time, but whether Peel became a licensee or evaded royalties by his own patent of 1779 is not clear.[10] A second building was erected in 1784 on the edge of the town at Bond End and connected with the Trent by a canal known as Peel Cut, across Burton meadows. The surviving building suggests a warehouse for raw cotton brought up the Trent, perhaps housing a few manually operated machines such as jennies. The building was extended in 1791 by the installation of a 30 hp Watt engine. However, before this time, probably in 1787, a second water mill was built on the Trent below Burton bridge and adjacent to Lloyds' foundry.[11]

The partners at Burton were the same as those for the Church concerns: Robert Peel senior, William Yates, and Peel's three sons, William, Jonathan and Lawrence. The younger Robert Peel was not a partner but, as we shall see, benefited from his father's connections at Burton when he moved to Tamworth. The evidence of the Sun insurance valuations that the first two Burton mills were on the pattern of the earliest mills built by Arkwright, is supported by the evidence of the surviving building on the site (known as Winshill (Table 10)). Jonathan Peel was the managing partner after his father retired to Ardwick Green but he does not appear to have maintained the momentum of the early growth at Burton although he did move into power-loom weaving, using Radcliffe's patent, about 1804.[12]

Table 10 Valuation of Peel, Yates & Co.'s cotton mills at Burton-on-Trent, 1795

Mill	Buildings (£)	Machinery (£)	'Millwright's work' (£)	Steam Engine (£)	Stock (£)	Mill total (£)
Weir mill (1780)	1,254	1,590	244	0	126	3,214
Winshill mill (c. 1787)	1,000	1,280	256	0	150	2,686
Bond End mill (1784, 1791)	2,118	2,762	570	1,500	300	7,250
Total	4,372	5,632	1,070	1,500	576	13,150

SOURCE: Sun CS: 7/640034, 21/674492, 21/676405; Royal Exchange Co. Registers: 30/144536.

The elder Peel was clearly conscious of the difficulties of establishing a new centre of the cotton industry and recognised the need of investment on a considerable scale. When Lord Paget suggested a cotton mill to employ 50 or 60 people on his estates in Anglesey, Peel observed that 'to do such a small business in a new country will be attended with so much expense and difficulties as not to produce the desired effect'.[13] The Burton development was successful in the sense that several local entrepreneurs were induced to divert capital into cotton and the town became a minor centre of the industry.[14] But more telling is Peel's decision in 1787 to build a new and integrated concern eight miles from Manchester.

The emphasis which has been placed on 'Parsley' Peel's migration into the midlands has served to divert attention from what was certainly a much more significant development – the building of an integrated spinning, weaving and printing works at Mill Hill, Bolton, from about 1787. In the 1780s improved techniques of dyeing and bleaching were being introduced in Lancashire, thus rendering quite obsolete the methods on which Peel's business was founded.[15] The introduction of Lancashire-made muslins resulted in a further development in calico printing, as these finer cottons began to be printed, doubtless representing the most lucrative sector of the industry. All these innovations took place in Manchester, Bolton or Stockport, reasserting their position as the major centre of technical innovation as well as the commercial hub of the cotton manufacturing region.[16]

The Manchester Literary and Philosophic Society was founded in 1781 and shortly emerged as the north of England's forum for diffusion of new ideas on dyeing, bleaching and calico printing, and the main platform for the application of scientific method by pioneers like John Wilson, Charles Taylor and Dr Henry.[17] The Peels and their partners were not closely connected with this vigorous development, but no doubt benefited from the rise of new methods in the town.[18] It is not known when bleaching by sulphuric acid was introduced into Lancashire but this technique could not have been used on an extensive scale until the first lead chamber plant in the region was built on the Bridgewater Canal at Eccles, four miles from Manchester, in 1783,[19] shortly to be followed by several others in the locality.[20] When Berthollet demonstrated the bleaching properties of chlorine the Manchester trade immediately recognised its possibilities and in 1788 the Peels joined numbers of other manufacturers in petitioning Parliament against the spurious claims of a French firm for a British patent.[21] Among the first to experiment with chlorine and with non-toxic solutions of the gas were Peter Ainsworth of Haliwell (Bolton) and his son Richard. They employed a Frenchman called Vallette, from the famous Javelle (Paris) chemical works, to build experimental plant for them.[22] It was at just this period that 'Parsley' Peel commenced partnership with Thomas Ainsworth (1759–1831), Peter's youngest brother, as muslin manufacturers and calico printers at Mill Hill, Bolton.[23] The Mill Hill works were 'Parsley' Peel's most ambitious venture and the decision to divert the major investment programme to Bolton clearly represented a turning point in the history of the family business necessitated by the need to keep abreast of technical developments. Peel, Ainsworth & Co. also built a new steam-powered mule spinning mill by the Mersey at Warrington, doubtless to take advantage of the cheap transport from Liverpool, but for some reason this was shortly given up.[24]

Peel's works at Bolton were evidently planned as an integrated manufacturing colony to compete with Arkwright's Cromford, Strutt's Belper, and others established by pioneers of the cotton industry. Characteristically, however, Peel did not contrive the kind of spectacle that Arkwright sought at Cromford. At the period of Peel's retirement it included joiners', turners' and blacksmiths' machine shops, three cotton spinning mills, a muslin picking shop and extensive mule spinning rooms. The watch house provided security for the acres of fabrics tentered in the fields about. Peel provided 53 houses for his workers on the site, 42 of them in a development known as Bengal Square, with weaving shops under the domestic accommodation. The cost of this workers' housing, taking into account the industrial use of the basement, suggests a better standard than that at several factory colonies of the period.[25] Thomas Ainsworth had a large house on the site, and he evidently managed the whole enterprise. Satellite to the concern were seven warehouses – at Manchester (Peel Street), Burnley, Colne, Chorley, Middleton, Hindley, Warrington and Paisley (Scotland), with additional spinning mills erected at Latchford (Warrington) in 1787 and at Stockport in 1795. It appears that the warehouses were used as yarn distribution and calico receiving depots for weavers employed by Peel in country districts.[26] Some yarns were also sent to Paisley to be woven. The valuation of the Bolton works in 1794 is set out in Table 11. The total valuation reached £10,000 in 1790 and 1791 and then shot up to £31,000 in 1794, perhaps partly as a result of the enterprise of the second generation who were admitted to partnerships at this time, and partly as a reflection of the rapid expansion

Table 11 Valuation of Peel, Ainsworth & Co.'s property, 1 May 1795

Item	Value (£)
Spinning factories and shops	
Latchford, Warrington workshops	2,300
Bolton old mill	3,000
Bolton new mill	1,450
Little Bolton mill	2,000
Bolton workshops	1,450
Stockport (and warehouse)	1,200
Total	**11,400**
Warehouses	
Friars Green, Warrington	300
Burnley	500
Chorley	1,000
Middleton	400
Hindley, Wigan	200
Turton	100
Paisley, Scotland	1,500
Peel Street, Manchester	10,800
Total	**14,800**
Printworks etc. at Little Bolton	
Printworks	4,265
Bengal Square (42 weavers' houses, looms and stock)	1,340
11 other cottages and smithy	250
Watchhouse, counting house, etc.	2,200
Thomas Ainsworth's house and contents	1,045
Total	**9,100**
Policy total	**35,300**

SOURCE: Sun CS: 9/640809. For previous developments, see OS: 369/572748, 374/580715; CS: 3/627272. For subsequent developments, see CS: 13/653286.

characteristic of the Lancashire cotton industry during these years.

Table 11 serves to direct attention to the large amount of capital invested in country warehouses. Investment in spinning was relatively modest and individual units were on a small scale, only three out of five using mechanical power. The valuation of the printworks seems quite small, certainly by comparison with those of Sir Robert

Peel at Bury. Summarily, it emerges from the analysis that 'Parsley' Peel's business at Bolton was more dispersed than that of 'factory patriarchs' like Arkwright, Strutt and Oldknow, and that his factory colony was founded almost as much on domestic calico weaving as factory spinning and printing.

From the late 1780s until the closing years of the French Wars the Peels' early site at Church Bank (opened in 1772) was the starting point for vigorous new initiatives under the direction of the second and third generation. New printing works were opened on water mill sites in and about Church, at Foxhill Bank, at Accrington and at Sawley (to the north-east of Clitheroe), while a further works at Oakenshaw (Clayton-le-Moors) was held for a short period in the late 1780s. Machine printing was being used at Church Bank by 1795.[27] The rapid growth of calico printing soon put strains on the output of the handloom weavers and new sources of supply had to be sought. According to a contemporary the general practice of the industry at this period was for manufacturers to 'establish their weaving ... in all the little villages about [their works] in some of which they put a manager and take apprentices and also give out work to the inhabitants at their houses.'[28] The Peels built on this practice by opening what they called 'manufacturing warehouses' around Church. The largest of these centres was at Burnley, where the Peels also opened a large cotton mill in 1790, as well as the printworks already referred to. By 1793 there were also country branches at Lower House (near Burnley), Padiham, Harewood and Ribchester, and by 1798 Altham was revived and Gisburn and Sawley added.[29] The printworks were also the focus of colonies of houses which were probably built for weavers as well as journeyman printers. Certainly the building in squares (Nelson Square consisting of 37 houses at Church Bank and Duncan Square of 22 houses at Foxhill Bank) is reminiscent of 'Parsley' Peel's weavers' colony at Bolton.[30] The isolation of Church and the satellite works from their main markets in London and abroad was eased in 1790–1 when the narrow and tortuous old road was replaced by a turnpike from Bury to Haslingden, Blackburn, and Whalley, the district in which the Peels' more northerly works were located. Several Peels were trustees. The Leeds–Liverpool Canal, 128 miles long and commenced in 1770, finally reached Liverpool in 1816 and Manchester in 1821. The route passed through Church valley and in 1810 an arm was cut to the Church Bank works.[31]

But before the opening of the Canal was joyously celebrated, there were clear signs that the Church Peels had reached their climacteric.

Table 12 Valuation of the Peels' industrial property in the Blackburn district, 1787–1811

Date of valuation	Church printworks (£)	Branch warehouses and mills (£)	Manchester warehouse (£)	Total (£)
1787	13,260	2,300	8,000	23,560
1789	13,260	2,300	10,680	26,240
1791	23,710	1,500	13,000	38,210
1795	20,495	13,325	13,000	46,820
1798	20,495	20,775	13,000	54,270
1809 } 1811 }	42,070	15,610	13,500	71,180

SOURCES: Sun OS: 347/535221, 360/554227, 376/582862; CS: 7/640034, 21/674492, 87/837725, 100/8650121.

Although the total investment continued to rise until *c*. 1810, there was a fall in the numbers of manufacturing warehouses soon after the turn of the century; by 1809 only five years were being insured (see Table 12). Then some of the smaller printworks were sold off: Burnley in 1808, Sawley and Lower House in 1812, and Foxhill Bank in 1813.[32] Burnley mill was destroyed by fire in 1798 but not rebuilt.[33] The Church Bank works and remaining manufacturing interests in the locality would have been sold at this time if suitable customers could have been found. In the event, the Church works remained in family ownership until 1836, the last of their manufacturing interests to be disposed of, but this was only because it proved difficult to find a buyer with adequate capital. The concern was advertised for sale in 1811, 1822 and 1835, when the buyer could only afford to occupy part of the extensive site and buildings.[34] Meanwhile the second and third generation Peels followed Sir Robert into the ranks of the country gentry, a succession of them functioning as squires of Accrington.[35]

Chapter 4

The Structure of Sir Robert Peel's Enterprises

The only informative source on the early life of 'Parsley' Peel's most able son, Robert II (or Sir Robert, as we shall call him) is an anonymously written work called *Public Characters of 1803–04*. The approach is characteristic of the flattery of eminent men of the age, but makes a substantial point:

> The comparatively rude state of this infant [cotton] trade at that time [*c.* 1760] furnished a wide field for the display of the inventive faculties and persevering industry of Sir Robert Peel. He devoted himself very early to explore the powers of mechanical combinations ... [and] soon became sensible of the improvements to which machinery was susceptible ... The contemporaries of his youth are unanimous in their testimony that he discovered a precocious attachment to books, and an insatiable thirst of knowledge ... The hours that others dissipated under pretence of recreation were employed by him in books and the midnight lamp incessantly witnessed the patient labour with which he cultivated his intellectual faculties.

Sir Robert clearly inherited his father's mechanical ability, but he was not limited to the empirical knowledge of his forebears. A prospering father gave him access to education, so that familiarity with machinery and trade practices was united with a notable erudition, a distinction that placed him in a class above most – perhaps nearly all – his contemporaries in the Lancashire cotton industry. All the early accounts pay tribute to the younger Robert Peel's abilities and energy as an entrepreneur. His father provided him with important initial advantages: an education at Blackburn

Plate 1 The first Sir Robert Peel, from a portrait by Sir Thomas Lawrence (Earl Peel's collection)

Grammar School, where he probably acquired some knowledge of French and German as well as classical languages, and an apprenticeship to one of the Blackburn Yateses, followed by a period of commercial experience in London and on the Continent.[1]

Sir Robert Peel's nephew has left us a revealing account of his uncle's drive: 'He was an ambitious man. He loved money, but he loved it principally as an instrument of power.... He was a man of untiring energy', constantly working out new schemes for the development of his business.[2] He carried his boundless energy into every branch of his organisation. Like Arkwright he 'introduced among his operatives that order, arrangement and subdivision of employment which form the marked characteristics of the factory system ... he insisted on a system of punctuality and regularity which approached the discipline of military drill', and no doubt this organisation covered his army of apprentices, whose health, cleanliness and clothing was strictly attended to at work-houses at Radcliffe and Hinds, near Bury.[3]

'Peel was to calico printing what Arkwright was to spinning: a man of iron mind and frame, possessing great mercantile talent and application', apparently a very rare quality amongst the early printers.[4] Peel's keenness and drive as an entrepreneur is also revealed in a family recollection of him as 'a man of invincible perseverance in business. He formed all the plans and his partner Mr Yates carried out the details.' His scheming mind proved to be the taskmaster of a long sequence of later partners.

Like other well-known entrepreneurs of the period Peel believed passionately in 'self-help' and preached his faith by practical ways of encouraging frugality, providence and self-reliance among his workers. He established friendly societies at Bury, allowing them five per cent interest on their funds and making periodic donations to them. Worthy employees often received gifts and legacies and institutions like the Sunday Schools and Methodist Chapels enjoyed the partners' patronage. In later years Peel tried to persuade Pitt to adopt a scheme for a new national insurance company to safeguard the funds of workers' benefit societies.[5]

The foundations of the future Sir Robert Peel's fortune and fame were laid in a dozen years of 'silent industry' following his move to Bury in 1772. It was precisely the period at which Arkwright was winning his battle for pre-eminence in the spinning sector of the industry, but by no greater degree of devotion to business than that shown by the young Peel. He lived on the job, married his partner's daughter and, being 'a very indifferent and unintelligible writer', employed her to write the firm's most important letters. Meanwhile she bore him four sons and two daughters. Once a week he sat up all night with his pattern-drawer waiting 'to receive any new patterns which the London coach, arriving at midnight, might bring down.' If bad weather threatened he would be up from his bed to make the nocturnal round of his bleachfields to assure himself that all was secure. The combination of total dedication to business, stamina, perception and planning demanded success, and he rapidly attained it.[6]

The choice of Bury for the site of the Peels' most important works was a characteristically perceptive one. The mills on the Chamber Hall estate were only nine miles from Manchester which was just beginning to emerge as the northern centre for calico printing (see p. 26). Bury printworks, like other Peel concerns, began in a modest way. 'Parsley' Peel is reported to have given his son £500 to commence business on his own account and perhaps this matched the contribution of the other two partners. The original site at Elton was at first rented but in 1780 the opportunity was taken to purchase some 74 acres – an invaluable addition, for much land was needed at calico works to dry the washed and printed fabrics. For the first 15 years or so Peel and his wife lived in a small house with two living rooms and a scullery and two bedrooms above. The rapidly growing family compelled them to move to Chamber Hall in 1787 but Peel still only had to walk across a croft to reach his works.[7] Although Robert Peel formally separated himself from his father and brothers when he moved to Bury there are clear indications that close business collaboration was maintained.[8]

Some of the technical achievements of the Bury printworks have already been noted (see Chapter 2). They were accompanied by an equally impressive rise in production so that by 1784 Peel could say that he employed at least 6,800 people and paid an annual excise tax of £20,000. An easy calculation indicates that he was already producing one-eighth of British output of printed textiles, an output second only to that of Livesey, Hargreaves & Co. (Table 13).

After the collapse of Livesey, Hargreaves & Co. the Bury works became the largest manufacturing unit in the Lancashire cotton industry, virtually employing the whole town. Dr Aikin, whose lengthy *Description of the Country from Thirty to Forty Miles around Manchester* (1795) seldom mentions the names of cotton manufacturers, singles out Peel and the Bury works for a flattering commentary:

Table 13 British output of printed textiles, 1784

Firm	Output (million yards)	% of total
Peels and partners	1.37	12.5
Livesey, Hargreaves & Co.	1.78	16.2
Other British firms	8.03	71.3
Total	**11.18**	**100**

SOURCES: *Gentlemen's Magazine*, LV, 1 (1785), pp. 448–9; T. S. Ashton, *An Economic History of England: the Eighteenth Century* (1955), p. 248, for total output.

The articles here made and printed are chiefly the finest kind of the cotton manufactory and they are in high request both in Manchester and London. The printing is performed in the most approved methods, both by wooden blocks and copper rollers, and the execution and colours are some of the very best of the Lancashire fabric.... Ingenious artists are employed in drawing patterns and cutting and engraving them on wood and copper, and many women and children in mixing and pencilling the colours, etc. The company has several other extensive works in the neighbourhood, as well on the Irwell as on the Roch. Some of these are confined to the carding, slubbing and spinning of cotton; others to washing the cottons with water wheels.... Boiling and bleaching the goods are performed at other works.[9]

The Sun insurance registers contain a detailed catalogue and valuation of the Bury works, as well as Sir Robert Peel's other interests in the area at the period at which Aikin wrote the description quoted above. (A summary of these details has been made for the compilation of Table 14.) When Howarth's sons opened their own works Peel promoted one of his employees, James Halliwell, to a partnership and brought in a Manchester merchant, Thomas Tipping. An adjustment was made about 1790 when Tipping left to establish his own works at Manchester and Edmund Yates, eldest son of Peel's partner and father-in-law William Yates, was made a partner.[10] About 1783 Peel, Yates & Co. started a second printworks at Ramsbottom, a valley site further up the Irwell, 13 miles from Manchester, and in this connection promoted Henry Warren, who was another trusted employee, to a partnership.

Table 14 Valuation of Peel, Yates & Co.'s works in the Bury area, 1795

Location and item	Fixed capital (£)	Stock and utensils (£)
Bury centre		
Elton Print Works, 27 buildings	5,060	27,020
20 cottages	600	
Cotton mills at Bury, Burrs (2), Heywood, Ratcliffe, Summerseat (3) and Hinds	14,200	3,700
13 cottages	520	
Hinds Dye Works	850	6,100
Total	**21,230**	**36,820**
Ramsbottom centre		
Ramsbottom Print Works, 17 buildings	**2,545**	**14,865**
Warehouses		
Peel St, Manchester	1,500	15,000
Yorkshire St, Rochdale	100	800
Total	**1,600**	**15,800**
Policy total	**25,375**	**67,485**

SOURCE: Sun NS: Vol. 7: summary of policy nos. 640,035, 640,037, 26 Mar. 1795. Some workers' cottages were probably insured with another company, as *MM*, 14 Jan. 1806, refers to 'many cottages for work people' in an advertisement for the sale of the Ramsbottom works. For the full inventory see Appendix B, pp. 217–19.

In 1795 the fixed capital at the Bury works was insured for a little over £5,000 while the Ramsbottom works was valued slightly in excess of £2,500. The Bury works was evidently the largest in Britain at the time, being almost twice the size of its nearest rivals in London and the north of England according to the insurance registers. Nevertheless the size and arrangement of the buildings at the Peels' calico printing centres was fairly conventional. Bury consisted of some 27 small, cottage-like buildings that had gradually replaced the wooden sheds that Peel & Yates first used. They were scattered round the water mills that originally occupied the site and formed a straggling and far-extended collection of workshops. Ramsbottom consisted of 17 similar buildings surrounded by 40 acres of tenter fields. Some of the buildings housed a single function – notably printing – but most were divided among several. All the indications are that they were erected in an *ad hoc* manner as need dictated, a development already noted as characteristic of the London calico printing industry by *c.* 1775. The only advance in physical arrangements that can be discerned is that, unlike the pioneer factories at Church (Blackburn), the manufacturing operations were focused on a single site rather than being scattered round the town. The Bury works were not rationalised in one building until 1821–2, and the organisers then were not the Peels but their successors, the Grant Brothers. It is interesting to notice that this rationalisation was undertaken just 30 years after that at Jouy and 50 years after the building of Schuele's celebrated 'palace factory' print works at Augsburg.

The Bury and Ramsbottom works were supported by nine cotton mills in the locality, only the Radcliffe Bridge mill being built on as large a scale as Arkwright's. Two of the nine did not have mechanical power so they were evidently used for manually operated jennies and mules. (Power-assisted mules were only just coming into use in Lancashire at this time.) In fact it seems likely that all but Radcliffe Bridge were mule spinning workshops. By 1803, when the Peels had 15 small mills in the Bury and Church areas, these units were still small. The reason can be readily understood from a general appreciation of the structure and development of cotton spinning at the end of the eighteenth century. The centre of the manufacturing region – Bolton, Manchester, Stockport and the satellite villages – came to specialise in the finer mule-spun yarns, while the Pennine periphery, where power was more abundant and cheap, retained the trade in the coarser, Arkwright-mill yarns.[13]

Nevertheless it may seem surprising that the Peels made so little an attempt to invest in the multi-storey mills that other Manchester merchant families were building in the closing years of the eighteenth century. Did the family lose contact with the rapid advance of steam power technology at this time? Or was their commercial success followed by a more conservative policy than that on which the family fortunes were built? It is worth turning aside for a moment to examine the justification for Peel's preference for the smaller unit in spinning.

The Peels certainly kept themselves abreast of technical advances in steam power. 'Parsley' Peel studiously followed Arkwright's attempt to apply a Newcomen engine to cotton spinning at Manchester in 1783 and rightly concluded that its motions were not smooth enough. Peel's friend at Burton, Joseph Wilkes, contacted

James Watt to enquire after a patent engine for his Measham mill, but Watt was discouraging and the purchase of a patent engine was deferred until 1787.[14] In the same year Thomas Ainsworth asked to see the Albion flour mills that Rennie was erecting and equipping with Watt engines, after which his partner (Peel) took the plunge and bought a 14 hp Boulton & Watt engine for the Warrington mule spinning mill, probably the first time that steam and mules had been married.[15]

In 1790 Peter Drinkwater opened the first mill in Manchester to rely solely on steam power, to be shortly followed by Philips & Lee at Salford. Peter Atherton, the Warrington machine builder and former partner of Arkwright, began to furnish plans for the erection of steam mills, buildings of six storeys containing 3,000 spindles driven by 30 hp Boulton & Watt engines. John Peel visited Atherton at Liverpool to consult him about 'a steam engine or two' which he proposed to erect at Burton, and in the same year, 1791, he bought a 30 hp Watt engine for extension on the Bond End site.[16] The engine did not, however, fulfil expectations and within a year John Peel was complaining that it had not been properly constructed.[17] One might be inclined to blame Peel's workmen but for the fact that other cotton spinners were making similar complaints at the period.[18] Their disgust with the steam engine patentees is indicated by the sale of the Watt engine at Warrington in 1792 and their purchase of a Sherratt & Bateman pirate engine for the Bolton mill and Burnley calico works.[19] The truth is that the substitution of the steam engine for water power was a gradual process and those who were on good mill sites found the negligible running costs offered a decisive advantage. It has been calculated that on a prime site the water wheel was capable of competing with the steam engine until the mid nineteenth century.[20] Sir Robert Peel, the most successful of the second generation, continued to rely on water power alone at Tamworth with mills built very close to the Arkwright pattern.[21] There was indeed little change in the pattern of mill buildings until after 1830.[22] Consequently, entrepreneurs with modest capital continued to enter the industry and up to the end of the century numbers of successful firms, like the Peels, grew by multiplication of small spinning, printing and bleaching units. In the opening years of the nineteenth century a handful of the most technically advanced Manchester firms established their leadership of fine spinning on the basis of multi-storey steam-powered spinning factories, but the typical manufacturing unit remained much smaller.[23]

There is one very important feature of the structure of Sir Robert Peel's business that finds no reflection in the earlier insurance policies but is made clear in the 1803 policy. Reference has already been made to 'Parsley' Peel's country warehouses as centres for the employment of calico weavers, and the greater size of his son's printworks at Bury and Ramsbottom leaves no doubt that, directly or indirectly, he must have provided employment for many more handloom weavers. A contemporary writer records that the Bury works 'had at one time some thousands of handloom weavers in Darwen, in Padiham, in Bacup, and in Burnley, and also put out by their agents in many parts of Lancashire.'[24] In 1803 there were 15 of these agents, with stock varying from £100 to £900, insured by Sir Robert Peel, and a warehouse owned directly by Peel and his partners at Stockport. The agents were situated as far north as Colne, as far west as Walton, Liverpool and to the east as far as Chapel[25] (see Fig. 2). There was nothing unusual about the dispersion of managers and agents. Other merchants like the Greggs of Styall, and Daintry, Ryle & Co. of Macclesfield employed weavers and trained apprentices in more remote parts of the Pennines.[26] The insurance records, however, which include numerous policies of Lancashire merchants, contain no hint of any comparable scatter of agents attached to another concern.

After Sir Robert Peel moved to Tamworth the printworks at Bury and Ramsbottom were not expanded any further, and they may be regarded as having reached their meridian about the time of Dr Aikin's visit. The inventory of 1795 was little changed in 1803 and there was a slight decline in the investment insured at Ramsbottom.[27] However, Peel continued to expand his interest in cotton mills in Lancashire by multiplying the small water-powered units. The nine mills of 1795, including one at Tamworth, had increased to 10 in 1797 and 14 in 1803, five of them on the same site at Summerseat. Transport and communications between the Bury printworks, the mills and the Manchester and Liverpool warehouses became easier after the opening of the Manchester, Bolton and Bury Canal at the end of the century. The Canal was routed by the Bury works and linked in with the national network, and there was a direct water route to Tamworth.[28]

Sir Robert Peel's purchase of the pocket borough of Tamworth and his entry into Parliament in 1790 is a familiar story for it has rightly been recognised as a milestone in the rise to power of the manufacturing middle classes, as well as a preface to the political career of his son, the future Prime Minister.[29] However, most

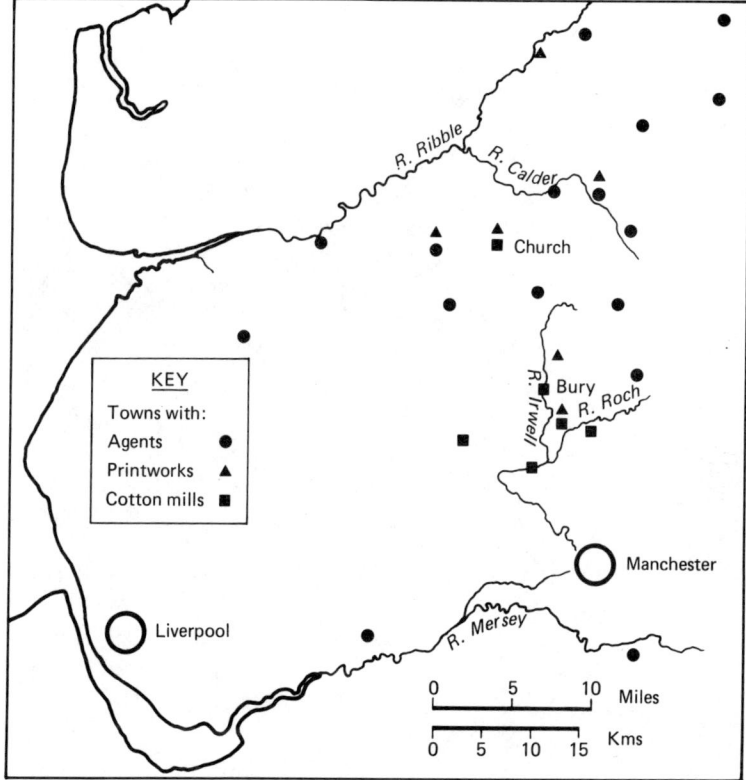

Fig. 2 Dispersion of the Peels' printworks, cotton mills and putting-out agents in Lancashire, c. 1805

historians have been writing about Prime Minister Peel rather than his father or grandfather, and the first Sir Robert's motives for entering politics, as well as his economic reasons for migration into the midlands, have been left in some obscurity. A proper examination of the Peels' business demands that some analysis of this development be attempted.

Even before the collapse of Livesey, Hargreaves & Co. in 1788 the Peels were taking the leading role in trade politics in Manchester. It is said that 'Parsley' Peel was the instigator and most active promoter of the protracted legal proceedings of 1781–5 which finally led to the termination of Arkwright's patent rights.[30] If this is true it would account for his popularity, for Arkwright was widely regarded as a tyrant in the trade. In the same period Peel became

Plate 2 Summerseat cotton spinning mills, from an old print in Manchester Public Library

The Structure of Sir Robert Peel's Enterprises 65

a spokesman for the Lancashire campaign against the newly-imposed fustian tax. In spring 1785, when petitions were pouring into the House of Commons from all sections of the Lancashire textile industries,[31] Peel and Josephus Smith represented the trade's plight to MPs.[32] The repeal of the tax must have brought Peel further status in the cotton trade, and in 1786 he was elected to the chair of the calico manufacturers and printers at a public meeting in Manchester.[33] Although Arkwright and his Nottingham partners had secured the repeal of the Calico Act the industry still laboured under a heavy excise duty, and the younger Robert Peel and his Manchester friends took up the cause of freedom from taxation. It was in the same cause that he entered Parliament and supported William Pitt, whom he regarded as an enlightened protector of industry.[34]

In 1790 a similar leading group of calico printers entered into a trial of strength with the block printers' trade union. The earliest block printers in Lancashire were highly paid artisans who had migrated from London and their union tried to maintain members' incomes at a metropolitan level.[35] The gradual introduction of roller printing was an obvious threat to their security of employment and the preliminary skirmish in 1786, already noted, was followed by a struggle lasting 13 weeks in summer 1790. The Peels and nine other leading firms published an ultimatum to the 'Journeyman printers, block cutters and drawers' threatening to instruct new workmen and to prosecute those on strike for forming a combination and the apprentices for breaking their bonds.[36] They made good their threat by taking on a great number of workmen as trainees, and women to work at the tables as pencillers. This finally broke the union's resistance.[37] But the continuing militancy of the union induced the Peels to move the foci of their printing operations into outlying districts where they could train up a more docile labour force.[38] William Peel and his Church Bank partners opened one of their new works as far away as Sawley, near Clitheroe, 34 miles from Manchester, and Peel, Yates & Co. planned to move the centre of their operations to Tamworth, 70 miles from the centre of the industry.[39]

If 'Parsley' Peel had recognised the drawbacks of location in the midlands, as we suppose, it follows that Tamworth was chosen without a realistic appraisal of its long-term economic possibilities. Certainly the peripheral situations of the new Peel works placed them on the edge of, and in the case of Tamworth, outside, the penumbra of the technical and commercial growth area. However, it could be argued that this was not something that could be foreseen in 1790 when the cotton industry was still expanding geographically. And in some respects Tamworth possessed important advantages to a textile manufacturer. It was a centre of an old, woollen-cloth industry, specialising in 'tammy' (a heavy worsted fabric in popular demand), and it had excellent communications. When Arthur Young visited Fazeley soon after Peel and Wilkes's purchase he thought that the site was 'probably the first situation for an inland town that is to be found in Great Britain, for here is the junction of the Birmingham and Coventry Canals, which unite Hull, Liverpool, Bristol and London.' The locality also offered cheap coal, plenty of water and labour at half the wages paid in Manchester (see Fig. 3).[40]

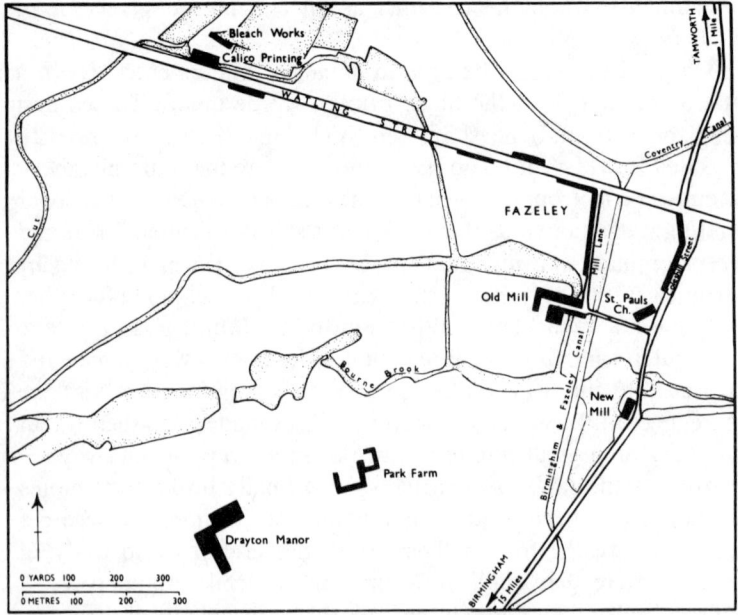

Fig. 3 Plan of Fazeley (Tamworth) as developed by the Peels, 1790–c. 1805

All the evidence suggests that Robert Peel put all his resources, financial and technical, into the Tamworth development in its early stages, and his workpeople enjoyed the idea of establishing a centre of the cotton industry rival to Manchester. His purchases were by no means limited to the £15,500 for the 120 houses needed for his election to Parliament. In partnership with Joseph Wilkes he also bought over 4,000 acres, including the hamlets of Drayton Bassett,

Sherrold, Fazeley and Bonehill, for £120,000. In a third deal he bought Drayton Manor for £74,880 and thus acquired a seat in the locality for himself.[41] The total purchase of landed estate dwarfed that being made by Arkwright at Cromford at the time.[42] Three able lieutenants, who had already worked their way up through the firm to partnerships, moved to Tamworth to establish the print works. With them went a journeyman from each of the departments to train a new labour force, all of whom were recruited locally. The new foremen were provided with houses and coal as well as their wages.[43]

Initially, Peel lost no time in exploiting his interest at Tamworth, for the first cotton mill was opened in Fazeley in spring 1791, an impressive 20 hp water mill which represented an investment of some £5,000. Joseph Wilkes of Measham, the most dynamic entrepreneur of the period in this part of the midlands, was a partner in the mill.[44] Tamworth Castle, a late Tudor house on a hillock overlooking the Tame bridge, and the Castle Mills were used for calico printing and machine building while more permanent buildings were being erected, and printworks were opened in Lady Meadow (Tamworth) in 1795 and Bonehill in 1797 at a cost, respectively, of £5,400 and £2,950.[45]

Circumstantial evidence suggests that the Peels may have found it more difficult to train up a labour force than they had anticipated. The experience of Charles Hulbert who left Manchester in 1803 'to obtain labour at a lower price than was then given in the vicinity of that and other manufacturing towns' seems to parallel that of the Peels. At Shrewsbury, like Tamworth an ancient centre of the woollen industry, he found difficulty in recruiting and retaining labour as 'the great portion of the young people willing to be employed in manufactories were engaged' to an existing works. Young people in the surrounding country areas, less habituated to industrial practice, were slow to learn, while:

> many of our instructed workpeople, notwithstanding all were engaged at regular wages for three years, left us for Manchester, Stockport &c.... We soon found that if business must be carried on to any great extent where hand labour was required, it must be in the neighbourhood of like manufactories, where an advance of wages would speedily obtain the number of hands required.[46]

The developments after 1791 were certainly not very impressive for a manufacturer whose net profit was said to be running at over £70,000 a year at this time, but there may have been other reasons. There is evidence to suggest that Peel almost over-reached himself

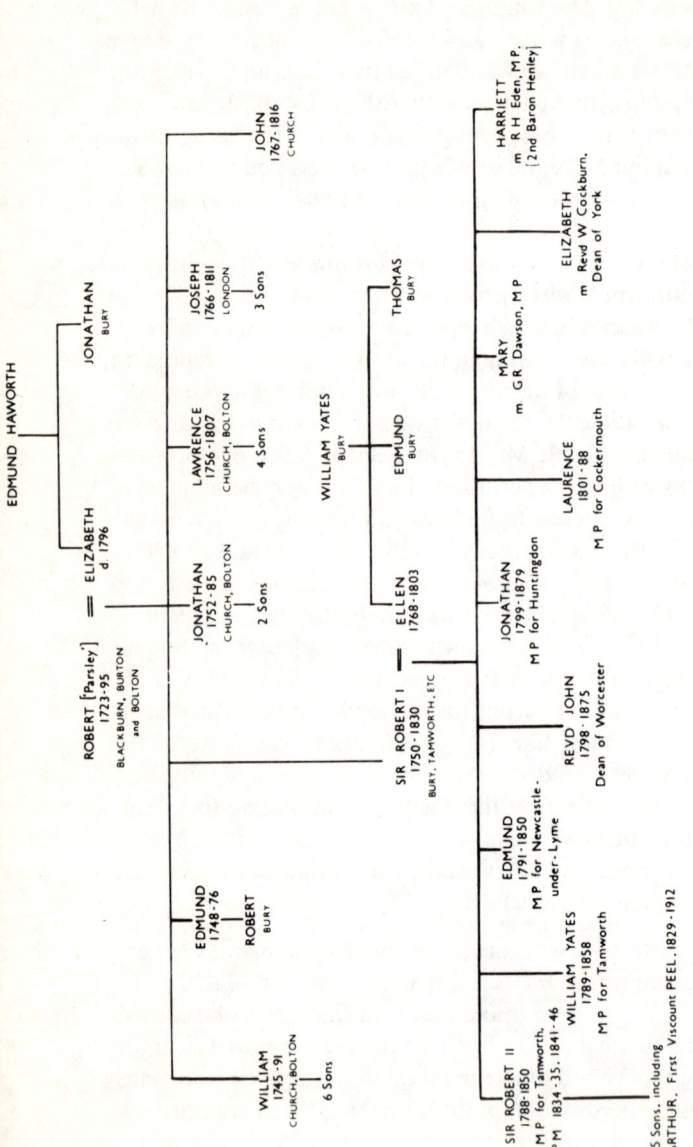

Fig. 4 The Peel family pedigree showing the principal marriage, business and political connections (SOURCE: *Gentleman's Magazine*, June 1830, p. 557.)

in the early 1790s, much as Samuel Oldknow, the pioneer muslin spinner, severely strained his credit in buying the Mellor estate.[47] Sir Lawrence Peel had no doubt that Sir Robert and his father retained their frugal habits to the end of their lives, and the plain buildings at Burton and Tamworth, without so much as a pediment, cornice or cupola to relieve the endless brick, seem to bear witness to their asceticism.[48] But these economies were not sufficient to make up for the 'disastrous year' that Peel's bank suffered in 1793.[49] Although there was a marked recovery by 1797 the bankruptcy of the Howarths in 1799, and of Peel, Wilkes, Dickenson and Goodall in 1806, probably restrained any grandiose scheme that Sir Robert had worked out for Tamworth.[50] From this period he began to run down his industrial interests and his brothers followed suit. Before turning to a closer examination of the various aspects of his industrial policies, it is worthwhile rounding off the story of his spectacular rise by taking a final glance at his social and political achievements.

Sir Robert Peel's purchase of Tamworth and his consequent election to Parliament was not merely an advertisement that he had won a fortune and now claimed to represent his industry and trade at Westminster. It also marked, both for him and his family, their entry to what the British call the 'Establishment', the rich landowning class that had traditionally expected to govern the country in both State and Church from generation to generation. Having secured a place for his family in the governing élite, Peel confidently expected their future to be there and not in the arduous and precarious life of manufacturing and merchanting. The full achievement of his ambition can be read in his obituary in the *Gentleman's Magazine*, part of which has been illustrated in Figure 4. Of Sir Robert's nine children, five became MPs, two daughters married MPs, one son became a Dean in the Church of England and one daughter married a clergyman who became a Dean. His most able son was twice Prime Minister and one of his grandsons entered the peerage as Viscount Peel, a line that still survives. The textile industry and trade was completely repudiated. Among the first generation of cotton mill owners, only the Arkwrights and Strutts were able to match this spectacular elevation up the social scale.

Chapter 5

Capital, Managers and Partners

Sir Robert Peel had some initial difficulties in recruiting capital for his works at Bury. Sir Lawrence Peel records that the first Sir Robert was wont to state that at the beginning of his business career 'the greatest difficulty which he had to surmount was the want of capital to keep pace with his schemes of extension. The profits of the business were exceedingly great and it admitted of great extension, but for some time the firm were hampered by the limited amount of their capital and credit....'[1] The Peels solved this problem by two strategies that are fairly familiar to students of the industrial revolution in Britain. First, they acquired buildings and power units quite cheaply by occupying existing water mill sites (often corn mills), buying a leasehold rather than freehold tenure. The old mills were demolished and rebuilt on a more appropriate scale and the leasehold converted to freehold tenure as and when profits allowed.[2] Buildings, as we have seen, were kept to economical standards. Second, they drew credit from established Manchester merchants. Their principal contact at the centre of the regional industry appears to have been Thomas Tipping (1747–1815), a yarn and cotton merchant who is said to have advanced 'thousands of pounds' to them, and became a partner in the Bury printworks soon after it was started. A connection of this kind was absolutely essential to a country *verlager* in the period before banks were established in Manchester and when firms were too small to have direct contact with London sources of capital. It is almost certain that Tipping was only the best-known of a number of established merchants and capitalists who advanced money to the Peel partnership, for it was said that when the first Sir Robert was at 'the height of his splendour and in his loftiest station in Bury', i.e. in the late 1780s, he made a virtue of his early indebtedness, often remarking 'the farther a man is in debt and the richer he is'.[3] This deliberate and repeated mockery of the conventional wisdom of the age was clearly the product of confidence derived from long success in working his business on credit. In the matter of trade credit, as in so many other matters, Sir Robert Peel was the successful heir to the policies of Livesey, Hargreaves & Co. (See pp. 28–33). The large profits of the early years of textile printing in the north of England (1770s–c. 1808) assured creditors of timely payment.

Apart from investment in land and buildings capital was needed for the purchase of raw cotton and 'drugs', i.e. dyestuffs and gums. In the formative years of the Peel family business the network of European international merchant houses had not yet extended to the north of England and the Peels had to rely on the system evolving in Manchester and Liverpool. In the early years at Bury the firm's wagon left every morning with calicoes for Manchester and returned in the evening with supplies from the merchants, and we may guess that Tipping was the major supplier and creditor. Later, one of Peel's most trusted managers, Hamer, travelled regularly to Liverpool to buy cotton from the new and rising class of brokers like Walton & Sons and Nicholas Waterhouse, and he is said to have sailed as far as Portugal to buy 'drugs'. The Liverpool brokers were accustomed to accept six-month bills on London banks or merchants in settlement of debts, and this period of credit helped to finance the manufacturing operations of Peels' and numerous other Lancashire firms. The Peels in turn granted extensive credit to local supporting tradesmen, especially in the textile and corn trade. We know all too little of the army of itinerant dealers who traditionally conducted much of the home trade but it is significant that the Grants, one of the families who migrated from Scotland without capital, did sufficiently well in Bury to purchase Sir Robert Peel's concerns in 1807.[4]

In so profitable and rapidly growing a business, the principal problem in the longer term was not the recruitment of capital but the training and retaining of managers to keep the numerous works under control. The Peels' first instinct, like that of their contemporaries, was to keep the business under family direction. Consequently, 'Parsley' Peel established a sequence of overlapping partnerships based on himself and his seven sons. They in turn expected dynastic control to continue into the next generation. The family outlook is no doubt epitomised in a Bury folk memory dating from about 1788 or 1789. The first Sir Robert Peel:

annually called his managers, drawers, cutters and calico printers together upon the green plat before Chamber House, where they ate and drank, sung and made flattering speeches to Mr. Peel. On one of these occasions Mr. Peel came to the front door with [his son] the present Sir Robert Peel in his arms and said, 'Gentlemen, I have long been a father to you, and this child which I have in my arms will be a father to you when I am gone hence'.

But the rapid growth of the business in the next decade, combined with the family's political ambitions, soon put strains upon family leadership. Nevertheless, means to control the business were evolved. At Bury the long-established practice was for the partners to meet every Monday morning for breakfast to discuss business policy, and as the business grew new managing partners were invited to join the founders at Chamber Hall. A policy of promotion within the business brought several capable men to share in the direction of the various branches. Again, according to local memories, the Bury company had three employees 'who held high situations in their cotton mills, calico printing works and compting houses, Mr. Hamer, Mr. Norris and Mr. Hardman, and they had the power to direct, suggest, and control the men, from the highest to the lowest, throughout the whole of these extensive manufactories'.[5] In other words, the day-to-day running of the Irwell Valley factories in and about Bury was entrusted to three supervisors, leaving the principals free to deal with the larger policy issues. Without such delegation it would have been impossible for Sir Robert to contemplate taking a seat in Parliament and leaving Bury for the new developments at Tamworth. Below the supervisory level, it was said, Sir Robert depended upon the trustworthiness of his Methodist workmen. As early as 1787 he wrote 'I have left most of my works in Lancashire under the management of Methodists, and they serve me excellently well.'[6] In practice, the trust in managers was limited for before the end of the century the Peels were demanding bonds of up to £500 from recruits to the ranks of their financial management.[7]

A recent writer suggests that the number of partnerships in which the younger Robert Peel was involved also points to his difficulty in raising capital.[8] The various Peel concerns were certainly built up on a complicated network of partnerships but, as we have seen, this was not for reasons of capital shortage alone, and it is important to distinguish the different categories of partners. Various records enable us to identify the different kinds of partners in the different branches of the Peel empire and to attempt an analysis of the reasons for their association with the family.

The lists of Peel concerns in the late eighteenth-century directories disguise the fact that at 'Parsley' Peel's manufacturing centres of Church and Bolton the three partners after himself were his sons, while Sir Robert's status as head of the business dynasty was recognised by a partnership in the Church, Burton and Bolton concerns after his father retired.[9] In due course Yates brought two of his sons into the concern, and the family interest was jealously guarded into the third and fourth generations. At Bury, Ramsbottom and Tamworth, Sir Robert Peel was initially the only representative of his family, but his partners in each case were his brothers-in-law, William and Edmund Yates, and in course of time he continued his father's policy of drafting sons, nephews, sons-in-law and grandsons into the concern.[10] The economic justification for this practice was the need for managers who would link the dispersed empire into a concern responsive to the policy of the principal partners, but not all the second-generation Peels were equal to the challenge of their calling. In particular, Jonathan, 'Parsley' Peel's second son, took over the Burton mills but failed to expand the concern. He quarrelled with Boulton & Watt, bringing the family to the brink of patent litigation,[11] and Joseph Peel, the youngest brother, saw the London merchant house with which he was associated slip into bankruptcy.[12] In 1799, Yates's third son went to New York to 'get up a large business for Peel, Yates & Co. but he fell into debt and ended up in gaol.

It was no doubt the recognition of these weaknesses, and also because of the extent of their concerns, that 'Parsley' Peel's sons found it necessary to offer partnerships to some of their able managers, particularly those with specialised skills, as in the sales, financial and technical aspects of the business; the importance of Hamer, Norris, and Hardman have already been explained. James Halliwell, who was ultimately a partner in the Bolton, Bury and Ramsbottom concerns, was 'originally a menial in the warehouse at Manchester', who rose through the positions of packer, traveller, and then agent at the Cannon Street (Manchester) warehouse, to his partnership.[13] James Greaves of the Manchester banking house of Peel, Greaves & Co. began his career as a bank clerk.[14] John Roberts was an engraver at Peel & Yates's Bury works before he became superintendent of their machinery and engravers and then a junior partner. With Sir Robert he moved to Tamworth, where he was a senior partner for a few years, before leaving to establish his own firm with Henry Warren, who had made his way up through the Peel business to a partnership at Ramsbottom.[15] James Thompson, who had the advantage of an education at Glasgow University and a family connection with the Peels, served in the London warehouse before becoming chemist and then manager at the Peels' Church Bank works.[16] These interesting instances illustrate the variety rather than exhaust the list of promotions to partnerships.[17]

In a rapidly growing industry there was inevitably a more or less continuous loss of managers and partners who left to establish their own concerns. Several of these became leading firms in the industry. James Thompson left the Peels in 1811 to establish his own print-works at Clitheroe, and his laboratory work on dyeing soon established him as the technical leader of the industry, a position which he retained until his death in 1852. In cotton spinning, former servants of the Peels also scored some notable successes. Robert Duck and Charles Potts left Sir Robert Peel in 1792 to open a cotton mill in Manchester, and their Boulton & Watts engine was one of the first to be installed in the town; in 1797 their factory was insured for £8,500.[18] A similar development took place when Richard Thompson, the superintendent of Peel's cotton mills at Burton, left to establish his own mill at Newcastle-under-Lyme.[19] These successes strongly suggest the Peels' discrimination in the selection of managers and the importance of their training with the parent company. Moreover, in the last two instances, surviving letters show that the Peels were ready to help the new firms with credit, and the new partners made no secret of their debt to their former employers.

The third category of partners owed their association with the Peels to a major advance into a new district where both capital and local connections were needed. Only three partners were recruited on this basis, but their connection with key developments gives them a crucial role in the Peel saga.

Thomas Tipping came into the business in the late 1770s when Peel & Yates were simultaneously developing their printworks and first cotton mills, and Howarth had withdrawn to open his own concern. Clearly, the intention was to develop the Manchester end of the business, and Tipping's experience was necessary to the country manufacturers at Bury. The association of the Bury partners with an established merchant reflects the common tendency of small but promising firms or individuals to find a 'patron' with trading connections and capital. Arkwright found Need and Strutt, Peter Atherton found first William Harrison, a Manchester fustian merchant, and then J. & T. Hodgson (Liverpool merchants). John

Smalley's sons attracted William Douglas and other Lancashire merchants to Holywell, and McConnel and Kennedy began their Manchester business in partnership with Sandfords, the fustian merchants.[20] The better documented histories of these other firms suggest that Tipping may have played an active role in the rapid development of the Bury works before leaving to open his own calico works (c. 1790).[21]

Tipping is also said to have been in partnership with Thomas Ainsworth of Halliwell (Bolton), who became a partner of 'Parsley' Peel in the Bolton works, as already noted, about 1787. But there is an important difference between Tipping's and Ainsworth's relations to the Peels, for while the former remained in Manchester as the commercial wing of the Bury works, Ainsworth was resident manager of the Mill Hill (Bolton) printworks. No doubt his family connection, rather than capital, secured him the partnership.[22] Nevertheless, the basic motivation of the elder Peel was the same as his son's: he used an established local manufacturing concern to gain a foothold in new territory.

Joseph Wilkes of Measham (1733–1805) played the key role in the accommodation of both Robert Peels in the midlands, and his spectacular career helps to explain some of their success in the area. Born of farming stock, he rose to prominence as a merchant at Burton-on-Trent, a collection centre for Derbyshire cheese and other farm products, and played a prominent role in the development of the Trent Navigation. In 1777 Wilkes and his two brothers purchased most of the manor of Measham (1,900 acres) for £56,000 and embarked on a programme for its exploitation by draining, irrigating and manuring the land, introducing new animal breeds, building roads, tramways and canals, and opening collieries and brickworks, a corn mill, a coaching inn and a barge-building depot. From the perspective of the present study the most interesting development was an agreement made between the Wilkes brothers and the Peels, at the end of 1785, to build a cotton mill for weft spinning (i.e. jennies and/or mules) at Measham, at this time a 'mud and stud' village being rebuilt in brick. The Peels provided one-third of the capital and, it is reasonable to suppose, most of the technical knowledge. A second and much larger mill, and calico weaving shops for nearly 300 looms, were built in the next few years with £20,000 lent on mortgage by Peel & Yates, so that Measham and Ashby-de-la-Zouch became minor centres of an entirely new textile industry in the locality. Joseph Wilkes 'was possessed of a strong, intelligent, original and active mind, and whatever he took in hand was conducted with a spirit which overcame all obstacles'. Within a few years the capital value of the farming land alone was raised to £120,000.[23]

Wilkes's success in developing this area between Ashby and Tamworth, and his experience in raising capital for land purchase and development, clearly made him a valuable partner for the younger Robert Peel when he turned to the midlands. Eighteenth-century Tamworth, like Measham, was isolated and somnolent, and ripe for development by energetic industrialists who could command capital. Peel and Wilkes bought 4,755 acres for £123,000. Of this sum, £50,000 was raised on mortgage and the rest contributed in cash: £46,000 by Peel and £27,000 by Wilkes.[24] The need of further capital is suggested by the formation in 1790, the year of the Tamworth purchase, of the new London banking house of Peel, Wilkes, Dickenson & Goodall. The London house was linked with the partners' provincial banks – Peel, Greaves & Co. of Manchester, Dickenson & Goodall of Birmingham, and Wilkes's banks in Ashby, Burton and Measham.[25]

Joseph Wilkes was a partner of Sir Robert Peel in the Fazeley cotton mill from 1791 to 1798 when his place was taken by Edward Dickenson, another experienced capitalist who had risen to fortune in Burton-on-Trent.[26] Dickenson was a brewer in Burton with important connections with Birmingham where William Dickenson, probably his brother, was a dealer in porter and Burton ale and a banker.[27] Dickenson clearly had connections with the Burton cotton mills for in 1793 he wrote to Boulton & Watt on behalf of John Peel.[28] He played his part in the purchase of the Thynne estates around Tamworth by buying land and a colliery at Dosthill and Wilnecote, adjacent to Peel's purchases.[29] It is not difficult to see that Peel, Wilkes and Dickenson were partners in a grand strategy for the economic development of Tamworth and its district, based on their experience at Burton.

It was a relatively easy matter to lay down rules for the management of small country mills and printworks, where the processes were largely mechanical and the 200 or so employees were mostly juveniles and young women engaged on repetitive work. On the banking and merchanting side, delegation presented much more difficult problems and, despite the experience and financial standing of the partners, the connection with Joseph Wilkes, Dickenson and Goodall did not last for long. The partnership of Peel, Wilkes, Dickenson & Goodall apparently assumed the merchanting function of Sir Robert in London, and the senior partner became Joseph Peel, who had opened a Manchester warehouse for his father and brothers in Cheapside in 1789. The London partnership was declared bankrupt in 1805 when, according to one of Wilkes's descendants, two of the junior partners absconded.[30] The shock is said to have brought on Wilkes's death. To add to the confusion, his will could not be proved and his affairs took several years to unscramble.[31] Shortly after, Joseph Peel left London for Tamworth to manage one of his brother's mills, a post which was probably more consonant with his abilities.[32] Although the resources of the Peel family bore the financial strain, the damage to the prestige of King Calico was permanent, and it may well be that it was for this reason that in 1806 he went so far as to advertise the fact that he was contracting the scale of his business.[33] Certainly the Peel empire had become too unwieldy for Sir Robert Peel to control now that he was heavily involved in Parliamentary affairs.

Chapter 6

Domestic and Overseas Markets

During the 1780s the Peels were the principal rivals of Livesey, Hargreaves & Co., and when they collapsed the Peels took over their emergent techniques. A perceptive contemporary wrote that Sir Robert Peel:

> seems to have profited by adopting similar modes [to Liveseys], and by attending to quality as well as quantity he has in some cases exhibited respectable work, but without a compliment to the Principal, his labour, attention, investigation and systematic arrangement of the business, as well as his concept of trade in general, must have been very great to reach the heights to which he has now arrived....[1]

In other words, Peel's genius was that of the entrepreneur rather than the engineer, chemist or designer. In these departments he recognised and employed the ability of others, but always subject to the overriding consideration of his conception of popular market demand.

There is all too little detailed evidence of the Peels' commercial policy, but what there is points to their assiduous cultivation of the popular market. The elder Peel was in the chair at a meeting of Manchester calico printers in 1786 when it was urged that 'three parts out of four of printed goods are consumed by the lower class of people', and it was this highly elastic popular market that the Lancashire producers set out to exploit.[2] The Peels' patterns were simple and 'generally consisted of leaves variously disposed, small circles, pippins, clubs, dice, diamonds and spots, and flower heads of a daisy or buttercup form, which ... stared the beholder full in the face.' They were mostly printed in one colour on white. In furnishing fabrics a simple five-inch sunflower pattern was the Peels' best-selling line. 'The simplicity and stiff awkward appearance of some of the earliest patterns designed and printed at the Ground would now excite a smile', the Bury folk recalled in after years. 'The style of the earlier patterns continued the same, almost invariably, from year to year; the high price readily obtained for them making it not so strictly essential to obtain newer, richer, or more original designs.' Much of the earlier printing was on linen of rather coarse texture, 'and it was the very limited supply they were able to obtain of this material' that first directed their attention to cotton, the same local source insisted. The Peels' policy seems to have been to exploit a few popular designs, of which the famous parsley leaf was the earliest success. In the 1780s experience showed that a design that caught on would justify a production of 20,000 pieces (of 28 yards in a piece) *per annum* for several years, and the piece retailing at £4 to £5 (3s. to 3s 6d. a yard) would give a clear profit of a guinea to the manufacturers.[3] The maximum output attained by Sir Robert Peel was 70,000 pieces manufactured a year, and the usual output 50–60,000 (half of it blockwork), so it is apparent that three or four designs accounted for most of the annual production.[4]

Invariably, designs were copied directly from the most popular London productions, at any rate until the time of the shortlived Copyright Act (1787). Five or six of the dozen or so London printers drew their own patterns or employed their own designers, an expensive undertaking for such original work cost them as much as £1,000 a year and copper plates commonly cost £10–20 each. They employed the finer Indian fabrics and best quality dyes. The provincial producers in the Manchester area, Carlisle and Aberdeen justified their plagiarism by insisting that the London manufacturers were chiefly employed in printing foreign (i.e. oriental) muslins and calicoes adapted for the consumption of people of fashion while they were 'extensively concerned in manufacturing and printing calicoes for the lower class of people' from which they deduced 'the necessity to copy and imitate the patterns worn by their superiors'. This was at least true to the extent that, as a London draper explained in 1793, the 'prepossessions' of the 'higher wearers' was still against muslins of British manufacture despite their high standard.

For some years after the commencement of the Bury works there was no 'drawing shop', and the sole draughtsman on the payroll, a man recruited in London, worked alone in a small office. The London printers were all too familiar with Robert Peel's commercial policy, observing bitterly that '.... of the vast quantities [of prints] he himself has thrown into the market, a great part is well known

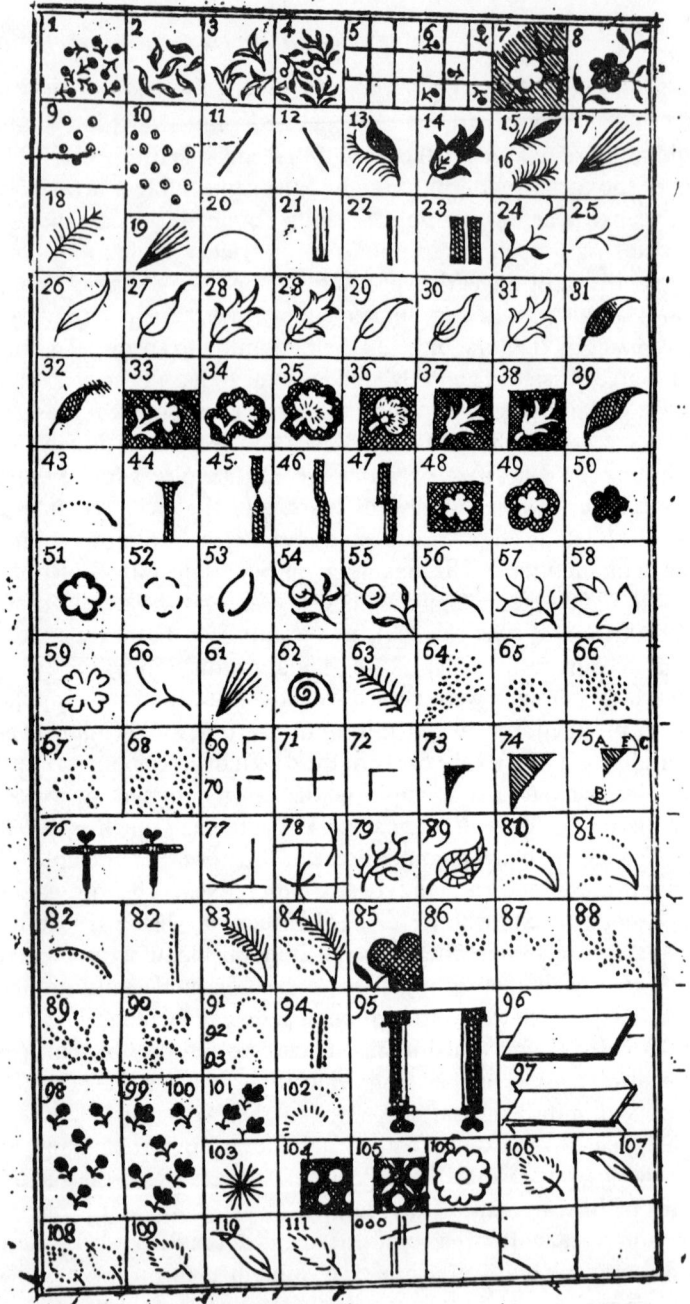

Plate 3 Frontispiece of C. O'Brien's *The ... Callico Printer's Assistant* (1790), depicting typical wood block patterns used in eighteenth-century Britain. Nos 64–72, 86–93 and 108–9 suggest the early development of *picotage*.

to have cost him little on the score of design and execution, the sale at the time being undoubted'. An instance of a common method of piracy was disclosed to a Parliamentary enquiry in 1787. Ralph Yates, a London warehouseman who dealt in popular prints, sent one of the most attractive new designs from the Wallington printworks, retailing at 6s. 9d. per yard, post-haste to Bury one Saturday. On Wednesday week Yates had a copy with instructions to sell at 4s. 6d. per yard. William Kilburn, Wallington's owner and designer, not unreasonably complained that such systematic piracy brought him frequent losses from dead stock, and his campaign led to the earliest British Copyright Act for cotton printing designs.[5]

In fairness to the Peels it should be added that systematic piracy of London designs was nothing unusual in the period. For instance, the pioneer Glasgow calico printers, Archibald Ingram & Co., developed their trade year by year 'by stealth from the working printers in London, where the manager was supposed to resort in the winter, and return to work in the spring, as full of information in his art as a London dancing master from Paris, with half-a-dozen new lessons at his heels.' The attractive simile probably refers to the early decades of the Glasgow industry, the 1750s and 1760s, but London leadership is still evident 50 years later. Even at the height of the Napoleonic Wars the most insistent demand at the embargoed Frankfurt fairs was for muslins and printed calicoes *sur les dessins et modèles venus de Londres*, but often produced by Swiss or Alsatian manufacturers.[6]

More expensive prints were often designed to reflect political and patriotic themes. At military and naval victories, the conclusion of peace or royal anniversaries, Peel, Yates & Co. printed scarves, sashes, flags and escutcheons containing the names and titles of the heroes, 'thickly enclosed with emblems and encircled with motoes relating to liberty and patriotism', and produced in 'gorgeous if not very delicate emblazonment'. Some English printers of the period, possessed of a greater sense of market opportunity than patriotism, printed cottons bearing portraits of Washington and Franklin for the American market, but in view of the Peels' passionate patriotism it is doubtful if the Peels took part in this trade, despite their early links with the US merchants.[7]

A number of the invoices that the Peels sent to Philadelphian merchants which have survived provide further detail about the firm's export goods. The principal American demand was for the 'low-priced common sort' of prints, which Lancashire was able to supply at a competitive price. (London leadership of quality printing was not relinquished until the depression in the industry that followed the French Wars.) In the period 1785–91 the Peels' sales to North America consisted of prints costing between 1s. 6d. and 3s. 6d. a yard, but was most commonly in the 2s. to 2s 6d. bracket. The cheapest prints were decorated with various kinds of stripes, small spots and flowers, running sprigs, branches and vines, and sometimes with small or large figures, probably in profile. The American preference was for 'lively' patterns and those 'very full of work', presumably to look exotic and expensive. Strong colours such as purples and chocolates were frequently ordered. The limited range of patterns was varied by printing on a variety of grounds, stormont, laylock (i.e. lilac), mosaic, 'Pompadour' and 'Devonshire' being most frequently mentioned.[8] The last two descriptions recall the names of the best-known aristocratic beauties of the eighteenth century – the Marquise de Pompadour (1721–64), famous mistress of Louis XV, and Georgina Cavendish, Duchess of Devonshire (1757–1806), the idol of London society in the last quarter of the century. The Marquise gave her name to a conspicuous shade of crimson, the Duchess to a striped cotton cloth woven with dyed and plain colours.[9] These details serve as a reminder that suppliers of the popular end of the market, whether in the north of England or the USA, were compelled to interpret the fashion trend set in Paris and London.

A surviving account of the origin of one of Peel's most popular innovations in design provides an illustration of the firm's more imaginative response to movements of fashion. In the late 1780s Sir Robert Peel saw a style of work called 'Stormont Pins' and rightly anticipated that it would have a long run. He decided to imitate the irregular spotted design and ordered a large broom of fine twigs which he used to spirit the cloth after it was printed with blocks. One of his mechanics, Roberts, improved on this simple device by making a circular brush of bristles to obtain continuous production of the same effect, which was then superimposed on the work of the block printers. According to a contemporary in Manchester, 'many thousand pieces were done in this way which was considered a great improvement'. At this period the production of blocks for printing had been cheapened by tracing the design by small pins hammered into the wood. Roberts improved on his earlier contrivance by covering his wooden roller with a design in pins. Peel approved the idea, experimented, and succeeded beyond his or Roberts' expectations.[10]

There is no doubt, however, that after the Copyright Act the Peels'

Plate 4 A page from one of the Church Peels' Pattern Book, in Bolton Museum

most characteristic response to fashion movements was to adapt patterns the partners had seen in Manchester or London. The precise way in which this was done can be read in a pattern book belonging to the Church (Accrington) Peels, now in the custody of Bolton Museum. The pattern book refers to the period 1807–20 and contains instructions and samples sent by Lawrence and Joseph Peel and a few later partners to their pattern drawer. The record is a little late for our purposes, but the same partners and drawer were working together from at least 1792 and it seems likely that similar practices were maintained throughout the period. The most frequent instruction was to copy particular samples with variations of 'grounds' and motifs, or of the direction, emphasis or size of the pattern imposed on the 'ground'. Usually the market demanded novelty, but sometimes a reversion to styles that were popular up to 15 years earlier. The range of samples collected in the book suggests that the main emphasis was still on the simple, well-cut motifs on which the family had won their reputation. A small selection of the more articulate instructions may serve to illustrate the relationship between partners and pattern drawer: 'Draw about six patterns of chain work in imitation of 421 for light work and draw it bolder a little [and] such as you can print on rollers ....' (July 1807); 'Enclosed you have a pattern of one of the Bury House's plate furnitures. Joseph Peel desires you will draw up and engrave two or three patterns similar, they must be showey and full of work' (August 1807); 'This pattern is considered by the Trade as one of the best black and whites ever printed: a few patterns in this style would be useful....' (June 1808); 'If you were to cut blotches to these patterns they would be favourites for this course [i.e. type] of work which in our opinion will be favourite for Autumn ....' (February 1811); 'Try something in this colouring on a smaller scale and with more novelty in the figure. You must do your utmost to get novelty. You may as well do nothing as draw old figures' (June 1812).

The price of cotton yarns fell continuously through the late 1780s and early 1790s as more and more merchants and *verlegers* crowded into the spinning sector of the industry. It was followed by a steady decline in the price of muslins, calicoes and printed fabrics. By 1797 the outcome, according to a memorandum sent to the Prime Minister and signed by Sir Robert Peel and other leading Manchester manufacturers, was that 80 per cent of the output was sold for under 2s. 6d. a yard and 11 per cent sold for 1s. or under. Fabrics in this price range might be printed with up to five colours. The 'lower class of people' were indeed enjoying the fruits of industrialisation.

All too little is known of the Peel's selling techniques, but the limited evidence once again emphasises the family's originality and drive. For most of the second half of the eighteenth century the centre of Manchester's commerce was the neighbourhood of King Street and St. James's Square where the most prosperous merchants built proud Georgian houses and kept their warehouses. Even at the end of the century such eminent textile merchants as Peter Drinkwater maintained a residence in King Street. The Peel's leadership was powerful enough to break this continuity and to create a new focus of trade in a locality which until then was 'quite remote from business'. As Joseph Aston explained: 'The active genius of Sir R. Peel, Bart. effected the change. The superiority of the goods manufactured in the house of which he was the head forced his customers to follow him wherever he might fix. He erected a warehouse in a situation where land was cheap but which immediately experienced an unprecented advance...' The warehouse, which was approached by an avenue of trees later called Peel Street, united the family's commercial interests in one building. With characteristic enterprise Peel had created a prestige location at the most economical price.[11]

A Hull draper who travelled to Manchester to buy his printed calicoes recalled the method of selling at the end of the eighteenth century:

> The cart was in the habit of bringing a load of prints on three mornings a week – Tuesdays, Thursdays, and Saturdays – from the works. The warehouse doors were not opened till nine o'clock, by which time the prints were all arranged in the saleroom. A crowd of drapers was generally waiting for the doors to be opened, when they would rush upstairs to the saleroom, and a scramble for prints would ensue, each draper making a pile on the floor of such prints as he had chosen, and waiting for the entering clerk coming round to look them over and enter them.[12]

If this scene was typical the Peels had little difficulty in selling all the calicoes they could print. Nevertheless, they kept four travellers at work constantly touring the home market.[13] When the trade became more competitive it was one of Peels' successors, the Grant brothers, who made the running by introducing the system of 'hookers-in' to entice the country drapers into the fast-growing number of warehouses in the Cannon Street area of Manchester, and inviting foreign buyers to visit their country works at the weekends.[14]

In overseas commerce the Peels were once again pace setters. They were amongst the handful of London and Manchester merchants who sold direct to American merchants.[15] The American connection is said to have been established before the War of Independence (i.e. before 1774) and, according to a tradition that was popular in Bury, it was the chintzes of Peel & Yates that the American colonists prohibited their wives and daughters from wearing. If this is true – and oral tradition is usually found to be reliable in the main point – the Peels were among the very first Lancashire manufacturers to sell direct to merchants in the American colonies.[16] Exports, apparently, were channelled through the firm's Liverpool warehouse, and sent to merchants at the American centres of the trade in New York and Philadelphia. In the early 1790s the main consignees were respectively Isaac Cooke and Phillip Nicklin.[17]

Table 15 Amount of goods sent by Peel, Yates & Co. to North America, 1797–1800

Year	No. of customers	Total sales (£)
1797	47	32,531
1798	28	21,254
1799	25	21,763
1800	14	12,116
Average	28	21,916

SOURCE: New York Historical Society, New York; Bolton, Ogden & Co.'s Mss., letters of Samuel Ferguson.

The importance of the Peels' North American business at the end of the eighteenth century can be estimated from the data assembled in Table 15. At this time output was of the order of 50–60,000 pieces a year (see p. 79), each piece worth about £2 on average, so North America may have taken a share fluctuating between 10 and 30 per cent of the Peels' production. This estimate needs some qualifications, however. By this time, it should be noticed, the family's London house, Joseph Peel & Co., was also trading to North America, although probably on a much smaller scale than the Manchester partners. The disaster of young Yates's bankruptcy[18] may have been a factor in the partners' determination, expressed in letters to their Philadelphia agent, to contract the scale of their North American business.[19] It seems probable, therefore, that the 1797 figure is more representative of the proportion of their sales to America in the 1780s and 1790s than those for 1798–1800.

The Peels suffered from the usual problems facing exporters to America at the period: control and direction of their overseas agents, slow returns on sales, increasing competition and erratic trading conditions – particularly during the French Wars. After protracted difficulties in recovering debts from US merchants, they tried to solve the first two problems by appointing a young émigré Yorkshireman, Samuel Ferguson, to manage all their business in North America, binding him closely to their business with a tightly worded contract.[20] But there were still problems. Within weeks of the signing of the contract Ferguson wanted to undertake some trading on his own account, much to the Peels' disgust. Like any other inexperienced young merchant his principals accused him of accepting orders on credit without adequate knowledge of the men he was dealing with. The Peels had enough bad debts without incurring further ones. In 1799 they still had 'a great many accounts that have not been settled for seven or eight years', despite repeated exhortations to Ferguson to use every means to secure payment. The experience drove them to the conclusion that 'the trade to America for sometime past has been in such a disagreeable state that in future we intend to do business with very few houses, only those who have made their payments punctually...'[21] The underlying problem was increasing competition as more and more Lancashire printers tried to sell in the North American market. By the late 1790s the Peels felt compelled to send the latest patterns for American buyers to select. In 1798 they wrote 'we have ship'd twenty trucks of the newest and most fashionable prints we had in the warehouse, ... the patterns being generally such as have not been seen in the country before ... they are far superior in taste to anything we ever sent out [before] ...' The Peels recognised that the growing number of American merchants calling at their warehouse were looking for better quality and that this improving taste and purchasing power would soon be transmitted to a wider public. However, it seems that at the turn of the century they were unwilling or unable to cut their prices down to the level necessary to meet the competition in North America and some determined English rivals, so that the prospering Ferguson wondered whether to continue his commission despite the general attractiveness of the trade in printed calicoes.[22] The connection was in fact maintained but Ferguson's doubts show that the Peels had lost the keen edge of their earlier challenge in their most important overseas market. Other markets were even more competitive, at any rate in quality if not in price.

As late as 1786 Sir Robert Peel and other Manchester manufacturers stressed their continuing fear of Continental competition, but for the most objective account of English standards we must consult the Continental authorities of the day. Ryhiner of Basle, in 1766, had no doubt that the English producers led the field in both the elegance of their designs and the clarity of their execution. Schuele of Augsburg was reckoned to be their only equal on the Continent, with the Dutch and Swiss a little behind, but themselves well ahead of the French. However, 20 years later, French colours and designs were considered at least as good as any others in Europe. François de Rochefoucauld, who visited Manchester manufacturers in 1785, observed that 'their dyes are not very high quality and they do not finish them on cotton any better than we do, there are some which lose their colour by exposure to the air'. Another shortcoming was explained by a German visitor, F. A. Wenderborn, in 1790:

> it is said that the English manufacturers, particularly those who employ themselves in articles of luxury, do it with less taste than some other nations, particularly their neighbours the French .... they show this want of taste much in their drawings, their designs, and patterns. For this reason they have been obliged to procure these things from abroad or to engage Frenchmen to work for them. I myself have known some who for such purposes were employed and well paid by English manufacturers in the cotton and calico printing, or the silk weaving business.

Despite the institution of the Royal Academy to meet this need the problem was still remarked on after the French Wars, and at regular intervals during the first half of the nineteenth century. There can be little doubt that the migration of textile printing from London to the provinces led to a permanent deterioration of design.

Giving evidence on the proposed Eden Treaty in February 1786, Peel maintained that 'we are excelled ... in Switzerland both in execution and cheapness, and from what I have seen of their own [French] productions I have no reason to believe that we are their superiors', but he concluded cautiously that he thought the existing trade might be 'beneficially maintained'. The principal advantages of the Lancashire producers, Peel thought, lay in the production of plain calicoes and the 'extent to which the printing is carried on in this country and the many printing works already established ... [which] enable us to produce a greater variety of patterns than any other nation and execute immediate orders to any amount'. In other words, the Lancashire producers led on organisation rather than techniques. Another witness, Josephus Smith of Livesey, Hargreaves & Co., offered a little more detail. He said that there was a negligible export of English printed calicoes to France, either directly or indirectly, and that he was afraid of the competition of Indian printed goods imported through France. 'The export trade in our manufactures has increased within these last fifteen years [1770–85], though not to a considerable degree. It is very different in different years, principally owing to the variation in prices in the East India calicoes, which sometimes differ 100 per cent in their prices'. But, probably because of his greater knowledge of the work of the London printers and of recent developments at Livesey, Hargreaves & Co., he insisted that English spinning and printing machines were both cheaper and better than the French and saved half the colours. Samuel Salte, a wholesale linen draper well-known to economic historians as Oldknow's London correspondent, struck an even more optimistic note on muslins. 'There was a manufacture in Switzerland formerly, but of late years we have heard nothing of it. The Swiss first introduced the method of dressing and making up muslins in the Indian manner and we are indebted to the Swiss for that improvement', but now there was no serious competition to fear.[23]

At the beginning of the period covered by this book the great international fairs at Hamburg, Frankfurt, Leipzig, Bremen and other German towns still conducted most of the trade of central and eastern Europe, and if the Peel's sales were representative they were particularly interested in middle-quality prints in the textile sections.[24] In 1781 the British Consul at Hamburg reported that 'some of our manufacturers from Manchester and Leeds do send a vast quantity of their manufactures' to Leipzig for sale, and it seems likely that the Peels, being a leading house in the trade, were among this number.[25] However, as the international trade in cottons accelerated in the 1790s, merchants from both sides of the North Sea began to by-pass the ancient practices to establish a more regular system of buying and selling.

Some details are available to illustrate the origins of this development. The traditional method of supplying the more distant home markets was by employing itinerant agents called 'out-riders', who worked for a commission and usually served several firms.[26] By degrees, the system was extended to cover European markets. In 1788 Charles Taylor & Co., a Manchester firm of merchants and manufacturers chiefly engaged in foreign trade, appointed a German called Uhde (or Ulde) as an out-rider in Holland and Germany, and in the early 1790s he began to travel for the Peels and other firms as

Table 16 British consumption of printed textiles, 1797, analysed in price ranges

Price range (pence per yard)	No. of pieces	Total consumption (million yds.)	%
12d. or under	100,000	2.8	11
12¼d. to 18d.	450,000	12.6	48
18¼d. to 2s. 6d.	180,000	5.4	21
2s. 6¼d. to 3s. 0d.	60,000	1.8	7
3s. 0¼d. to 3s. 6d.	40,000	1.2	5
3s. 6¼d. to 4s. 0d.	30,000	0.9	3
4s. 0¼d. to 5s. 0d.	30,000	0.9	3
Above 5s. 0d.	20,000	0.6	2
Total	910,000	26.2	100

SOURCE: PRO: 30/8/301, Chatham papers, p. 252.
NOTES: 1. The piece measured 28 yards long in the two lowest price brackets and 30 yards long in the other six price ranges. 2. The official output of printed goods charged with duty in 1797 was 27.2 million yards: T. S. Ashton, *An Economic History of England* (1955), Table X, p. 248. The lower total given here was perhaps provisional. 3. It was possible to print up to five colours for 12d.; see S. D. Chapman, 'Rothschild'. p. 106.

well.[27] But in the meantime more direct connections were being forged.

To judge from the comments of the pamphleteers it was the commercial crisis of 1788 that induced British manufacturers to make more intense efforts to penetrate the Continental market. 'Let it once be known on the Continent of Europe that every article of decent apparel necessary for the lower ranks of females can be furnished of a beautiful fabric at a sum not exceeding fifteen shillings and the consumption will be immense', one writer proclaimed. Another insisted that 'the British have since last year [1787] acquired an indisputable pre-eminence, proved on the spot by accurate comparison, over the Swiss in a similar [cotton] manufacture'. The continuing decline in the price of British cottons, united with such feelings, may have broken down the Peels' earlier reservations about the Continental market. At any rate it appears that they began to send consignments of prints to Frankfurt through the agency of a London commission merchant from about this time. The recipient was Mayer Amschel Rothschild, one of 15 Jewish dealers who specialised in English textiles in this period. According to the

Reminiscences of Baron Ferdinand de Rothschild, Mayer's most able son, Nathan Mayer, was sent to Manchester and 'directed to arrange that the firm of Peel should make their consignments direct to Frankfurt, so saving the commission'. This sounds convincing and is consistent with N. M. Rothschild's own account of his reason for moving, but unfortunately there is no clear support for the story in the archives of his firm. However, it is clear that young Rothschild was sent to England in 1798, as soon as he was 21, and that in Manchester he bought from the Peels as well as a number of smaller *verlegers* and printers. His successful enterprise proved to be the forerunner of numerous other ones run by sons and junior partners of German textile merchants.[28] Novel enterprise, together with the continued decline in prices, is sufficient to explain why foreign imports of printed calicoes fell from ten to five per cent of the home-produced output in the 1790s (see Table 17). Once again the record is hazy, but it seems that the Peels were in the forefront of a crucial innovation in marketing.

Table 17 British consumption of home and foreign produced printed muslins and calicoes, 1790–1800 (million yds.)

Year ending 5 July	British produced (1)	Foreign produced (2)	(2) as % of (1)
1790–1	15.01	1.59	10.6
1791–2	16.96	1.79	10.5
1792–3	17.00	1.55	9.1
1793–4	16.65	1.37	8.2
1794–5	20.08	1.21	6.0
1795–6	24.36	1.75	7.2
1796–7	21.87	1.99	9.1
1797–8	23.45	1.78	7.6
1798–9	27.09	1.72	6.3
1799–1800	28.69	1.58	5.5

SOURCE: London Excise Office, quoted in PRO: 30/8/301, Chatham papers, p. 247.

NOTE: Small quantities of silks, silk handkerchiefs and 'linen and cotton stuffs' were also printed and included in the Excise Office's final total for goods charged for duty.

This claim is supported by evidence from the Swiss sources, which show that towards the end of the eighteenth century the Neuchâtel printers began to suffer from the lower prices of Manchester goods at the great international fairs in both Germany and Italy, their principal markets outside France.

The Lancashire manufacturers were not only anxious about competition from the Swiss and Alsatian producers. They also feared the continuing competition of the hand-painted Indian textiles, together with hand-made muslins, calicoes, nankeens and other Oriental specialities. The British East India Co. was not optimistic about the possibility of increasing the exports of any home-produced textiles because in India 'millions of ingenious and industrious manufacturers ... work for one-fifth part of the wages given in England.' An attempt was made to introduce English printed piece goods to the Indian market in 1786 by sending out some patterns, but a Company committee reported that 'it appears to be the opinion that none of them will answer for the general consumption of the natives; ... some Manchester goods to a trifling amount might be sold.'[29]

When the Company's charter was coming up for renewal in 1792, Prime Minister William Pitt invited the trade interests of Manchester, Glasgow, Birmingham and other manufacturing towns to send delegates to Downing Street to represent their interests. The two MPs for Lancashire, together with Peel and four other Manchester manufacturers, pressed for a total prohibition of sales of Indian textiles in the British home market, an increase of raw cotton supplies from the Orient, and direct access to the Indian market. This was at first agreed, but the loud protests of the London wholesale dealers in Indian piece goods resulted in the cancellation of the proposed concession. The pinacle of London society still preferred genuine oriental prints.[30] In the difficult trading conditions of 1788 and 1794 Peel and numerous other northern manufacturers claimed that their trade was in decline due to 'the immense importations' of piece goods from India and said that families were being reduced to insolvency and the poor to starvation.[31] The available statistics show that the fears and prejudices of the northern manufacturers were exaggerated. The East India Co.'s total sales of coloured piece goods about 1790 (five-year average, 1788–92) was not more than 8.4 million yards a year,[32] a figure that must be compared with total British production of 15 or 16 million yards, a large proportion of which went to export to North America and Europe (Table 16).

The Peel's precise position was revealed in the next period of trading difficulty for the northern manufacturers, in 1798–9, when there was considerable unemployment in Lancashire. The two houses of Peels petitioned the Court of Directors of the East India Co. for permission to send out 'an adventure' to India, and they shipped

5,000 pieces of printed calicoes 'selected according to the best information they could obtain from the captains of ships and mates who had carried out small quantities before.' Unhappily for the Peels the venture was an almost complete loss, but whether this was primarily because of price or of design is not recorded. Lancashire did not begin to capture the Indian home market until the period of steep decline in prices and dislocation of European markets following the French Wars.[33]

Chapter 7

Labour and Industrial Relations

Some reference has been made in Chapters 1 and 2 to the recruitment of a labour force for new industrial processes introduced by the Peels, but detailed consideration of the problems and processes adopted has been reserved for a separate chapter. Very little in the way of business records has survived but the importance of the Peels in their period led to the recording of memories, traditions and political material from which it is possible to discern the elements of the story.

The voice of the London printers, O'Brien, maintained that the 'country works', i.e. provincial printing workshops, had been established by putting '50 or 100 rude country hinds' to printing and that 'at the great country [calico printing] houses the subordinates have been used to look up to the principals as a superior kind of beings, and were therefore held as much as possible in a state of mental subjection ...' He acknowledged that 'perhaps the school at Bury is an exception', but then added disingenuously, 'who can judge the founder's view?'[1] There is almost an allegation here that Peel built the success of his concerns on a cheap and deferential semi-rural labour force, and this needs to be investigated.

The traditions preserved among the work people at Bury in the middle of the last century leave no doubt that when Peel came into the area 80 years earlier he and his partners occupied a country valley populated by a simple, uneducated people. The local population was gullible and superstitious, quite ready to believe in stories of demons haunting the meadows (taking the cows' milk) or the bleachfields (stealing the cloth) and with implicit faith in spells, divinations, astrology and magic. One of the best-known villagers was a 'herbalist and cow-doctor', an old man with the reputation as a seer and caster of charms who was ready to cure a quinsy by hanging toads' legs (cut from the unfortunate reptile at sunset) round the throat of the sufferer. The villagers entertained themselves with the traditional Lancashire pastimes: bull-baiting, and the celebrations of Mayday eve, Restoration day (commemorating the return of Charles II, 20 May 1660), bonfire night, the Christmas festivities (which always lasted a week) and the Robin Hood festival. Strangers to the area were few and far between and liable to be the subject of ribald remarks from the locals.[2] In short, the locality exhibited all the features of a traditional local society in which there was little sense of economy of time or progress, and in which the rationalism of the eighteenth century had made little impact on the parochialism of these remote, moorland valleys.[3]

Inevitably, it was difficult to attract skilled outsiders to such a place. Unfortunately, the Bury local records are not adequate to make an analysis of the geographical and occupational origins of the labour force as M. Chassagne has done for Oberkampf's Jouy, but all the indications point to the local recruitment of all but a handful of highly skilled workers. Several of the pioneers of the cotton industry chose sites where there was cheap surplus labour, and Bury and Tamworth were further examples of what became a familiar practice. Livesey, Hargreaves are said to have employed a number of London designers at their Mosney site, but for some years after the commencement of the Bury works there was only one 'drawer' as he was called. He came from London and apart from the partners, was the only man on the site addressed as 'Mr'. This pioneer, whose stiff and awkward productions were referred to in the last chapter, eventually built up a team of practitioners in his art, a local élite that was regarded by the rest of the Bury population as:

> a very high and fashionable body of men.... At 'loosings', dances, or other festivals of a similar nature they appeared in breeches, white silk-stockings, silver buckles on the shoes and at the knee, ruffles at the wrist, soft cravat of fine muslin ties round the throat with long ends falling on the breast, and often embroidered, and hair powdered. Their earnings were considerable (or thought so then) and extremely regular.... 40, 50 or 60s. weekly.

Indeed, the only workers whose earnings approached theirs in the period were handloom weavers, whose output was much at a premium in the late 1780s and 1790s.[4]

Although the Peels trained most of their own artisans there was sufficient appreciation of the status of their metropolitan antecedents for the drawers and block printers to retain aspirations of status far above that of other workers. In London, in the middle of the eighteenth century it was said that 'the printer who cuts nicely may earn while employed half a guinea a day during the printing season', though from October to March they were 'but little employed'. The most skilled men, it seems, could earn about £80 a year.[5] Edward Clayton & Sons, the first Lancashire printers, are said to have paid about one guinea a week to the men they drew from London,[6] but there may have been other benefits such as long contracts, regular employment and, possibly, housing. The Bury works, which 'never was a place noted for giving large wages', paid their engraver £2 a week.[7] In the last decade of the century wages were continuing to rise despite the introduction of roller printing. Around 1790 there was such a shortage of skilled men that employers are said to have offered premiums of five, 10 or 15 guineas for each man recruited. An analysis of the wage books of 14 leading firms at the end of the century shows that the highest paid journeymen were paid £103 *per annum* and the lowest £51 12s. 10d., an average for three years being £1 8s. per week. The hours of work were relatively short for the period, $10\frac{1}{4}$ in summer and seven to eight in winter. It was said that 'It is a fact that there are now many masters in the trade and carrying on much business who were enabled to begin by a capital they acquired by the good wages they earned while journeymen.'[8]

At Bury, Peel & Yates exerted themselves to keep their wage costs as low as possible, principally by employing large numbers of apprentices who could undertake the 'plain and easy work', in which they specialised, 'at moderate expense', a practice much resented by their London competitors.[9] Copper engraving was slow and expensive – a complicated pattern could take as much as three months to cut and cost £25 in wages alone – so in the place of engravers the firm employed numbers of women as block pinners, a process 'which consisted in inserting small lengths of brass wire or pins of different degrees of fineness into a wooden block to form the pattern required, which was delineated upon the block by a putter on or dresser'. The work was quite delicate; one unusually large block was said to contain as many as 63,000 pins. A woman pinner could earn 12s. to 14s. weekly after her apprenticeship. A great number of females were also employed as 'pencillers' (i.e. hand painters), working in long terraces of cottage-like workshops under the superintendence of mistresses. 'In the shops each woman had her piece suspended before her with a supply of hair pencils of different degrees of fineness according to the size of the object ... to be touched, and saucers containing colour, of red, green, blue, yellow, etc. of each variety of shade, according to the pattern required ... a good workwoman might sometimes earn £2 a week', though it seems likely that most earned a good deal less.[10] As noted in the last chapter, the style of the earlier patterns changed little from year to year, so the first generation of pencillers had plenty of practice on each design.

Before chemical bleaching was introduced juvenile labour was largely employed in the tenter fields. 'Many little boys were employed whose duty it was to peg these pieces to the ground at each end and afterwards pin them together side by side, to stretch and expose the surface to the sun and air.' A corps of boys was also used as messengers, running the 13 miles of tortuous road from Bury to the Manchester warehouse, or perhaps to Blackburn if urgent needs arose after the carrier's wagon had left in the morning. When the Peels began to build cotton mills on the Arkwright plan, women and children again constituted much the largest part of the labour force. By this time the local supply of labour was so short that children had to be imported from London workhouses and orphanages. The 200-mile journey took several days in carriers' carts. Many arrived wearing the uniform of the charities from which they came, and their strange southern accents made them the object of Lancashire raillery. At the end of the century Peel employed more than 1,000 pauper apprentices, dispersed in several cotton mills round Bury and Blackburn. Although 'regular hours' were said to be the rule at Bury, the cotton mills suffered from want of immediate supervision of the proprietors and the children were overworked, an unhappy development that soon led to political scandal.[11]

In later years, Peel had the candour to admit his former neglect. 'Having other pursuits, it was not often in my power to visit the factories ... The hours of labour were regulated by the interest of the overseer, whose remuneration depending on the quality of the work done, he was often induced to make the poor children work excessive hours, and to stop their complaints by trifling bribes'. However, Peel soon organised improvements in the thorough way characteristic of him. Apprentice houses were opened at Radcliffe and Hinds to accommodate juvenile workers. They were superintended by 'mistresses' and strict attention paid to their health, cleanliness and clothing, in accordance with their apprenticeship indentures. Youngsters stayed until they were 21 years old and Peel saw that they were taught to read and prepared to earn their own living. The Peels' own family doctor, Ellis Cunliffe, was paid £300–£400 *per annum* to attend the children who were employed at the mills.[11]

The employment of such large numbers of women and juveniles guaranteed a labour force that could readily be accommodated to the new work discipline. According to local folk memory in Bury the traditional revelries and entertainments in the village simply 'faded away before the approach of trade and regular unremitting employment, for they were incompatible with it'[12] – an indication of easy acquiescence of the majority in the ways of the new masters. The only problems created by employing women and children were raised by outsiders and not from the ranks of such employees.

The political issues introduced by Peel's employment of pauper apprentices in his cotton mills must be considered, but for the moment we are concerned only with the internal consequences of labour policy and, in particular, testing the truth of O'Brien's allegations. Despite the high wages attained by a handful of highly skilled artisans, and the peaks of earning power retained in folk memory, it is clear that the *average* wages earned at Peels' works and mills were remarkably low. In 1785 the branches in which his labour costs were highest – the manufacture of cottons and calicoes, employing about 6,000 hands, and printing, which employed about 800 – averaged only 8s. a week (about £20 a year), a figure not very much higher than the wage of agricultural labourers in full work.[13] Part of the explanation of the low wages of the handloom weavers is that numbers of them retained a residual interest in farming, but it seems more convincing to suggest that, scattered over a wide rural area, they lacked the opportunity to unionise and press the economic advantages of the rapidly growing industry.[14]

The handloom weavers made a contrast with the calico printers who had formed a strong trade union in 1785 or 1786. The union was started by a group of 'expensive and insubordinate' workers that Livesey, Hargreaves had brought to Lancashire from London. When their new masters tried to dilute their skills 'by means of machinery and apprentices' they found it necessary to protect their position. As the Peels had increased the scale of their operations principally by recruiting apprentices, they were obviously exposed to conflict, and when Livesey, Hargreaves collapsed in 1788 they were left in the front line. Moreover, 'Parsley' Peel strongly opposed the union as he thought it represented the same spirit and had the same object in view as that of the rioting country weavers in 1780, and his feelings may well have deepened the hostility felt by his sons.[15] The initial collision of 1786 (see pp. 31–2) was followed by a 13-weeks win-or-die struggle in the summer of 1790, which is said to have cost the union members £5,000 in funds and £10,000 in lost wages. The strikers were not easily intimidated by the employers' ultimatum,[16] and some of the employers proceeded against a few of the union leaders but, according to an early historian of labour relations in the industry, 'this had no influence on the great body of the men'.[17] So it was that, as we noted in Chapter 4, Sir Robert Peel felt 'under the necessity at this time of establishing print works at Tamworth ... free from the restraints and control of this combination', and for the next 20 years or so he printed 40–50,000 pieces a year – about the same number as he had printed at Bury at the time the union was formed[18] – 'principally by machinery and apprentices'.[19]

The conflict was by no means ended at the end of the 1790 strike. In 1807, 7,000 calico printers, block cutters and designers petitioned Parliament to regulate their industry, and a Bill was proposed to limit the number of apprentices and to introduce other restrictions in the industry.[20] In the following year Peel used his experience in Parliament to oppose Sheridan's Bill for limiting the number of apprentices, as well as Rose's proposal for fixing a minimum wage to be paid to cotton spinners.[21] He attacked these measures with reference to the principles of free trade, omitting to recognise that his first entry into the political limelight, in 1785, had been to oppose free trade between Britain and Ireland.

Returning to O'Brien's charge, it seems that the Peels were at first compelled to recruit and train up their own skilled workers because of the difficulty and expense of inducing highly-paid block cutters and printers to leave London for the 'new frontier' of industrialism. Peel & Yates found cheaper ways of manufacturing the simpler and more popular varieties of painted and printed fabrics by building up a corps of women block pinners and pencillers. The success of this policy enabled Livesey, Hargreaves, the Peels and other Lancashire firms to win much of the cheaper end of the market from the established London firms. The rapid progress of the northern firms seemed unassailable until the artisan printers determined to introduce the restrictive practices already familiar at the metropolitan print works. Sir Robert Peel responded with characteristic vigour by moving the centre of his activities to Tamworth where, after some initial difficulties, he almost attained the level of his output at Bury. Nevertheless, this peripheral location cost his firm the technical and commercial advantages of operating at the centre of a rapidly developing industry. It seems fair to conclude, therefore, that O'Brien's view that the early country manufacturers benefitted largely from a deferential labour force was largely true for the first

20 years or so in which the Peels were most active in the industry, but that thereafter they faced a trade union as strong as any thrown up in the early factory age.

Sir Robert Peel's later involvement in the problems of industrial relations was staged in Parliament rather than in Lancashire and thus falls outside the province of this book. However, it is worth commenting on his political opponents for the light this sheds on his sincerity and determination as a reformer. It is believed that Peel's Health and Morals of Apprentices Act of 1802 slipped through Parliament without raising much hostility, but the letter books of Edward Smith Stanley, MP for Preston (1796–1812), reveal the existence of very angry opposition, particularly from Peel's fellow manufacturers, and an energetic campaign was mounted to repeal it early in 1803. Fear of further, more incisive controls was sufficient to rally the support of all the major manufacturers against Peel's Act, including the likes of Richard Arkwright II, the Strutt family and Davison & Hawksley of Nottingham, who are believed to have been more liberal in their political and social ideals. Peel stood alone against the united interest of the trade lobby and won his case. It was a further demonstration of the confidence in his own judgement and the tenacity of purpose that brought such outstanding success to his family firm.[22]

PART THREE

Oberkampf of Jouy

Chapter 8

French Textile Printing and Fashion before 1759

Indian printed cottons made their appearance in France at least as early as 1587. The earliest imports were called *pintas* (Portuguese: 'spotted cloths') so it is fair to assume that they were brought to Marseilles by Portugese merchants or, at any rate, forwarded by them from the entrepôt ports.[1] The growing demand for Indian printed textiles and for other Oriental goods such as spices and porcelain reflected the passion of the affluent classes for the products of the East, and regular adventures began to supply the market. The peculiar attraction of Indian textiles can also be attributed to the lively colours which contrasted with the monotones produced by the Western textile regions, and the cultivation of exotic dress as a way of social differentiation. By c. 1650 the passion for *toiles peintes* and *chintzes* had grown to such dimensions among the wealthy that it was known as the 'Indian craze'. For Europe's leisured classes the new styles appeared indispensable to their way of life.[2] Colbert's establishment of the *Compagnie Française des Indes* in 1664, following the institution of the English, Dutch and Danish East India Companies – formed respectively in 1600, 1602 and 1616 – was merely a belated recognition of this fast-growing market.[3] Only systematic research on an international scale would allow us to trace the distribution network of these imports from the principal ports of entry, notably Lisbon, London, Amsterdam and Rouen.

The continuing growth of European demand and the prospect of profit which it offered inevitably stimulated the foundation of a local industry to imitate the Indian products. Despite the convoys from India and the enterprise of Armenian and Turkish traders the art of painting and then of printing cottons made its appearance in Marseilles as early as the 1640s. There is nothing surprising about the choice of the French port nearest to the East to inaugurate the manufacture of *indiennes*. The dyers of the period were accustomed to working on wool or silk but were ignorant of the qualities of the new vegetable fibre, and for long they struggled to imitate the Oriental technique. They were in no way discouraged by the growing import of Indian printed fabrics which around 1680 began to rival the *étoffes nationales*, the Norman cloths and Lyonnais silks, in the first rank of importance. The problem was so serious that the effectiveness of Colbert's mercantilist policy of supporting domestic industry was placed in some doubt, for they were the centre of his attempts to develop France's external trade.[4] After his death his rival Louvois, Director of Industry and Domestic Commerce could no longer procrastinate. The *arrêt* of 26 October 1686 forbade all import of painted and printed fabrics, and another of 1692 prohibited all wearing and use of these goods throughout the Kingdom. Whatever the truth of the arguments advanced to justify these prohibitive measures, they had two important consequences.[5] First, they stopped dead the early, tentative development of the calico printing industry in France, thus allowing to the Dutch and Swiss republics and the free cities of Germany the opportunity to nurture the new industry with the aid of French refugees.[6] Second, they restrained what the *arrêt* called the 'carrying and use of *toiles indiennes*', but the fashion was too well-established to be banished at the king's command.[7] The abundant prohibitive legislation – two edicts and 80 *arrêts* between 1686 and 1748 – shows the inability of the monarch to compel his subjects of the *meilleur partie* (literally the 'saner part') to obey. The severity of the penalties for contravention – heavy fines and prohibition from trade of merchants found transgressing – did not drive the trade underground for the administration was lax, particularly with reference to the dominant social classes.[8] In Britanny people of 'the first rank' led the way in flouting the law and in 1752 the Rouen *intendant*, officially charged with the execution of the law within his district, personally sent for a bale of Indian fabrics, but unfortunately for him it was seized at Caen.[9] The actual administration (or, rather, lack of administration) of the prohibitory legislation provides a splendid example of the limits and contradictions of the *ancien régime*: an authoritative facade behind which the dominant social classes and their loyal following mocked the King's laws.

In the middle of the eighteenth century the situation appeared absurd to the political economists, i.e. the free traders, the forerunners of Adam Smith, who were pressing for the liberation of productive resources to accelerate the development of French industry. 'The fashion for printed calicoes is nothing strange: they

French Textile Printing and Fashion before 1759   105

provide furnishings [i.e. furnishing fabrics] which are attractive, inexpensive and easy to wash', explained an Inspector of Industry to the members of a Chamber of Commerce at the time of the first campaign to repeal the repressive legislation.[10] The *intendant* for commerce, Michau de Montaran,[11] acting within his authority in regulating such matters, declared 'that it is obvious that our industries cannot produce anything that can substitute for these furnishings, the colours of our *siamoises* [linen and cotton fabrics in Siamese design] and *toiles flambées* [fabrics woven with a flame design] and *brochées* soon lose their colours, so the goods produced are not much use'. However, the political economist Véron de Forbonnais, a protagonist of prohibition, estimated that the average annual national consumption of printed fabrics was worth 16,000,000*l*, excluding the exports which were procured by them from 'the trade with the sugar islands [West Indies], where the heat or the climate does not allow the women to wear silks because they do not last long, nor woollens because they are too heavy'. As early as 1749 Montaran judged that 'it will be a great benefit to the kingdom if we can satisfy these two needs'. A practical administrator, he proposed to allow the printing of fabrics woven in France but to exclude all imported cottons, thereby discouraging the smuggling trade which was impoverishing the French excise. His scheme had the immediate support of the *députés* in the ports, but the announcement allowing only printing on cotton was more in the interest of shipowners and colonialists who were concerned with the cultivation and trade in cotton.[12] Nevertheless, the opposition of the Normandy Chamber of Commerce led to the rejection of the proposal, and Montaran himself feared the consequences for the linen industry and for the lighter woollen goods. 'How far would it be harmful? It is difficult to guess, and would it be wise to risk the present prosperity for an uncertain future?', he wondered.

The important point is that in the middle of the eighteenth century the central administration was unsure of its basic policy.[13] The prohibitive legislation continued to be ignored, and a widely dispersed industry survived the period of persecution by successful evasion of the law. The technique employed followed the original Indian, and consisted of preserving white places on the cotton by applying a gum or kaolin to the surface. When the cloth was immersed in a bath of indigo the dye only adhered to the unmarked parts. Until the work of the chemist Dufay was published in 1737 the application of indigo remained forbidden in France, as was the production of pastel, a dye only suitable for woollen fabrics. It was only at the end of the 1730s that the process was completely developed, when the indigo was mixed in a cold alkaline solution with iron sulphate added to it.[14] In 1744 Jean-Rodolphe Wetter, a Swiss manufacturer established at Marseilles since 1736, was the first to attempt to obtain a patent 'to manufacture printed calicoes by the method of those made in England'. The Chamber of Commerce rejected his request without discussion because, they said, textile printing was not restricted in the town.[15] In the following year an Avignon manufacturer, Claude Julien, sought permission to establish a factory for printing handkerchiefs, tablecloths and serviettes. The Chamber resisted but a favourable report by Hellot, Government inspector of dyeing, persuaded the members to abandon their opposition. Wetter tried again for a patent in 1746, restricting his claim to printing on linen. Toleration was not far away, however, even though the Bureau refused, in 1749, to allow a cotton printing workshop at St. Denis, Paris.[16]

In late 1749 the Danton brothers of Angers wrote to the *intendant* at Tours soliciting permission to 'dye in blue all the kinds of *toiles* made in France either of linen or of linen and cotton mixtures ... with different designs of flowers, stripes, or other motives for women's and children's dress, handkerchiefs, and other things in public use.' Unfortunately, the samples furnished did not give satisfaction when washed in hot water so the *intendant* declined their request. However, two years later the Dantons tried again, submitting a stronger case both to the *intendant* at Tours and to Vincent de Gournay, who had been appointed intendant in charge of commerce at the beginning of that year.[17] With the support of a distinguished Angevin they refuted objections to their proposals and in March 1752 obtained permission 'to dye in blue in good quality and workmanship the linen fabrics made in Anjou and the locality, but *without permission to supply from elsewhere*, nor to employ *any cotton fabrics* in this work [our italics].' The words of the regulation are printed in italics here because within a few months the Dantons extended the meaning to cover printed fabrics. Some months later, several bales of 'preserved' dyed cottons were seized at the homes of Parisian dyers. How were the regulations to be applied? After debate the Chamber of Commerce determined in May 1753 on freedom to dye *toiles*. The decision was a progressive one, but it left the practical problem of how the Government inspectors were to distinguish between the *toiles teintes à la réserve* (i.e. dyed goods that were pencilled with indigo on the Indian technique) and *toiles imprimées* (i.e. printed with mordants on linens or cotton and linen mixtures). 'It is easy to see that the freedom to make *toiles teintes* [dyed fabrics] was coming to France, but the *Conseil* did not seem to have recognised it',[18] a perceptive contemporary wrote.

In July 1754 Jacques-Daniel Cottin, a former Parisian banker, in partnership with a textile printer called Cabannes, 'inventor of a secret process of dyeing *toiles*', and five Parisian businessmen set up a factory to dye *toiles* with indigo. They leased buildings for six years within the Arsenal from the officer commanding the artillery. A man called Bernier was engaged as *directeur* of the factory with a financial stake in the company of three sols out of twenty. All the dyers he employed were trained in the principles of Cabannes, using only the indigo dyeing technique. The directions of Roussel, the master dyer in blue, were so neglected that numerous pieces were spoiled and had to be re-dyed in black, but this did not prevent Cottin inserting two public announcements and pictures of his products in the *Journal Oeconomique* of April and June 1755. He boldly presented his works as 'authorised by the [King's] *Conseil* and protected by the Chamber of Commerce.' His initiative induced some merchants to order several pieces which were seized by the tax officers responsible for regulating the trade.[19] Perhaps it was for this reason that Bernier turned to printing in 'oil colours', thereby threatening the maintenance of authority by the 'Establishment', while his partners terminated their association with him. Cottin then 'searched everywhere for people who had special secrets' which penetrated the oriental techniques.

The existence of a strong potential demand, demonstrated by various seizures of illegally printed goods, continued to promise profit to anyone who could exploit it. Cottin hired the first cotton printers from Geneva and Neuchâtel in spring 1758.[20] It was at just this moment that the son of the Dantons' partner Pierre Daviais, an Angers mercer, attempted to launch his own concern on the outskirts of the town. He was helped by a 'colourist', a former *imprimeur à la cire* from the Arsenal factory who had left to seek his fortune in Nantes. The earliest factory in Nantes for producing printed *indiennes* (cotton fabrics printed in the Indian style) was built by Jean-Baptiste Ferey at the beginning of 1758. Disagreement broke up the partnership but the rapid equipping of a second factory on the banks of the Loire, opened in summer 1759, followed directly after the arrival there of a young Neuchatel engraver, Jean-Francois Landry.

In May 1758 Landry and his friend Henry Sandoz, who was several years older, were planning to go to Paris when they were engaged by a man called Morlet from Colombier, 'who was looking for good workers'. Morlet told them that if they would like employment with Cottin's company then he would tell them how to get there. They agreed, were paid for their journey, and set out on 1 June 1758. Landry remained for barely four months at Cottin's and then went to a competitor who wanted him to join his own 'conspiracy'. Prosecuted by the Arsenal Court at the end of February 1759, he blamed his previous employer for the arrangements of his workshop and demanded to be either paid in accordance with the agreement between them or else allowed to work wherever it suited him. This is why he soon left Paris for Nantes.[21]

These quarrels and different initiatives are all evidence of the impatience of those who wanted to profit from the relaxation of the law after 1753. Each in turn, whether established entrepreneur or skilled worker, was restless with the existing situation and felt that the hour of emancipated enterprise in manufacturing had arrived. Vincent de Gournay and the polygraph Abbé Morellet prepared the way for repeal of the law by publishing various tracts, as well as by the publication of prospective legislation related to the printing of different types of *toiles* and fabrics. On 21 January 1759 restrictions on the printing of silk were lifted, but those on *toiles* and cotton fabrics were removed only in the following September and confirmed by an *arrêt* of 28 October. In order to protect the new-born industry and 'the freedom of pencilling and printing,' duties were laid on all imported *toiles* – 15 per cent on plain goods and 25 per cent on printed ones. On the other hand, all exports were free of tax. The boldness of several administrators, inspired by liberal principles, in drawing up people's rights in this matter finally freed the new enterprises. This emancipation was the signal for the invasion of the French market by genuine *indiennes* smuggled in by Swiss and Genevan traders.[22] The evolution of the market is strikingly illustrated by the supply record of a leading Montpellier merchant house, Ittier & Reboul (Table 18).

In France, as in Britain and Germany, the early textile printing works varied much in size, but taken as a class they represent an unusual concentration of fixed capital. Here, as elsewhere, there is no comprehensive collection of data, but Table 19 assembles details from different sources to illustrate their size. The *livre* was worth $10\frac{1}{2}$d.–11d. sterling so that fixed capital invested in these protofactories varied, on this collection of information, from £400 to £170,000, with a lot of concerns around the £750 to £1,000 mark. The largest French printworks, that is to say, represented a greater

Table 18 The development of the supply of fabrics by Ittier & Reboul of Montpellier, 1751–61

Year	Cottons (%)	Woollens (%)	Silks (%)	Printed (%)	'Swiss' (%)	Total (l.)
1751	68.88	12.90	18.20	0	0	45,320
1752	60.23	16.12	23.65	0	0	33,659
1753	78.70	7.96	13.14	0	0	56,383
1754	69.59	12.80	17.62	0	0	76,549
1755	68.68	20.25	9.00	2.00	0	45,393
1756	75.76	12.71	11.53	0	0	52,551
1757	49.06	14.85	11.37	24.72	1.75	40,157
1758	67.50	10.52	7.40	14.58	7.44	49,527
1759	4.90	4.80	0	72.85	17.45	34,383
1760	5.20	2.75	0	92.16	77.52	72,451
1761	11.11	0.96	0	87.68	83.55	128,153

SOURCE: AD, Hérault: 8: B444.
NOTE: 'Swiss' means printed fabrics supplied by Swiss traders.

Table 19 Assets of some French textile printing firms, 1767–89

Factory	Location and date of foundation	Total assets (l.)	Fixed capital (l.)	Date of inventory
Jacques Baron	Essonnes, 1762	nd	19,989 (P)	1768
Danton & Moreau	Angers, 1752	688,270	115,000 (PB)	1769
		402,193	70,314 (PB)	1771
Sarrasin & Oberkampf	Jouy, 1760	1,472,220	122,223 (PB)	1769
		5,682,787	345,553 (PB)	1781
Daguet & Moll	Coye (Oise)	104,856	15,000 (P)	1772
Seimandy & Liquier	Montpellier, 1772	128,075	22,500 (P)	1778
Brenier & Cie	Paris, 1771	118,480	14,800 (P)	
Garnier, Danse & Thévard	Beauvais, 1777	2,534,775	244,320 (PB)	1781
Imhoff	Melun, 1776	129,360	14,700 (P)	1778
Paris & Chaland	Vernaison, 1785	176,411	57,250 (PB)	1787
Lesourd de Lisle	Angers, 1785	154,707	18,000 (P)	1787
Josserand *frères*	Lyon-Vaise, ?1780	33,565	18,057 (P)	1788
Keittinger *père*	Montpellier, 1786	55,571	8,680 (P)	1786
Rother & Koechlin	Nantes, 1786	251,908	75,572 (PB)	1786
Simon, François	St. Denis, ?1762	28,500	12,000 (P)	1767
			15,000 (P)	1774
J. J. Mollien	Rouen, ?	nd	5,000 (P)	1780
Albert, René	Gentilly, ?	131,244	18,000 (P)	1777
Denize, Nicolas	St. Denis, ?	45,617	12,000 (PB)	1778
Perrenod, Siméon	Melun, 1776	547,064	144,367 (PB)	1789
			43,630 (P)	

SOURCE: S. Chassagne, 'Du nouveau sur un atelier de toiles teintes à la reserve à Angers ...', *Annales de Bretagne*, LXXXIII (1976), p. 170. Archives de Paris: D4 B6 (bankruptcies). Archives Loire-Atl: B5564, L suppl. 458; EXII/105.
NOTE: (P) = plant only; (PB) = plant and buildings.

concentration of fixed capital than the most celebrated textile factories of the day, the Arkwright mills, but the more numerous small printing works evidently fell below this standard.

Chapter 9

The Making of an Entrepreneur

In autumn 1759, when the prohibition on the printing and selling of printed calicoes was finally repealed, the young Christoff-Philipp Oberkampf had been working for more than a year at Cottin's workshop in the Arsenal. He was one of a colony of German emigrés employed in printing and cabinet making who drank together in the taverns of the Arsenal *quartier*. They talked about how to stave off the threat of wage cuts or unemployment with the coming of winter and swapped information on new jobs being offered in their trade. From the previous autumn there had been a trickle of departures to other workshops. Dissatisfaction dated from Cottin's complaint to the Arsenal court that some of his employees had violated the royal decree of 2 January 1749 which forbade any worker to terminate his employment, and any master to engage a new workman without written leave.[1] Cottin's plea to the court had led to the imprisonment of two Swiss printers, and by this means he hoped to arrest the flow of skilled men who were being seduced away to new competitors, now multiplying fast.

Oberkampf heard of various opportunities. Legrand & Hermel, a partnership between a printer and dyer that had enticed away one of the imprisoned men, was followed by a partnership between one of Hermel's workmen and a well-connected law student who planned to open a workshop together. Some months later Morlet, the colour foreman at Cottin's, joined this new rival.[2] Then two Zurich printers at the Arsenal followed one of their countrymen to Daviais's factory, near Angers. Consequently, in June 1759, Cottin applied for and was granted a court judgement which renewed the restraints on artisan mobility under penalty of heavy fines for deserting workers and offending masters.[3]

The threat does not appear to have deterred Oberkampf since,

Plate 5 Christoff Philipp Oberkampf, from a contemporary print (Musée Oberkampf, Jouy)

as early as July, he was considering breaking the three-year contract into which he had entered only three months earlier. 'I advise you to terminate your agreement as soon as possible', his father recommended to him. 'Concentrate on doing your work well and, with God's help, you will overcome this difficulty'.[4] Christoff first thought of leaving for Spain, then he looked round for an opportunity of settling in Paris. Fourteen months after his arrival in the capital he had managed to master French sufficiently well to run his own concern. In December he learned of an opportunity to enter into a partnership with three bourgeois capitalists from Paris and Versailles who were taking an interest in a new printing factory. At only 21 years of age Oberkampf was so sure of his technical abilities that he was ready to consider running a new factory alone, a factory in a miserable, unheard-of village called Jouy, two miles from Versailles. How could he have acquired so much confidence at such a young age?[5]

The answer lies in young Oberkampf's family background and experience. Christoff-Philipp was descended from a family of Wurtemberg dyers settled in Vaihingen-an-der-Enz, 17 miles northwest of Stuttgart, since the end of the Thirty Years' War. His great-grandfather Stephan, his grandfather Matheus, his great-uncle Johannes Schindler, and his father Philipp-Jakob, were all dyers (see Fig. 5). Two of his father's sisters married local craftsmen: a baker and a saddler, both guild members. Twenty-one cousins were all master craftsmen, five of them dyers (*schoen- und schwartzfärber*), The Oberkampfs of Vaihingen and their marital connections constituted an homogeneous and endogamous social group.

When he was 18 Philipp-Jakob left the family workshop 'in order to improve his art', as was the usual practice at the time. Three years later he married a *Kunstgärtner*'s daughter, Anna Magdalena Sehm, whose father was the gardener of the Court of Hohenlohe. The young couple settled at Wiesenbach, near Ansbach, where four children were born: Johannes-Albrecht (died soon after in 1736), Christoff-Philipp (1738), Friederich-Stephan (1740) and Sophia-Dorothea (1742). In the following year the father gave up his earlier vocation, for reasons unknown, and joined a flannel copper-plate printing factory at Heilbronn as a dyer. In 1745 he sold his workshop to his younger brother Stephan and brought wife and children with him to Heilbronn. According to the brief biography written by his son during the Napoleonic Empire, whilst staying in Heilbronn Philipp-Jakob would have 'discovered how to print blue on a white ground, or brush-application.'[6] This was the English 'China blue' method introduced in Bremen around 1740 and known, as early as 1745, at Ryhiner's in Basle,[7] precisely the same factory where Oberkampf's father entered on a three-year contract at the end of 1749.[8] By that time he had most likely acquired a thorough knowledge of blue printing.

Sixty years later Christoff-Philipp still remembered that he walked with his father from Heilbronn to Basle when he was eleven-and-a-half years old. It was here that he started learning drawing and

114 *European Textile Printers in the Eighteenth Century*

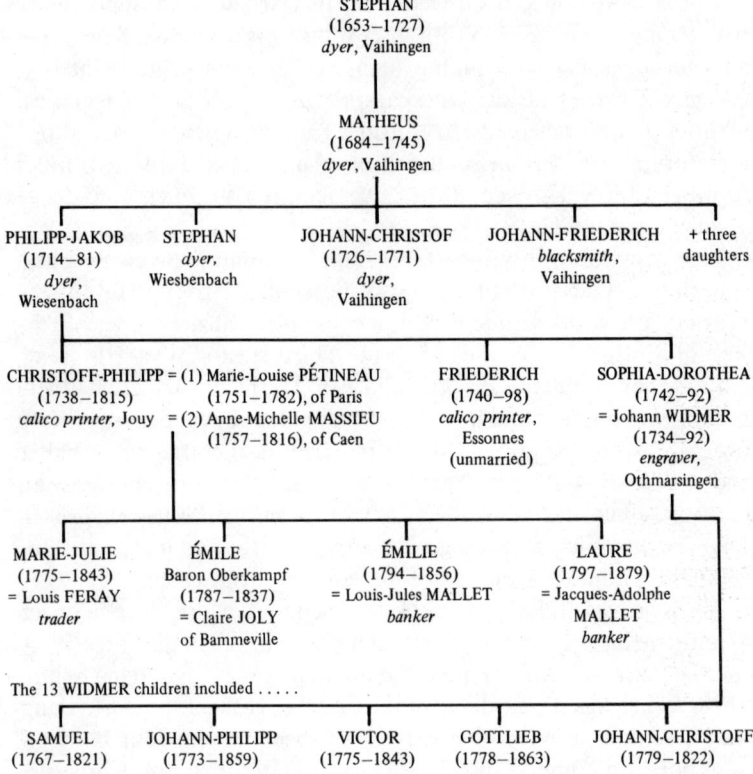

Fig. 5 Simplified pedigree of the Oberkampf family of Vaihingen-an-der-Enz (near Stuttgart), from 1653 (SOURCES: Jouy parish registers, diverse sources) (NOTE: only C.-P. Oberkampf's immediate forebears and members of the family who were connected with the business are included)

engraving. Then he worked as a *tireur* with a printer, with whom he kept in touch. In January 1752 Philipp-Jakob suddenly left Ryhiner's factory, curtailing his stay because he believed he had little opportunity to set up his own concern. The Margrave of Baden-Durlach was offering various legal and fiscal advantages to any Protestant who could set up a trade or a factory in three of his towns (Lörrach, near Basle, Emmedingen and Mülheim, near Friburg). In the following April Philipp-Jakob was allowed to settle as a *schutzbürger* in Lörrach and to establish a calico printing enterprise. He subsequently rented a former paper-mill and, at the beginning of

1753, sold his goods 'easily in Frankfurt, Karlsruhe, and in the Palatinate, as well as in Lörrach and the neighbourhood'. But his financial means appeared inadequate to the authorities who soon withdrew his privileges and gave them to an exiled printer from Bern, Friederich Kupfer, who was believed to be better able to increase local industry.[9] Oberkampf's father then moved to Switzerland and engaged himself for six years as head of the Brütel brothers' factory at Schafisheim, near Lenzburg, in Aarau. He stayed for barely two years 'because he always fancied a workshop of his own', his son later explained. The Brütels' prosecution of their defaulting manager reveals his proud, irascible and violent character – personality traits which, we shall see, Christoff-Philipp inherited. The prosecution brought by the Lenzburg bailiff did not, however, prevent Philipp-Jakob from continuing the small workshop set up at Aarau, where he was 'partnered with some burgesses of the town'.[10]

Christoff-Philipp assisted his father for a while but then, when he was 18 years old, he asked for leave 'to travel and work in other factories'. This was refused, but 'After several postponements I took French leave', he later confessed. Like father, like son: beyond his legitimate wish to improve his knowledge, this unlawful departure, encouraged by the mother, confirms the incompatibility of two fierce tempers. Young Oberkampf arrived at Mulhouse and joined the Cour-de-Lorraine factory as an engraver.[11] He stayed only six months, however, for his father demanded his return and threatened to put a curse on him. Nevertheless, he learned engraving and, returning home, taught his younger brother in the family workshop. He was waiting for a better opportunity to leave and extend his experience. One day in September 1758 a dyer from St. Gall, who was then employed by Cottin and at home to recruit printing artists, offered him an opportunity to go to Paris. 'I never welcomed anybody more than Mr Franz [Simon]. My father promised to let me go and I left a few weeks later.' After a six-month trial he signed on for three years as a colour-maker, being paid 24 *l.* a week for colour making, besides engraving which was paid extra. This represented a wage nearly four times that of a good worker and twice that of Neuenburger printers engaged by Cottin in the previous year. It is easy to see how much this entrepreneur appreciated him.

In Paris, trade was so prosperous for printers that Christoff-Philipp was soon begging his father to let his younger brother join him. The leave was granted, although with some reluctance for, as his father put it, 'you know his strengths', i.e. his limited abilities. Friederich was in Paris by the end of September, but instead of getting a job at Cottin's he obtained work as a master-engraver and overseer in a little workshop in the suburb of Saint-Marcel, set up some weeks earlier by three partners – a porter of the *Contrôle Général*, a burgess of Versailles and an officer of the King's House – who knew nothing about printing but its easy profits. The limited talent of the younger Oberkampf became obvious very soon. 'Unable to keep order in the works', he advised his masters to recruit his elder brother, who laid down his conditions and obtained what he wanted: half of all future profits for him and his brother and a bonus of 10 sols for each printed piece as a reward for engraving woodblocks. Their verbal agreement also forecasts the transference of the works from the rue de Seine Saint-Marcel to Jouy, a village along the River Bièvre – the river on which the famous Gobelins works stood – not very far from the dwelling of two of the partners. By the end of January 1760 they were jointly renting from a mason a small house named Stonebridge House. It had three lower rooms, one upper room, three stables and a yard behind that the owner promised to repair.[12] Meanwhile, Christoff-Philipp continued to work at Cottin's although he had obtained his leave for 30 December.

When his sons reported their business with Fritz's employer, Oberkampf's father recommended caution and distrust. 'Does your *patron* know the trade? Has he a family which he should work for? I hope that God blesses your enterprise,' he wrote to his son.[13] These brief excerpts from Philipp-Jakob's long letter reveal all his basic instincts and something of the education given to his children; first, 'think before embarking on any enterprise ... and you will avoid empty hands at the end', and secondly, 'call upon Almighty God to prosper you'. Material success and pietist morality cannot easily be separated in his mind. From the beginning, family religiosity placed the Jouy factory under Godly protection and clearly reveals Christoff-Philipp within the Protestant-capitalist tradition. It is, however, interesting to note that the religious language of his parents, nurtured with Holy Scripture and rich with hymn quotations, is in contrast with the dry and secular prose of the elder son. One instance, among others, illustrates Christoff-Philipp's lack of religious display. In June 1778 his father sent him news of the successive deaths of three grandchildren, all victims of smallpox. 'We are in the depths of misery, not because of these angels entering into Heaven, for there they are happy, but when thinking of the sufferings these dear children endured'. 'Were the three children well looked after?' was the only reply, apart from a statement that he intended to innoculate his family. This intention was acted upon

The Making of an Entrepreneur   117

in 1782 but unfortunately proved to be fatal for his first wife. We have to wait until post-Revolutionary times, almost exactly when the *Genius of Christianity* was published, for the first explicit mention of 'God's will' in his correspondence – after his 16 year old son's death from a pulmonic disease.[15] However, the Jouy master chose both his wives from the Parisian Protestant circle,[16] and twice married according to the Protestant rite (Lutheran first, Calvinist second), though his children were baptised at the Catholic Parish church like any other humble servant of the King.[17]

Oberkampf's education came mainly from his mother and it left an indelible mark on his deepest beliefs. His faith is shown most clearly in an undated profession but probably written during the Empire; that is, in the later years of his life:

> One can only know God by His works. It matters that everyone knows and fulfills the duties that God's law demands, both towards his neighbour and himself.
> The apparent happiness of this life is nothing, for there is another in the hereafter when the Supreme Being will reward the good and punish the evil. There is nothing useful to know but that which teaches us to do good. God is witness to all our thoughts and acts, good and bad. He rewards the first and punishes the second. We must do good works without ostentation because God likes it so, endure evil without murmuring because He will compensate for it, and live every day of our life as we shall be glad to have done when we appear before Him.[18]

Oberkampf practised the traditional family virtues. A grateful son, he honoured his parents by his regular money remittances from 1766 onwards, notwithstanding the occasional scoldings he gave to them. 'I don't understand where you put your money, except living in luxury.' And he threatened 'no remittances at all' if they stayed at Othmarsingen 'against his will'.[19] In 1777 he reluctantly paid 18,000 Bern florins in buying the Binzenhof's[20] for his father in order to provide his parents with an income from rents in their old age. They were acknowledged as burgesses and citizens of the Bern Republic shortly before his mother's death.[21] An affectionate brother, he surely suffered from knowing that his 'dear sister' was married to a lazy, intemperate and violent Swiss, who made her pregnant 15 times between 1761 and 1786.[22] When their father died in June 1781 he committed all his properties in Switzerland to Sophia-Dorothea so she would lack nothing and could bring up her children with ease. An attentive uncle, he looked after his nephews' education, although his primary motive in this case lay in the fact that at that time he still had no son. In 1778, after his mother's death, he called the elder Widmer boy Samuel, born in 1767 and fresh from local school, to see him. His undisclosed aim was to prepare him to become his eventual successor at the head of the Jouy enterprise.

Oberkampf's family background and standards are reflected in his relationship with the adolescent nephew. He sent him to a boarding school in Paris for three years to learn French. Samuel there revealed not only considerable intellectual gifts but also a very disobedient temper, close to rebellion, perhaps against his father. In 1781 he began his printing apprenticeship by drawing and engraving but he hardly acquired more sense. 'I pray you, dear Samuel, for God's sake, behave as a virtuous man', his mother wrote to him. 'Be meek and obedient with my dear brother'. 'Though he is sixteen, he is still a child', his uncle complained, 'he is lazy and does only what he is compelled to do. I am always in conflict with him'.[24] Continued trouble impelled Samuel to desert the factory. For two days he wandered through Paris looking for a cousin who might help him to return home. He finally gave himself up in the Parisian office of the Jouy factory where Mme de Maraise set him on the right path, which led back to Jouy. The just wrath of the master-uncle insisted that the delinquent confess 'his sincere repentance' in a letter and to promise that he would never offend him again. Three months later, however, he was caught 'playing in a gambling-den,' and was given his first 'smack' by his tutor-uncle. Indeed, he dared 'to buy on credit a hat, a pair of stockings and another of shoe buckles, to go shooting in spite of my forbidding', and worst of all, 'to steal gun powder from a wardrobe', the key of which he also obtained without authority! Oberkampf prescribed the penalty: 'I'll give him only three pounds a month from now onwards', instead of six as before. 'The biggest risk', Oberkampf explained to his sister, 'is that I am his uncle, and he thinks that I am rich enough and that he need not try his utmost'. But the warning was heeded; thereafter Samuel did not make his 'poor uncle' angry any more.[25] From July 1784 he was engraving woodblocks and then drawing patterns for the works. When he was 19 his uncle finally made clear to him that his only ambition was 'that he become an honourable man'. He therefore insisted 'that he knows thoroughly all the functions of his rank' if he wanted, some day, to run a factory. The youth could only succeed by knowing all the technical operations sufficiently well 'to be able to teach the operatives and take the place of any of them. Otherwise you are subordinate to everyone, and

The Making of an Entrepreneur 119

obliged to believe what they say, without any means of checking the facts'. To reach this position, 'employ all your lost time ... to get knowledge about everything, including handwriting and accounting,' he was instructed.

'If my father had given me a better education', the old Oberkampf lamented in 1800, 'I would not have been compelled to share the fruits of 30 years continuous labour with partners'.[26] This was an inaccurate and unfair comment. Had he learnt French or even Italian as did his nephews Philipp and Victor,[27] because of his pressure, he would nevertheless have been unable to set up his own factory without the help of partners, i.e. without external capital. About 1760 the family patrimony was practically worthless.[28] Neither the 500 *l.* saved nor the help of friendly merchants were sufficient to cover the initial expenses of the new factory. The poor Wurtemberg immigrant only became a famous manufacturer and 'Patriarch of Jouy' because of the experience and capital injected into the concern by partners with capital and their social connections.

Oberkampf's earliest partnership was with the three partners of the Saint-Marcel workshop who agreed to move to Jouy, near Versailles, the eighteenth-century centre of French fashion and conspicuous consumption. The partners were soon short of capital to continue the factory and turned to the Paris merchant who supplied their raw materials and marketed the Jouy prints, Claude-François Levasseur de Verville.[29] Levasseur was already in partnership with a Lyons merchant called Dailly in the silk trade, but quickly recognised the possibilities of the trade in prints. He was soon in a key position in the new partnership and he contrived to allay Oberkampf's fears and to oust Tavannes, the last of the three original partners. In March 1763 he paid 6,200 *l.* for the business which he himself estimated was worth 'more than 15,000', and the concern became Levasseur et Cie.[30] Meantime, however, a sleeping partner, Joseph-Alexandre Sarassin de Maraise, had been enrolled into the partnership. He had been an advocate in the Dauphiné *Parlement* (i.e. High Court) and, previously, assistant judge in the Forest court at Grenoble, but was now living on private means in Paris. Levasseur described him as 'a very kindly bachelor, witty, well-mannered ... and well known to a wide circle of friends, some of whom are likely to be useful to us'.[31] He was introduced by the government official responsible for factory regulation in the *Contrôle Général* at Versailles, and contributed 50,000 *l.* (about £2,080) to the concern having 'no interest in commerce but an ambition to make his fortune'.[32] Levasseur later tried to push Sarassin de Maraise out of the partnership, but, as we shall see, it was the lawyer who survived, continuing as Oberkampf's partner for 27 years. As a creator of the Jouy enterprise he must be recognised as the equal of his artisan partner.

Maraise's legal skills were valuable from the first. When Cottin brought a prosecution against Oberkampf and Haffner for desertion he successfully defended them.[33] Then, when the other Bièvre river users, jealous of the new works, complained to the Forest Court in Paris, Maraise was again in court. The 'advocate without a practice' as Linguet called him, soon proved himself to be an excellent legal and financial adviser to the factory. But, not least, he was also Oberkampf's first and best friend in France. He was rapidly able to esteem his character – and not only for its market value – and his feelings were soon reciprocated. When Oberkampf fell ill (in spring 1763) and became depressed, Maraise realised Levasseur's deceit and he asked one of his medical friends to attend his young partner. At the same time Maraise prescribed the right course of action, gave comfort by his calls and letters, and maintained 'his interest' in the business as if it was his own. It would have been very easy for him to conspire with Levasseur to defraud 'the German' though not to get rid of him, for he was essential for the operation of the factory. But Maraise did not attempt to exploit the situation. After breaking with Levasseur he managed the factory's Parisian accounting office, while insisting that he lacked business ability. Moreover, he sacrificed his celibacy to the prosperity of the new enterprise. At the age of 42 he married Mary-Katherin Darcel, the daughter of a Rouen trader.[35] The 'dear partner's' wife soon became more than the 'half' of the partnership. She directed all the double-entry book-keeping, both of Jouy and of Paris, dictated and often wrote all the outgoing correspondence herself, welcomed and entertained customers and correspondents coming through Paris, and generally appeared for the partners before the public authorities, requesting an audience with Trudaire, for example, or, when her husband was away, answering an interview fixed by Necker, who was an intimate friend. Sixty of her autograph letters to Oberkampf[36] show the extraordinary personality of this dominant, playful, cultured, pro-Jansenist Anglophile, skilled in accountancy as well as in medicine, Tissot's friend and supporter of his advocacy of infant breast feeding.[37]. Every line of her letters reveals her wit and good sense. It is regretable that there appears to be no portrait of her.

This energetic woman took such care of Oberkampf's brother

Frédéric (Friedrich) that she found a wife for him, a woman that Christoff-Philipp found 'more suitable for himself', and asked his brother to give way. Miss Pétineau, a wine-grocer's daughter, appears to have been an honest middle-class match, bringing a 15,000 *l.* dowry.[38] Her death, eight years later in 1782, left Oberkampf 'quite empty-hearted, a vacuum which can be filled only by a good, wise and meek wife looking as far as possible like the friend I unceasingly pine for'.[39] He found such a wife in 1785 in Anna-Michelle Massieu, the daughter of a Protestant merchant from Caen and recently ennobled. 'She is 29, but she thinks like a woman of 40, she has the best possible reputation. . . . She will bring me 100,000 *l.*', Christoff wrote when sending news of his wedding to his sister.[40] Four children also came from this second union, three of whom reached adult years: Emile, his only son (1787–1837), Émilie (1784–1856) and Laura (1797–1879), who both married sons of Baron Mallet de Chalmassy, a founder of the Bank of France.[41] Between his first and second marriages Oberkampf had raised himself from the trading middle-class to the business élite, a social elevation confirmed by patents of nobility in March 1787, no doubt owing to the influential friends of his 'dear partner' Maraise, himself ennobled by a Chancery office bought in 1784, and father-in-law of a high servant at the King's Council.[42]

Four months after the conferment of his title Oberkampf notified Maraise of the end of their partnership because of his 'duty towards my children and relations [his nephews].' The displaced partner needed more than three years to come to terms with his fall. Nevertheless, he retired with some 4,500,000 *l.*, a handsome return for a 50,000 *l.* initial investment. 'You are right', Mme de Maraise wrote to Oberkampf on 19 July 1789, 'our fortune is adequate, perhaps too great, for our children do not surrender themselves to the shame, dangers and lethargy of leisure'.[43] Political circumstances afforded Maraise a good investment for his fortune in *Biens Nationaux* and finally removed his sorrow at being no longer at the head of the Jouy enterprise.

The Revolutionary period provides final evidence of Oberkampf's genius as an entrepreneur. The factory was only once at a standstill, in February 1814, and was successfully 'requisitioned' by a decree of the *Comité de Salut Public* in floréal II, but its master never lost his control over the local situation. Unlike Maraise, who was obviously reluctant to accept the events of 1789, he welcomed the changes that followed the States-General meeting. In February 1790 he became the first elected mayor of his commune and his nephew,

Samuel, was in command of the local National Guard, a military force made up for the most part of factory workers. In 1793 his elder brother-in-law, Pétineau, succeeded him as mayor, while the younger Pétineau was the first chairman of the Jouy Popular Society, which Citizen Oberkampf joined, pledging, as required, 'to maintain freedom, equality, safety and property... the unity and indivisibility of the Republic, mans' and citizens' rights'.[44] His Jacobism explains why he contributed some 300,000 *l.* to various voluntary or compulsory loans between 1792 and 1796. This was the price he had to pay to ensure his personal safety – perhaps his life – and to retain his enterprise.[45] Only one employee, an engraver, dared to challenge his power by denouncing him to the Parisian Committees and that came to nothing. The Jouy Popular Society removed him from his Government appointment as *agent national* and Oberkampf, with a great show of magnaminity, gave him his job back at the factory.

The pioneers of new industry in the eighteenth century were characteristically strong personalities who worked to establish a powerful control over their workers' whole lives. Oberkampf was evidently an entrepreneur cast in this resolute mould but his strategy seems to have varied from that of some of his best-known contemporaries. Under the *ancien régime* there is no trace at Jouy of the sponsored friendly societies which were such an established feature of industrial relations at several early British factories, not least those of the Peels. The idea was not uniquely British; a society was founded by the workers at Wetter's printworks at Orange as early as 1764 and another was launched at Morlet's works at Troyes in 1792.[46] But despite his autocracy Oberkampf never suffered from the labour unrest which gave so much trouble to the local authorities in Beauvais in 1778, in Vernaison (Lyons) in 1787, or – to take an English example – in Nottingham in 1792 and 1797.[47] So long as the master of Jouy made sure that everyone had a full stomach his authority would not be threatened, and that is why he dreaded a prolonged recession in trade. The collapse of the *assignats* at the beginning of 1792 gave rise to the first united action of the printers against Oberkampf. Keenly aware of the problem and of its political implication he met them with a statement reaffirming his authority and declaring his policy:

> Monsieur Oberkampf wishes to give full consideration to the petition that the printers have presented to him, and has made up his mind to grant the wage rise asked for, just at the moment when the prices of goods have fallen back to their normal level.

He hopes that this new sign of his attachment to his workers will persuade them to redouble their zeal in order to merit its continuation. It is in giving the closest attention to their work, in renewing their efforts every day to add to the soundness and high quality of their work, that Monsieur Oberkampf will be assured the means to constantly maintain the well-being of all those around him. He never separates his prosperity from that of his workforce, at the centre of which he continues to live like a solicitous father, increasingly occupied with their interests and always ready to render them the services which they have merited.

Their wives and children will find a secure employment in work in which they will lack nothing, and where their behaviour will be beyond reproach. If they become ill they will be paid the same wages as in good health. But these benefits can only be assured by their industriousness, their care and their diligence; they will soon be unemployed if they are allowed to become idle and undisciplined, for if the production which provides their livelihood falls below standard it will not be able to meet the competition of other manufacturers nor be sold at the same price. The merchants will put off buying, and a works which cost so much trouble and care to establish will soon be on the verge of bankruptcy.

How then will Monsieur Oberkampf find employment for his workers? Inevitably he will be forced to reduce their number and lower their wages, and in such circumstances what will become of Jouy and the country surrounding it? This calamity will never happen if everyone fulfills his task with zeal, obeys the law, respects the magistrates, and takes care to avoid the troubles that have agitated our neighbourhood. Fathers should set an example to their children so that they grow up to love virtue and their work, and are always happy ... It is violence that brings scarcity; food is in plentiful supply where markets are free and law and order prevails.[48]

In autumn 1797 there was a second explosion in prices, and again the printers petitioned Citizen Oberkampf. He replied with a signed notice insisting that 'It is just and also in the interest of everyone that I should be master of my own concern and give each worker what is convenient to me, for isn't that what you do for your children?'[49] Six months later the marriage of Oberkampf's elder daughter to Louis Feray was made an occasion to demonstrate the reunification of the master's family of workers. The workers paraded before him in groups – printers, painters, etc. – to present their allegiance and their bouquets to the bride, apparently with the greatest happiness and satisfaction.[50] Perhaps the most revealing illustration of Oberkampf's personal autocracy is contained in an anecdote recorded by Gottlieb Widmer.[51] The record is worth reproducing in full because it shows the Biblical overtones of the autocrat's thought patterns:

> About the year 1805 several new printing works were set up around Paris, and they looked for the best workers of Jouy and tried to attract them, chiefly the printers. Some of these allowed themselves to be tempted, and together asked to leave ... Victor Dubois, one of the oldest workers of the factory, gave Monsieur Oberkampf a list of deserters, including some 15 names. The master told him: 'The certificates will be ready in three days. Make good use of the time for thinking about what you are doing'. On the third day the printers returned, already less numerous, and their leader, with two or three others only, entered the office where Monsieur Oberkampf was signing his mail. Dubois came to him and said, with some difficulty, 'We have come to fetch our certificates'. Monsieur Oberkampf answered with simple words of emotion: 'Here they are. Go away. I hope you find a better master'. They came out without a word, but after some discussion with their workmates they all went back to the printing room to resume their employment.

Oberkampf was above all else the supreme autocrat of Jouy, unchallenged and feared within his domain, exercising power with unfaltering authority for well over 50 years before his death in October 1815.

Chapter 10

The Jouy Works, 1760–1815

The Jouy factory started production at the end of April 1760. At first the processes and techniques employed were rudimentary. 'I see that you have taken the opportunity to open a factory', the father wrote to his two sons when they had formed the partnership with Tavannes. 'Make every effort to produce good work, don't try to go too fast until you are well established'.[1] He did not spare them his advice nor did he cease to offer them help with both the raw material (white *toiles*) and the engraved block patterns for fine furnishings. When it first started the Jouy factory seemed like a smaller version of the father's enterprise at Aarau.

Problems immediately arose. Tavannes and his partners were soon out of ready money and the deed of partnership was never signed. Then the tanners and towers of Paris along with the manager of the Royal Gobelins factory formed a syndicate of river users on the Bièvre and opposed the new factory in the Forest Court.[2] Tavannes damped down this opposition with bribes, but his social connections began to desert him.[3] Just at this moment Cottin initiated his prosecution of Oberkampf and Haffner, as a consequence of which the future of the Jouy enterprise remained precarious for the next two years.[4] Then, in the third year, the parish priest tilted his authority against the enterprise. 'He pretended that I was a bad influence in the country, that neither I nor any foreign workers attended mass, and he didn't like my *toiles* being watered on Sundays', Oberkampf recalled some years later. The most serious threat arose in 1764 when the lord of the manor of Jouy gave permission for the cutting of a new leat (water course) to the new works and the other river users, furious with jealousy, sought revenge on the upstart firm. Tension reached such a pitch that the partners expected sabotage or an attack on their buildings, which in 1766 were already worth 600,000 *l* (£25,000). Even the manorial attorney and village notary joined the opposition in a violent storm of abuse addressed to Maraise in January 1766. 'It looks as if it is impossible to continue here and your great factory will have to be given up', the local official commented.[5]

Nevertheless, the business prospered. In March 1762 the Paris mercer Levasseur became partner in a new company (Levasseur & Cie) to provide half the capital, while the other half was provided by Sarrasin de Maraise, a barrister and *rentier*, with the result that the profits for the two years 1762–3 were 120,000 *l*. From an initial investment of 50,000 *l*. these profits represent an average increase of 120 per cent. It is easy to understand Levasseur's schemes for ejecting the unfortunate Tavannes to take complete control of the business, and it is equally easy to understand the resistance of Maraise and Oberkampf to his tactics. Despite brother Frédéric's departure in October 1760, although he returned three years later, Christophe was by no means short of work for 3,600 pieces were printed between May 1760 and December 1761. 'We work all day and keep the books at night', he explained as an excuse for failing to write to his parents.[6] The house *Pont-de-pierre* soon became inadequate and the work had to be dispersed around various buildings and rented hovels, which made supervision more difficult. The problem rose just at the time when a dozen similar concerns were trying to obtain accommodation for expansion. In July 1764, after protracted proceedings, the Duke of Beuvron at last leased to them four acres in the meadow behind the watermill. 'We can now stay here for the rest of our time in France', Christophe told his parents soon afterwards. He began building immediately, erecting a factory 137 ft long by 40 ft wide (41.5 m × 12.1 m) and three storeys high, intended for the printing and drying sections. It was finished in 1766 at a cost of 70,000 *l*. (£2,900). A second building, situated on adjoining grassland and acquired in 1765, was built between 1771 and 1772 and cost about the same sum. Then, in spring 1773, the partners made a further purchase from Beuvron, buying the old mill of the manor of Jouy with 12 acres of surrounding land for about 43,000 *l*. (£1,790). In this way they expanded their domain on the banks of the Bièvre. The next year the tenant miller installed a new water wheel, 9 ft × 2 ft, which also propelled mechanical beaters for washing the cloth. At the same time Oberkampf and Maraise, the sole owners of the factory after Levasseur was paid off enlarged their investment at various sales.[8] Gosset's houses and Reverend's houses were bought with three acres of meadow land at 'la butteaux-beurres' in January 1772, and a further 15 acres were purchased in the following year.[9] The walled factory enclosure progressively took shape, and with the construction of the constantly-guarded gateway and 'Swiss House', for the Swiss guards, it came to resemble a monastery or fortified manor. These defences were built to protect from predators and vandals the cloths laid out for drying and bleaching, but the monastic isolation from the outside world also served to reinforce the sense of work discipline.

Oberkampf's sales rose sharply between the end of the 1780s (25,000 pieces *per annum*) and 1791 (36,000 pieces), and he was induced to undertake major new building within the factory compound at Jouy. He wanted to assemble all the manual processes under one roof to secure tighter control of his workforce and commissioned a Parisian architect to draw up plans. In 1793 the building was completed, a huge block of four storeys, 111 m long × 14 m wide (343 ft × 45 ft), and 23 m (75 ft) high. As Figure 6 shows, it was lit by 52 arched windows, and each of the main

Fig. 6 The main building at the Jouy works, built 1793

floors must have been some six metres (18 ft) high. As far as we know it was the largest factory building in France or Britain at the time, though unlike the Arkwright-type mills it had no mechanical power. (The largest and most handsome mill completed in Britain at this period was probably Robert Owen's No. 4 Mill at New Lanark which was 156 ft × 33 ft × 70 ft high [47.2 m × 10 m × 21.2 m].) The building fulfilled a vision which Oberkampf had had in mind since 1764; namely, to bring the main manufacturing processes into large closely-supervised areas, with copper plate and wood block printing on the ground floor (231 tables in all), designers and engravers in separate workshops on the first floor, pencilling and sizing on the second floor and warehousing in the top (roof) storey. The completed building cost some 250,000 *l.* (£10,000) and this did not include machinery and equipment, which were largely

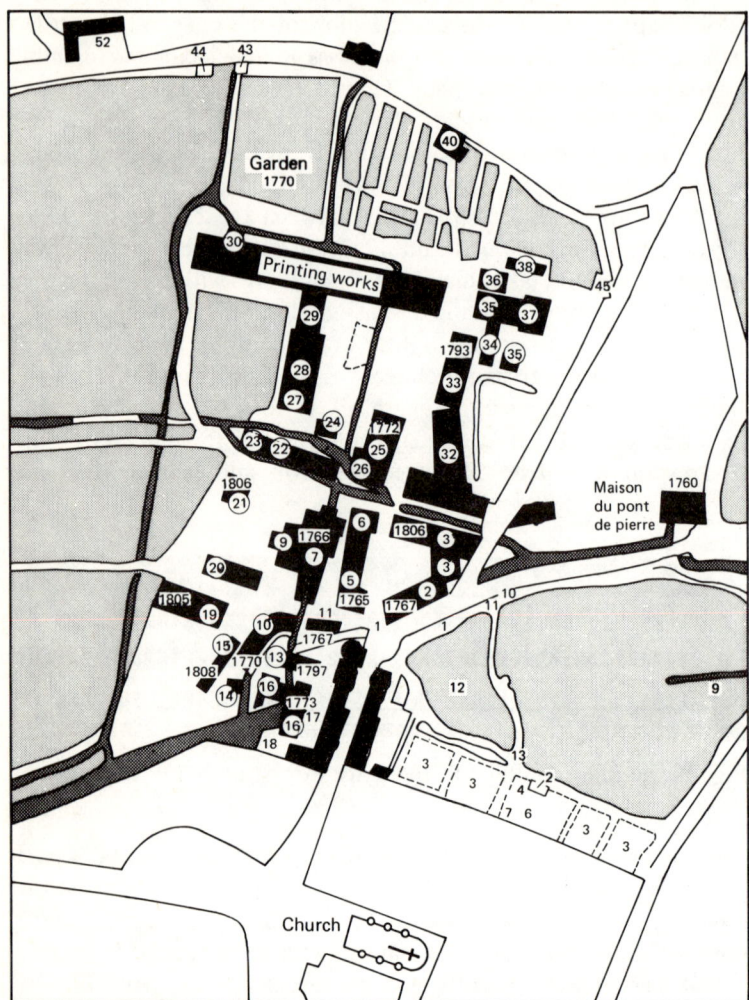

Fig. 7 Plan of the Jouy works under the Empire, 1803–15 (SOURCE: Arch. Communales, Jouy.) (NOTE: Oberkampf's house, no. 2, is still standing, currently used as the mayor's offices.)

KEY

1 Main gateway to the works (1766)
2 Oberkampf's dwelling house (1767)
3 The Widmers' house (1806)
4 Fountain (1767)
5 Office and shops (1765)
6 Drying rooms (1765)
7 Building on the leat (1766)
8 Tenter fields
9 Autoclave machinery (1805)
10 Shelter for rinsing cloths (1770)
11 Building for scrap iron (1767)
12 Shelter for washing cloths (1770)
13 Shelter for utensils (1770–97)
14 Wood store (for engraving) (1773)
15 Machine for engraving rollers (1796–1808)
16 Calendar house (1773)
17 Turret of the old mill (1773)
18 Watering place (for horses)
19 Building of the *croix d'honneur* (1805–8)
20 Joiners' and blacksmiths' workshops (1801)
21 Smithy (blacksmiths' furnaces) (1805)
22 Bleachery (1796)
23 Chlorine bleaching apparatus (1796)
24 Wash house (1796)
25 Building for white cottons (1772)
26 Drying oven (1800)
27 Chemical laboratory (1796)
28 Building for preparing colouring materials (1793)
29 Covered way and wash house (1793)
30 Training school for *bastringue* (1801)
31 Dyeing workshops (1776–1808)
32 Store for 'drugs' (1766–1808)
33 Shelter for carts (1793)
34 Store for the weld (yellow dye) (1796)
35 Store for coal and cinders (1798)
36 Stables (1793–6)
37 Latrines and dunghill (1793)
38 Watering place (horses) (1793)
39 *Jardin anglais*
40 Rordorff's house (1764)

NOTE: the shaded area on the left on the plan represents part of the walled tenter fields, at the far end of which stood the *maison des Suisses* (1772), the Swiss guards' house.

transferred from older buildings. The plan of Oberkampf's works shows how the site looked at the time of its maximum prosperity (Fig. 7). The spectacular development of Jouy depended in the first place on Oberkampf's technical expertise, so we must now turn to examine its development in some detail.

Oberkampf's first visit to London at the end of 1773 reassured him that his decision to extend the Jouy works was right.[10] All the prints that he saw in London and Amsterdam seemed to him to be inferior to his Jouy fabrics. It was fresh confirmation of what Frédéric had concluded in 1769 when he visited Mulhouse. 'According to what I heard, said and saw, I can speak with a clear conscience when I say that I have never yet seen a more beautiful cloth than that which we manufacture', he roundly declared.[11]

The technical success of the works at Jouy owed much to the father's expertise. From 1760 to 1772 he constantly supported his sons' enterprise with his advice and schemes, and also by sending them skilled technicians, patterns for *toiles blanches*, and dyes.[12] By their skill and devotion, Bossert the engraver, Rohdorff the designer and dyer, and Haffner and Schramm the printers, were responsible between them for building up a major part of the Jouy workforce. Perrenoud, a Neuchatel joiner, constructed and installed a 'polishing' shop, for finishing printed cottons, which was driven by a horse wheel on a plan similar to those at Berne and Aarau of which his father had sent details. When the father made his first visit to Jouy early in 1766, being in a strong position with his creditors at the time, he was able to have proof of the soundness of his technical knowledge.

By autumn 1769 the family business at Othmarsingen seemed to have got worse. Christoff decided to send his brother there, which pleased his mother and sister who were longing to see him. But above all it gave Frédéric the opportunity of looking at the quality of Swiss and Alsatian prints. He broke his journey at Mulhouse where he examined a variety of patterns, none of which he liked. He was unable to visit any factories, which annoyed his brother. Then he moved on to Basle where he enquired whether anyone printed in *bleu anglais*, but obtained no response. He collected more than 60 patterns which the local printers were going to risk sending into France. (Perhaps Christoff considered the possibility of becoming an importer of these smuggled goods?) At Aarau he met several engravers and examined them before confiding his recruiting mission. Again on foot, he visited the warehouses of Zurich, Soleure and Berne, and he would really have liked to have found out the composition of Kupfer's mordant. At Neuchatel he was honoured by an invitation to dine with the secretary of the great firm of Pourtalès and saw their new factory.[13] 'I can't say that I saw anything new', he recorded for his brother's benefit. However, a visit to assess the bankrupt stock of a firm at Greng, near Morat, the old fortified town to the south of Lake Neuchâtel, was more productive. Frédéric saw some copper plates offered for sale and was immediately enthusiastic. Moreover, he managed to recruit a young copper plate engraver he had chanced to meet on his travels. As Oberkampf's fame as a textile printer rests on the quality of his copper plate designs, and as his achievement in this field can be traced to Frédéric's discovery, it is important to explore this development at length.

The technique of printing fabrics with engraved copper plates had been perfected in Dublin and London in the middle 1750s but the secret was well-guarded and only slowly dispersed among the numerous Continental manufacturers. As far as we know the technique was known to just four or five firms outside Britain in 1769. It appears to have been introduced to the Continent at Sèvres by a London printer, Louis Beauford, with an English mechanic called Parsons. These migrants were known to Oberkampf's father who mentioned them in a letter in 1764. Frédéric wrote from Morat that the copper plate printing machine he had seen was built by 'an Englishman' and that 'two printers from Sèvres worked it, but I don't know their names'. There were also two copper plate printers from Sèvres working at Baron's factory at Corbeil in 1766, and Baron's probate inventory records 'a mill for copper printing, with its table and wheels, valued at 600 livres' and he had 'five engraved plates'. The technique had also reached Bourges, according to Frédéric's letters, and Wetter's factory at Orange in the south of France by this time. In 1769 a company applied to the French government to set up 'a factory for copper plate printing... on the English manner' at Haguenau, in Alsace. The applicants claimed that 'the Swiss factories do not have the secret of copper printing and print only with wood blocks', so it seems that the partners did not know about the short-lived Greng enterprise. From this survey it is clear that the London technique was still a novelty in France in 1769 and as yet at an early stage of development in those few localities where it was known.[14]

Oberkampf attached such importance to the new technique that he indentured three 'safe and faithful' wood block printers to serve him for six years to develop it. The workers promised 'not to disclose any information on their proceedings either by word of mouth or in writing, nor to make drawings of machines or parts of machines, nor to pass on drawings or samples, or let anyone come in'. However, the builder of Oberkampf's first copper plate machine, a Swiss joiner called Perrenoud, did not have to submit to such a stringent contract, no doubt because he was a treasure to be sought on almost any terms.

The new technique allowed Oberkampf to manufacture bigger and finer prints and so to catch up with the London producers. Moreover, he could adhere more closely to the topicalities and tastes of the period, directing his designers and engravers to respond to the events of the day. In this way such celebrated designs as 'The American War of Independence', 'Figaro's Wedding', 'Gonesse's Balloon' and 'The Processes of the [Textile Printing] Industry' were produced as early as 1783. J. B. Huet, perhaps the best-known designer of the day, drew designs for Oberkampf for some 28 years, from 1783 until his death in 1811. In the later years he was paid a standard price of 200 *l*. for each design.

The 'classic' designs of Huet and his contemporaries were not so expensive to produce as may be supposed. They were highly fashionable for wall hangings, bed sets, curtains and upholstery, but it is important to establish whether their sale can be described as genuinely popular or whether they were limited to an upper-class market. Unfortunately no data has survived for the period before the French Revolution, but some figures for 1795–1804 are helpful:

Year	No. of wood block prints (pieces)	No. of copper plate prints (pieces)	% of copper plate prints
1795	30,490	1,511	4.7
1796	20,069	5,827	22.5
1797	35,267	11,011	23.8
1798	36,022	5,626	13.5
1799	30,624	3,218	9.5
1800	38,080	7,479	16.4
1801	48,758	12,854	20.9
1802	32,284	25,438	44.1
1803	34,940	51,229	67.3
1804	27,296	77,294	72.9
Average	33,383	20,149	37.6

SOURCE: AN: 41 AQ 5.

During the French Revolution, demand from wealthy customers collapsed, so the early figures in this table cannot be considered typical. 'Normal' demand was restored soon after the turn of the century, perhaps with a strong resurgence to make up for the years of lost spending, so we may consider 1802 as closest to pre-Revolutionary demand. At any rate, we will surmise that something approaching half of Oberkampf's production was of copper plate pieces and rather more than half of wood block pieces, a division close to that chosen by the Peels at this period. Broadly speaking it may be said that the copper prints were for the upper-class market and the wood block prints for the popular one; in particular Oberkampf's blue 'picotés' *siamoises* were rather cheap. All Oberkampf's copper prints were high quality, compounded of the highest quality calicoes and the finest quality dyeing (*schoenfarber* or *bon teint* with metallic solutions), and Jouy's celebrity was based upon these consistently top quality productions, so the very name became synonymous with the finest copper prints. But it may well be that the fame of the Jouy label was sufficient to sell the cheaper half of Oberkampf's output. The contrast with British producers of the period seems obvious enough but we defer full consideration of the implications until the Conclusion. For the moment we return to the main chronological narrative, rejoining Frédéric on his tour of Swiss printing factories.

Before hurrying back to Paris, Frédéric again stopped at Geneva where he stayed for five days and visited eight factories, including Fazy's.[16] Then he went on to Lyons, from where he wrote that the factories at Marseilles and Montpellier should be very successful, and made his way to Villefranche-en-Beaujolais to see the works of their former supplier of *siamoises*, Humblot.[17] At Lyons he received another letter from his eldest brother informing him of the purchase of Corbeil, the works built in 1761 at a place named 'les Bordes' on a branch of the River Essonne by the Parisian haberdasher Jacques Baron.[18] When Baron died in 1768 the works were offered for sale because his feeble-minded widow could not keep them going. Oberkampf started negotiations for the purchase with the trustees of the estate despite the unpleasant legal proceedings still continuing with Levasseur. The acquisition, completed in December 1769, was not made official until the following August.[19] Oberkampf felt that Frédéric should have the whole property registered in his name and take half of the profits, that he and Maraise should have the other half, but that the whole transaction should be kept secret. The purchase of Corbeil, a just reward for Frédéric's hard work since 1763, marked the beginning of a new era in the history of the business.[20]

In December 1769, at the time of the tacit renewal of the partnership between Oberkampf and Maraise and the termination of the 1764 partnership with Levasseur, the registered capital was about 765,000 *l.* compared with 50,000 *l.* six years earlier. The business remained prosperous; the profits accumulated between 1764 and 1769 reached 1,229,320 *l.* and the profits for the four years 1770–3 were almost as high. Christoff was able to envisage the possiblity of giving his ageing parents some money and of setting his brother up at Corbeil.[21] The business was sound and already largely ahead of similar enterprises (Table 20). For most of the time that Maraise and his wife were involved in the partnership in the Jouy works, the enterprise, constantly buoyed up by growing demand, did not suffer any significant setback or financial difficulties. It functioned like a 'great machine' – the phrase used by Maraise in 1790 – to produce substantial profits and continuous increases in capital (see Tables 21, 23). From 1790 the account books maintained by Mme Maraise to demonstrate her sound management provide a continuous series of annual balance sheets, produced on 31 December each year. These summaries, established from the annual balance of all the accounts in double-entry book-keeping by the works' Paris office, make it possible to follow the growth of the firm's resources in detail – both their own and borrowed assets – and show the annual growth in profits as well as the allocation of working capital. The same picture emerges from the annual extracts of the stock accounts despite the absence of the general working accounts. In these extracts, what Oberkampf and his godchild[22] called 'profits' roughly correspond to the gross profit margin at the end of each financial year. Similar figures can be calculated by subtracting the 'capital' recorded in each annual inventory from that for the following financial year.[23]

The section of the accounts in which the annual surpluses of fixed and working capital were apportioned offers the clearest representation of the actual financial state of the business and allows us to make some interpretation of development. In 20 years (1770–1789) the recorded capital increased six-fold, reaching almost 9 million *l.* in the year of the Revolution. The only factories of the period to exceed this investment were the Royal Glass Factory at Saint-Gobain (13.9 million *l.*) and the Anzin coal mining company (9.2 million *l.*).[24] In making these comparisons it must be borne in mind that Oberkampf's company retained considerable hidden reserves and that the proportion was increasing all the time (Table 20). The strict policy of retention of profits within the business was adhered to

Table 20 Comparative structure of the assets of several calico printing businesses contemporary to the Jouy works

Entrepreneurs (with date of foundation)	Date of evaluation	Net total assets (l.)	Fixed capital (l.)	(%)	Working capital (l.)	(%)	Realisable capital (l.)	(%)	Liquid assets (l.)	(%)
Sarrasin-Oberkampf & Cie, Jouy (1760)	*12/1769*	*1,472,220*	*122,223*	*8.2*	*424,707*	*28.8*	*419,796*	*28.5*	*387,366*	*26.3*
	12/1781	*5,682,787*	*345,553*	*6.1*	*1,426,346*	*42.6*	*2,103,655*	*37.0*	*380,553*	*6.7*
Danton-Moreau & Cie.	7/1769	688,270	115,000	17.0	360,000	52.3	205,370	29.6	7,900	1.1
Angers (1752)	5/1771	402,193	70,314	17.6	120,788	30.0	24,860	6.3	1,784	0.4
Gillet & Montaut, Angers (1763)	3/1771	211,960	11,000	5.2	43,988	20.7	128,995	61.5	27,435	13.1
Seimandy & Liquier, Montpellier (1772)	9/1778	128,075	22,500	17.5	81,013	62.0	21,375	17.9	3,187	2.5
Guillaume Imhoff, Melun	6/1778	166,490	14,740	8.8	24,358	14.6	125,951	75.7	1,140	0.7
Gurnier, Danse, Thévard & Cie, Beauvais (1777)	12/1781	2,534,775	244,320	9.6	1,298,187	52.0	843,340	32.6	112,564	4.4
Paris. Chaland & Co.., Vernaison (1785)	11/1787	176,411	57,250	37.0	32,483	20.9	64,700	41.8	273	0.2
Le Sourd de Liste, Angers (1785)	11/1787	154,707	18,000	10.2	36,617	20.7	31,520	17.8	5,248	3.0
Keittinger *père*, Montpellier (1786)	5/1788	55,571	8,680	15.6	6,285	11.3	8,126	14.6	n.d.	
Perrenod & Cie, Melun (1786)	2/1789	547,064	154,395	27.7	225,323	41.1	136,932	25.0	10,865	1.9
Josserand Brothers, Lyon-Vaise (1780)	12/1788	33,565	18,057	53.8	1,500	4.4	1,793	5.3	n.d.	
Oberkampf, Jouy	*10/1815*	*6,271,027*	*438,136*	*7.0*	*3,110,836*	*41.0*	*1,931,364*	*30.7*	*515,035*	*8.2*

SOURCES: Jouy: AN: 41 AQ 14, 41 AQ 9; Angers: AD, Maine-et-Loire: VIB 242; Beauvais: AN: F12/1405; Vernaison et Vaise: AD, Rhône: 3E; Montpellier: A. Chante, Mem. Maitrise (1972); Melun: Arch. Paris: D4 B6, 104/7396.

throughout the period of partnership of Sarrasin de Maraise, Oberkampf & Cie, but when Oberkampf took over sole charge after 1790 it was necessary to spend more of the profits: first, to repay the share of his former partner, and then, after 1805, to finance the building of Chantemerle.[25]

The determination to finance the business out of retained profits explains the low level of the company's debts. After 1775, excepting one year (1779) when cloth purchases at Lorient were unusually high, the proportion of debts due for payment to total debts remained very low at six per cent, and fell as low as three per cent after 1782-9 (see Table 21). Another indication of the competent management of the business can be seen in the liquidity ratio (i.e. liquid assets ÷ liabilities due in the short term) which was only once, in 1774 – because of large purchases of cotton cloth in London – less than 50 per cent of what would be considered financially marginal today, although the ratio was exceeded several times after 1796. The profit-earning capacity of the company stock (i.e. the annual return on the partners' capital) followed the general downward trend, from 30 per cent in 1770 to 5.7 per cent in 1789, but there were also significant cyclical fluctuations (+ 20 per cent in the years 1768-73, 1776, 1791-2 and 1804-5), moderate fluctuations (15 per cent in 1774-5, 1779 and 1800-3) and weak profitability (less than 12 per cent). Clearly, Oberkampf profited considerably from fluctuations in demand by his skill in anticipating the estimated rises in price, taking advantage of any favourable opportunity to augment his profits.

What was to be done with the resources that accrued from the accumulation of profits? Apart from the contribution of 100,000 *l.* to a state loan and the purchase of 25 shares of 1,000 *l.* from the Senegal Company in 1785 – 'investment without exploitation' – the fixed assets remained small, continually below 10 per cent of the working capital, a demonstration that calico printing in the eighteenth century did not require large fixed capital investment but only land and some buildings.[26] The working capital on the other hand absorbed a large amount of money in proportion to the size of the business. Since the credit of the Jouy partners was well established after 1770, and particularly after the London trip in 1773,[27] and because international business connections lent them money, the proportion of the total capital invested in the works fell from 59 to 27 per cent of total assets between 1770 and 1789. The situation changed after 1790 because Oberkampf had to utilise large stocks in order to continue the works, the working capital thereby moving

Table 21 Evolution of capital recorded in the Jouy factory accounts, 1770–1814

	1770	1775	1780	1785	1790	1792	1796	1800	1805	1810	1813–14
Capital in the accounts	100	222	340	475	618	498	375	565	841	1,081	885
Actual capital	100	333	564	810	1,077	643	543	716	1,035	1,293	911
Actual capital as % of liabilities	52.6	50.3	74	83.4	78.5	66.3	75.5	66	64	63	54
Debts due as % of liabilities	32.0	12.4	6	2.5	7	12.1	27.4	18.7	41.2	34.8	42.5
Liquidity ratio	82	90.5	75.7	677	2,014	99.6	25.5	134	66	25.4	n.d.
Profit earning ratio	30	17.5	9	9.1	6	35.5	n.d.	12	21	6.7	−4.2
1. Fixed capital as % of total net assets	5.2	7	6.6	6.4	12.2	10.5	14.1	14	12	31	40.8
2. Working assets	59	39	54	34	45	55	60	49	51	35.4	30
3. Realisable assets	25	45	35	52	20	30	24	33	34	32	21.5
4. Disposable assets	10	9	3	7.6	22.4	5	1.9	4	3	1.6	7.7

SOURCES: The data for the period after 1796 are quoted in L. Bergeron's thesis, p. 701.

in the opposite direction. Between 1770 and 1789 it increased from 25 to 59.5 per cent, which explains the critical influence of credit in the commercial policy of the enterprise. More than once, Maraise and his wife had experienced the 'utmost difficulty recovering debts', but they learned to be constantly 'vigilant about it', a further demonstration of the importance of maintaining the liquidity ratio. After 1790 the realisable assets no longer held so important a place because Oberkampf did not want to increase the number of debtors who delayed payments or were of dubious credit, and who were consequently a drain on his capital. Maintenance of liquid assets, on paper rather than in cash, was the overriding aim of policy during the period of Mme Maraise's management. This brief analysis of the financial management of Sarrasin de Maraise, Oberkampf & Cie serves to emphasise the importance of the circulating capital and the relatively modest commitment to fixed capital whereby, throughout the period of the *ancien régime*, the financial structure of the enterprise appeared more commercial than industrial.

The available data on production costs at Jouy are set out in Table 22. During the period 1769–90 total costs of production remained remarkably constant, as did the component parts. The years 1791–2 are different because of the inflation that followed the Revolution. Half of the factory costs was attributable to labour and management (wages and salaries), and one-third to 'drugs' (dyestuffs, gums and chemicals). But these costs were modest compared with those of the 'raw material' used (the white *toiles*), which fluctuated between 82 and 92 per cent of the total costs of production. Unfortunately, no comparable data are available for any British calico printer of the period so it is not possible to take full advantage of this material in our Conclusion. However, it is worth making two points here. First, if the structure of the Peels' production costs was anything like that of Oberkampf, and we imagine it was, it helps to explain why the Lancashire firm concentrated so much attention on reducing the costs of the basic input (fustians) by cutting the cost of spinning, weaving and bleaching. Second, there is evidence to show that Oberkampf worked to reduce costs at various stages of the process of printing.

During the last years of the *ancien régime* some important innovations were made in the business. The earliest discoveries reveal Oberkampf's involvement in laboratory research. In 1784 the first attempts to heat the tanks and boilers with coal took place (bought from the Perier brothers of Chaillot), and then with peat sent from Mennecy, near Essonnes.[28] From 1788 the consumption of

Table 22 Structure of Oberkampf's costs of production, 1765–92 (thousand *l.*)

Year	Value of white cloths	% of total costs	'Drugs' used	% of total costs	Labour costs	% of total costs	Other manufacturing costs	% of total costs	Costs of production	Average cost of each piece
1765					36	5.6			645	
1766					46	5.7			789	
1767	n.d.	n.d.	n.d.	n.d.	52	6.3	n.d.	n.d.	809	n.d.
1768					78	5.6			1,390	
1769					78	5.0			1,549	
1770					77	4.7			1,636	
1771	1,453	83.4	130	7.4	82	4.4	76	4.4	1,741	2. 6. 5d.
1772	1,792	87.2	125	6.0	91	4.4	147	2.2	2,055	2. 4. 8d.
1773	1,950	84.4	138	5.9	116	5.0	104	4.6	2,307	2. 4. 9d.
1774	2,435	90.3			132	4.9			2,695	2. 6. 2d.
1775	2,339	90.8			127	5.1			2,575	2. 5. 4d.
1776	2,407	92.4	n.d.	n.d.	133	4.7	n.d.	n.d.	2,603	2. 6. 0d.
1777	2,839	90.8			147	5.0			3,123	n.d.
1778	n.d.	n.d.	n.d.	n.d.	177	5.0	124	3.5	3,508	n.d.
1779	3,116	87.7	133	3.7	177	4.8	87	2.4	3,551	3. 13. 1d.
1780	3,229	90.0	98	2.7	171	5.5	183	2.3	3,586	2. 17. 9d.
1781	3,164	89.0	113	3.2	194	5.2	79	2.2	3,555	3. 0. 1d.
1782	3,151	83.4	146	4.0	186	5.4	74	2.1	3,561	3. 1. 7d.
1783	3,022	85.5	135	4.0	184	5.2	82	2.2	3,415	3. 0. 0d.
1784	3,317	90.0	95	2.6	194	5.3	79	2.1	3,688	2. 17. 2d.
1785	3,316	90.0	134	3.6	198	5.7	94	2.6	3,727	2. 19. 8d.
1786	3,113	88.2	120	3.4	200	6.2	37	1.0	3,528	2. 19. 9d.
1787	3,190	89.4	119	3.3	222	6.8	39	1.1	3,567	2. 18. 1d.
1788	2,999	88.2	128	3.7	232	n.d.	n.d.	n.d.	3,399	2. 19. 0½d.
1789	3,310	89.9	138	3.7	n.d.	7.7	75	1.9	3,683	2. 17. 0½d.
1790	3,258	86.0	165	4.3	294	7.7	75	1.9	3,791	2. 17. 11d.
1791	3,546	85.3	182	4.3	315	7.6	114	2.7	4,158	3. 0. 2d.
1792	4,289	85.4	256	5.1	380	7.6	94	1.8	5,020	3. 8. 7d.

SOURCE: AN: 41 AQ 9.
NOTE: 'Drugs', 'labour' and 'other' columns together represent manufacturing costs, of which the greater part (more than three-quarters) is derived from direct expenses: labour, colouring materials and fuel.

coal, now bought directly from the mines of Decize, reached almost 300 tonnes.[29] 'The success of the dyed cloth depends principally on the preparation of the raw materials', Oberkampf emphasised to his nephew Samuel, with whom he carried out a sequence of experiments between 1782 and 1789. Oberkampf's early commitment to this principal is illustrated by his purchase, in 1769, of the first carboys of sulphuric acid produced at Holker's pioneer plant at Rouen, and during the next few years he experimented to establish the optimum length and temperature of immersions in acid to bleach his cottons. Oberkampf paid for Samuel Widmer to be trained under Berthollet, so that when the nephew began to take a hand in the technical direction of Jouy he introduced chlorine bleaching to the works, opening a plant in 1792. During the Revolutionary Wars, when imported materials became scarce, uncle and nephew experimented with techniques to economise on costly dyestuffs. It is said that both Widmer and Oberkampf enjoyed the friendship and esteem of the leading Parisian scientists of the period.[30]

Nevertheless, the most important innovation, printing with engraved cylinders, was hindered for several years by the turmoil of the Revolution. The idea of the machine was conceived by Samuel independent of Thomas Bell's invention in Preston and put to work in the Perier brothers' workshop at Chaillot between June 1787 and February 1788.[31] It experienced teething troubles; 'the greatest impediment was caused by the back which was making folds in the cloth'. 'While they were burning spinning machines in Normandy it would have been very unwise to offend the printers', Oberkampf explained in 1803 when public order had been restored and when nothing was preventing the working of the machine which had been installed at the Jouy works in October 1796.[32] In addition to its speed the great advantage possessed by the engraved cylinder for Oberkampf was its capacity to work continuously. But, he added, 'the biggest drawback that I can find is that I gave permission for the printing machine to be installed in the workshops at Chaillot, for as soon as the printing machine was on public view at Jouy there was a man in Paris who bought the design for it and was making machines for anyone who wanted one.' He stigmatised Benjamin Lefebvre, a mechanic of Rue Porte-au-foin in Marais who made similar machines, at first for Ebingre of Saint-Denis, then for the Wesserling factory and the manufacturers of Neuchatel. Oberkampf was in no doubt about his mistake in failing to patent his machine.[33] But as soon as it started production he was perfectly aware that 'this mode of printing would, in time, put all the others out of work,

Plate 6 The Jouy works, taken from a painting by J. B. Huet, c. 1806 (Musée Oberkampf, Jouy).

and the benefit would remain with those who could make them cheaper and in less time'. In spite of the protectionist policy of the Revolutionary régimes, which assured him sales within the national market, he continued to search for ways to reduce production costs. In March 1798 he asked his London contacts to obtain for him, at his expense, 'copies of the patents that had been granted during the previous 10 years relating to dyes and printing colours'. 'Also, get for me', he added, 'the book entitled *Experimental Research* by Edward Bancroft, in English, and the collection of the *Journal of Natural Philosophy, Chemistry and the Arts*, illustrated with engraving by W. Nicholson in quarto'.[34] Three months later he authorised his nephews, Samuel and Gottlieb, to visit their sisters at Aarau on condition that the trip would be useful for the works. Subsequently the two young men visited the works of their suppliers of madder at Hagenau and at Geiselbronn, 'which was a big favour for us as normally no one was allowed to go in'. The elder nephew made some drawings and measurements while the younger one studied the machines and their workings. They travelled during the night and arrived at Colmar the next morning where they visited Haussmann's factory.[35] Next day they were in Basle, where their local connections in the trade had been requested to arrange for the young men to see all the interesting factories in the town.[36]

Eleven years later, in July 1809, Samuel, the inventor of the *vert solide d'application*, returned to Aarau via Alsace accompanied by his brother Christoff.[37] He again visited the factory of Logelbach at Colmar which by that time had 200 tables.[38] After noting for his uncle all the preparatory processes for printing and bleaching, he concluded: 'nothing seems to be calculated in this workshop [the steam dyeing room], everything here is muddled and illogical.... There isn't a single roller in the factory but they nevertheless produce very beautiful cloths.' At Munster, he recorded the same day that 'the printing is carried on on the same lines as that of Haussmann. Despite my connections, they [the owners, the Hartmanns] showed me their machine, which is heavy and not very convenient; it needs twice as many people to work it as ours... it is powered by water... and in general I can assure you that they are still a long way from perfection'.[39] Two days later, at Wesserling, he wrote that:

> I have found a very large establishment (200 tables) which is extremely spread out. Monsieur Roman, the director, is no manufacturer, and the work shows the effects of this.[40] One notices everywhere signs of negligence, which contrasts greatly with the

order and care that I saw at the Munster factory. You can't imagine the stupidity of some of the operations, and I can assure you that if we ever want to perfect any of our methods of manufacture, you won't learn much if you come here ... They have two *bastringues* [nickname of the roller machine] of which they are very badly supplied.[41] In the same place I also saw a spinning-mill; it is impossible to imagine a dirtier stable, machines in such bad condition but they still manage to spin and weave excellent cloth.[42]

The next day at Thann he visited two printing works and a sulphuric acid works 'which didn't offer anything of note'.[43,44] The day after that he visited two more factories at Mulhouse: 'that of Nicholas Koechlin ... produce lovely cloths, very well, and they are without doubt the best in Mulhouse.[45] They've also got a *bastringue* made like all the others by Lefebvre of Paris and that of M. Heilmann where nearly all our rich designs are copied'.[46] In the morning, before leaving the town, he visited the factories of Dollfus-Mieg and Jean Hofer. 'They don't work very carefully at either of them, and I didn't notice anything special', he wrote. At this time Dollfus-Mieg was the most important manufacturer in Mulhouse![47]

'You can well imagine', he wrote to his uncle from Aarau,

that the *vert solide* and the steam heating system have been the subject of much discussion.[48] On the former I was constantly defending myself by saying that I couldn't remember anything more, while as for the latter, they would not understand without someone designing and even building a workshop for them. I didn't meet anyone who had even the minimum knowledge of physics necessary to understand the operation of a steam factory.

Samuel's scientific education and his close connections with Berthollet, Gay-Lussac and the members of the *Société d'Arcueil* evidently proved to be most fruitful.[49] He was sufficiently identified with the intellectual scientific community to allow himself a contemptuous comment on the Mulhouse manufacturers: 'sound reasoning is not, I feel, their strong point'.

The gold medal presented to Oberkampf at the 1806 Exhibition in Paris, the only one of the 25 prestigious awards which was presented to a textile printing works, demonstrated the premier position of the Jouy enterprise, whose products were reported as 'faultless and deserving the high reputation that they enjoy'.[50] This pre-eminence was partly due to Samuel's technical ability. After he had perfected an automatic washing machine in spring 1795, he went on to give practical effect to a device for engraving the copper cylinders that were beginning to be used in French textile printing. The idea was conceived by the Perier brothers at the turn of the century but it was first put into operation at Jouy. Samuel also improved copper plate printing to allow the printing of two or three colours simultaneously. Above all he discovered, in 1808, *vert solide*, the green dye based on tin peroxide, one of the most valuable chemical discoveries with an immediate industrial use. 'A neighbouring country, one of our rivals in trade, offered a prize to anyone who discovered this colour. The discovery was made in France and no prizes awarded in England', the advisory *Bureau* of arts and manufactures triumphantly reported to the Ministry of the Interior.[51] Samuel's role in these important improvements deserved a prize, although his personal achievement went unacknowledged except in profits from the works.

Table 23 Drawings of the Oberkampf family partners from the Company, 1793–1810 (in *f.*)

Period	Samuel (10%)	Pétineau Jnr. (8.3%)	Pétineau Snr. (5.3%)	L. Feray (6.3%)	Ph. Widmer (4%)	V. Widmer (4%)
1793–1801	108,000	108,000	108,000	66,000	0	0
1802–1810	584,597	487,162	365,373	365,373	148,055	66,451
profit bonus	175,314	172,594	136,469	279,189	48,409	10,229
Total	867,911	767,756	609,842	704,562	196,464	76,680

SOURCE: AN: 41 AQ 8.
NOTE: The 1793–1801 division was a lump sum. That of 1802–10 consisted of two parts, the contractual share of each partner and a profit bonus in proportion to their money left in current account in the factory.

From 1792 to 1810 the distribution of profits by Samuel's 'good uncle' yielded him a total of 867,911 *f.* (Table 23), which represented an average, for the nine years of the second partnership, of 84,400 *f.* a year, roughly 20 times the annual salary of men on the *commis* grade in the firm's employment.[52] The other members of the family firm – the two Pétineau brothers-in-law, Feray the son-in-law, and two other Widmer nephews – never completely reconciled themselves to devoting 'all their time and effort' to the development of the Jouy enterprise and so were paid less.

Table 24 Jouy's output and sales, 1771–1817

Year	No. of bleached pieces bought	No. of pieces printed	No. of pieces sold	No. of pieces in stock
1771	19,288		19,664	17,636
1772	27,304		26,541	18,399
1773	31,834		25,369	25,464
1774	34,432		24,054	35,845
1775	29,965		27,052	38,758
1776	39,658		26,097	32,319
1777	37,435		25,848	43,906
1778	19,942		30,549	33,299
1779	48,007		23,275	58,058
1780	15,328		23,400	50,646
1781	15,602		24,586	41,689
1782	22,648	n.d.	22,160	42,177
1783	17,808		19,806	40,079
1784	28,614		25,744	40,049
1785	25,424		27,552	40,921
1786	24,360		26,816	38,442
1787	30,888		27,244	42,086
1788	19,857		23,363	38,580
1789	29,646		25,866	42,317
1790	24,702		27,283	39,736
1791	38,032		36,347	41,421
1792	42,908		27,831	56,498
1797	52,932	46,278	40,596	66,944
1798	36,267	41,648	37,673	65,653
1799	35,169	33,842	31,625	69,598
1800	42,508	45,539	47,837	64,591
1801	56,036	61,612	45,911	75,041
1802	45,107	57,722	40,047	80,300
1803	40,354	76,169	41,904	78,354
1804	75,654	106,060	53,904	100,997
1805	61,986		52,007	111,879
1806	23,445		42,523	93,167
1807	48,220	n.d.	51,945	90,243
1808	42,752		57,558	76,072
1809	48,051		58,221	66,807
1810	48,980	53,100	46,829	69,687
1811	43,742	42,000	32,091	81,199
1812	22,324	33,100	27,703	77,357
1813	21,954	38,900	33,182	67,048
1814	16,838		30,856	53,901
1815	22,080	n.d.	26,293	50,305
1816	51,535		47,183	54,657
1817	54,942		33,924	58,777

SOURCE: AN: 41 AQ 8.

After his return to Glasgow Robert Hendry maintained a correspondence with the Oberkampf family, and especially with the youngest son Samuel. In May 1810, after briefly describing the progress of the British cotton industry, he warmly invited him to come and see for himself.[53] Samuel obtained permission from Oberkampf to travel and took Gottlieb, who could speak some English, with him. Oberkampf was glad to release him 'while I was still in a position to look after my works', as he explained to him. Armed with a French Empire passport and introductions to Sir Joseph Banks, the celebrated President of the Royal Society, signed by Chaptal and Berthollet, they sailed from Ostend in mid October. They stayed in London for five days and then took the mail coach to Glasgow, which took an exhausting three nights and two days. They stayed for more than a month in Glasgow where Hendry took them to see Tennant's St Rollox soda bleaching works[54] and a cotton printing factory at Paisley[55] where they bought cotton handkerchiefs printed in Turkey with red and white stripes. They also saw several mills with power looms driven by steam engines, still a new development at the time. On their way back Charles Brandt cordially received them at Manchester and gave them opportunities to visit various factories where they made drawings of various printing machines and others for cleaning and beating raw cotton.[56] Samuel found the Lancashire people more reserved than those in Scotland and compared them to the Swiss. 'Though they are devilishly skilfull, I hope that we will have to do business with them. If the Continental ports were open there would be great potential for the goods are at the lowest possible price, but as it is the whole trade is in a state of stagnation'. Eager to return home and cursing the terrible British weather, they made their way to Leeds, Sheffield and Birmingham, where they visited Boulton & Watt's works. At Soho, Samuel was impressed by the improvements made to the small (2 to 8 hp) engines.[57] They left London in the middle of February 1811 and reached Jouy a month later. Unfortunately the deteriorating economic and political climate prevented them from consolidating the knowledge they had acquired. The slump was already being felt in 1810, and unsold goods piled up. In June 1813 Oberkampf disclosed that he did not have enough work for his employees, not even on a part-time basis, and in November he decided to reduce output to a minimum 'until things looked more hopeful'.[58] But he died in October 1815, before France had begun to surmount the post-war depression (Table 24).[59]

Chapter 11

Markets and Sources of Supply, 1760–1805

In spite of the disappointments experienced by Sarrasin de Maraise and Oberkampf, Levasseur's participation in the 1762 company for the development of the printing factory at Jouy was, on the whole, beneficial to the enterprise.[1] 'Using a familiar and accredited name in the trade', Levasseur and Dailly, his partner from Lyons, intorduced 'the printed cloths made at Jouy near Versailles' to the Paris market. In less than two years they acquired such an enviable reputation that the mercers and their customers no longer talked about *toiles indiennes* or *toiles d'Orange* but only about *toiles de Jouy* as the phrase *toiles d'Orange de Jouy* proved too cumbersome for popular use.[2] This famous trade mark was always to remain theirs. In France *toiles de Jouy* is still, 150 years after the disappearance of the works, synonymous with printed fabrics or, more precisely, cloth with designs printed in cameo by copper plates in the period from 1780 to 1820. Oral tradition has preserved one of the most triumphant moments in the artistic achievement of the Jouy workshops.[3]

At the beginning of his time at Jouy, Oberkampf worked on commission printing, i.e. printing for merchants or private individuals, rather than for the general market.[4] This method of working to order saved on circulating capital since the customer provided the raw material for printing, the design and even the dyes necessary for their prints. Above all, Oberkampf's goods acquired a social cachet as his customers were obviously the most distinguished and influential people, notably the Duke of Gontaud (Lauzun) who boasted in the salon of the Duchess of Choiseul in 1776 of having given Oberkampf an oriental design to copy, and that when he succeeded in reproducing it exactly he had pretended the copy was a genuine Indian one and the court believed him.[5] (According to the snobbish values of the day, expensive oriental imports were devalued by local imitations, the more so if the local product was a faithful copy.) Two or three advertisements of this kind were sufficient to publicise the renown of the Jouy works throughout Parisian high society. The social mimesis in 'a society of the court' did the rest. In December 1776, while he was at Lorient for the sales of the *Compagnie française des Indes*, Oberkampf decided to cease working to special order. This was consistent with a decision taken seven years earlier to terminate his connections with the merchants who dealt in 'specials'. All his production was now destined for the general market but his policy was nevertheless oriented by his shrewd choice of designs, which he called the 'creation of a new taste', and he constantly assured himself that it was in high demand.[7] With the help of the Parisian designer Jean-Baptiste Huet (1745–1811) the 1780 models were printed in cameo (blue, violet, red or black, on a white background) of popular events of the day.[8] The 'American Independence', the 'Marriage of Figaro' and the 'Ballon de Gonesse' provide the best-known examples. The great increase in new designs engraved in the final years of the *ancien régime* can only be explained by Oberkampf's need of increasing sales, on which the prosperity of his firm depended.[9]

Because of the loss of the accounts and the commercial correspondence before 1790 the sales of the firm cannot be measured for the first 30 years of its existence.[10] It is unlikely, however, that it was much different than at the end of the *ancien régime*: mainly Parisian (52.6 per cent good debts; 51.3 per cent indexed correspondents in active correspondence; but 40.2 per cent of balances of current accounts)[11], and dominated by a small number of substantial customers, such as Jacquemart & Bichebois, who were assiduous buyers of the factory goods from 1762–64 (see Table 25).[12] Most of the Parisian customers, or those from the environs, were, in actual fact, former commercial connections, often reaching back to the 1760s. They were all recipients of a 'sales current account' balanced at the end of the year, and for a few 'privileged' people a discount of five per cent on total sales was granted – this was the reward of the wholesale dealers who advertised on their shop fronts that they dealt in *toiles de Jouy*, and firms like Girard-Descotils at Versailles or Meynier at Saint-Denis.

Second in importance were the debtors and correspondents (8–12 per cent) from Normandy, some of whom, from Rouen and Le Havre, reached the level of the Parisians. However, not a single Norman debtor attained the importance of the Lyons consignee Bouchard & Cie around 1770, and Pont, Rainaldi & Cie around

Table 25 Oberkampf's markets, 1790–1800: regional distribution of 'good' debtors

Region	1790 No. of debtors	Balance (*l.*)	%	1800 No. of debtors	Balance (*l.*)	%
Paris	71	177,330	*20.6*	103	293,057	*23.5*
Versailles	25	103,082	*12.0*	29	88,930	*7.1*
Region around Paris	62	64,788	*7.6*	63	75,598	*6.1*
Rouen	7	49,265	*5.7*	13	45,563	*3.6*
Normandy (other)	17	49,735	*5.8*	15	33,647	*2.7*
Britanny, the Loire	25	48,500	*5.6*	15	109,395	*8.7*
Champagne, Ardennes	24	68,550	*7.9*	28	99,645	*7.9*
Massif Central	22	31,800	*3.7*	25	30,510	*2.4*
Lyons	6	103,275	*12.0*	6	83,349	*6.6*
Lyonnais	8	11,200	*1.7*	4	2,184	*0.2*
Nord-Picardie	12	34,350	*3.9*	17	44,360	*3.5*
Franche-Comté	8	53,175	*6.2*	11	49,445	*3.9*
Aquitaine	5	18,590	*2.1*	7	41,000	*3.2*
Bourgogne	3	4,720	*0.5*	12	34,530	*2.7*
Provence	5	36,395	*4.2*	7	41,845	*3.2*
Languedoc-Rousillon	n.d.	n.d.	*n.d.*	20	228,540	*18.3*
Alsace-Lorraine	n.d.	n.d.	*n.d.*	7	23,465	*1.8*
Total	**300**	**858,860**	*100*	**382**	**1,245,855**	*100*

SOURCE: AN: 41 AQ 15.
NOTE: The figures represent the balance of current account at 31 Dec., not total sales for the year.

1790. Thanks to them, and to some other customers, Lyons became an important market for Jouy products in spite of the competition of the local manufacturers, one of whom in particular was the Genevan Picot-Fazy, who began in 1786,[13] or the neighbours of Vizille, Valence or Jallieu near Bourgoin.[14] The Lyons rebellion of summer 1793, which disrupted commercial communications between Paris and Lyons, was a temporary setback to Oberkampf's trade. In the long term, however, the situation did not significantly harm the business as Lyons later became the centre of the Mediterranean, Provence and Languedoc markets. Oberkampf never visited the Beaucaire fairs unlike his competitors Cambon of Montpellier or Lesage of Bourges.[15] To his consignee at Lyons, and to others at Montpellier and Marseilles, Oberkampf allowed sales 'on conditional account', whereby the customer undertook to return unsold articles while Oberkampf left his trusted agent free to fix the price beyond the level 'recommended' by him. This system offered the advantage of sending the *toiles de Jouy* to the distant rival markets without great transport or commercial costs. Moreover, regular correspondence with the warehouses frequently informed him of fluctuations in taste or prices in the locality. Finally, the system ensured a regular monthly return of capital, with bills maturing after three months.

The last two strongholds of Jouy sales in 1790 were both close to textile printing centres and near to frontiers where smuggling continued to be an important trade. At Rheims, one merchant enjoyed the advantages of a 'conditional account' while six others had current accounts, clear evidence of the importance of the town in the dissemination of the latest Parisian styles. Besançon, Oberkampf's other distribution point, seems an even more surprising success. It was far removed from Paris (420 km) and close to the Swiss calico printing towns of Basle, Neuchatel and Geneva. Clearly, Oberkampf was able to compete with the long-established Swiss manufacturers.

At the demise of the *ancien régime* 80 per cent of all the correspondents, debtors and creditors were situated north of a line from Rouen to Lyons. The line separated the France which was developed, or developing industrially, from underdeveloped, agricultural France. However, as early as 1774 the reputation of the *toiles de Jouy* was such that 'in a small village where you would not believe that anyone would have a notion about it, the salesman would be given the price he asked as soon as he showed the trademark'.[16] His clientele established, Oberkampf made no attempt to increase the number of his creditors.[17] Any new customer had to pay cash and was allowed the usual six per cent discount. Only when he had proved his solvency and when other creditors, tradesmen or bankers, had vouched for him could he be admitted to the select group of current account customers who were allowed to settle their debts at the end of the year. As Oberkampf did not have a sales room in Paris the customer was obliged to go to Jouy itself to make his choice.[18] The reception by the warehouseman or by the owner himself was always courteous, and often even hospitable for the provincial clients, for whom the journey to Jouy also invariably meant a tour to Versailles or a visit to Paris to see the tourist sights. If the customer did not wish to travel or delegate one of his relations the Jouy manufacturer could send him, at his own expense, an assortment of choice articles from which he could pick those that suited him and send back the rest within 15 days. Alternatively, he could be sent a 'card' with numbered samples of designs available at the shops, with the price per piece. The customer had to reply quickly if he wanted his order to be sent before the shop was sold out of the desired goods, although the factory could always substitute a similar item.

After 1790 Oberkampf again began to print to order, but solely in cameo by copper blocks.[19] He also agreed, for the well-established houses, to print to order the dimities, muslins or organdie that other manufacturers or merchants provided.[20] He also consented to print exclusive designs, but only on condition that the order exceeded 250 aunes (12 pieces), that he was provided with the design or the idea, and that the printing of these patterns did not slow down the current orders. All the work done to order was to be paid for after four months at a price dependent on the intricacies of the design or the difficulty of printing.

In 1790, employing this latter mode of production, Oberkampf initiated new but short-lived commercial connections abroad, notably with London.[21] Through his correspondence we can trace three London customers during the first year and a further four in the following year. All the same, none of them received more than 200 pieces a year, dispatched by the English commission agent at Dunkerque. These consignments were intended to show the un-challenged technical success of the Jouy manufacturer but they remained an insignificant proportion of the total sales, only 0.88 per cent of the pieces sold in 1791. Unlike the manufacturers from Mulhouse and Alsace, who were frequenters of the Frankfurt fairs and dependent on the German market, Oberkampf disposed of the whole of his produce on the home market, especially in the Parisian region before 1790 and after 1800 (Table 25 and Fig. 8).[22]

The Revolution hardly altered the geographical pattern of sales: Paris and the Île-de-France remained just as important in 1800 (51 per cent of good debtors, and 36.5 per cent of the debit balance). The customers from the east of France (Bourgogne, Franche-Comté, Lorraine) increased in number while the proportion of those from the south and Languedoc also grew. The outcome was a new development at the close of 1798 which consisted of the creation of entrepôts run by commission agents resident at Bordeaux, Lyons, Toulouse, Marseilles and Montpellier.[23]

From 1792 Oberkampf, on his own account, sent some pieces to a Frankfurt merchant who did not manage to dispose of them.[24] Another fruitless attempt was made in the autumn of 1795, with 85 pieces of printed *percales* sent to Friederich Empaytaz of Berlin for sale at the Leipzig fair.[25] The first exports to Hamburg were launched by the enterprise of Risler of Fixheim in summer 1799,

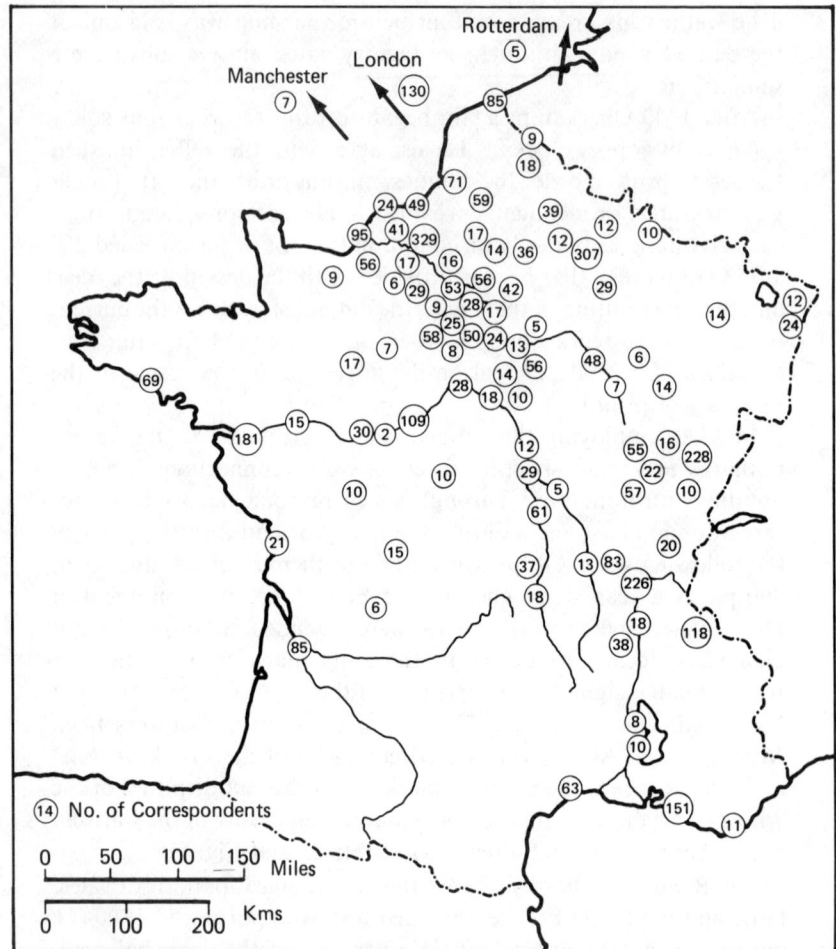

The business relations of the Jouy factory, 1790–92.

Fig. 8 Location of Jouy's customers, 1790–2

but the sales did not even reach 2,000 *f.* and were short-lived.[26] It was not until 1811 that any further attempts were made to get into the German market.[27] Several postal contacts of Gottlieb Widmer in 1815, made with a fresh exploitation of German outlets in mind, had no greater success.[28]

Markets and Sources of Supply, 1760–1805   153

The business had little more success in the Belgian markets. Several dispatches to a house at Ghent in October 1795, however, showed some potential, but the competition from Flemish manufacturers and smuggled English merchandise restricted the possibilities.[29] The depot at Lille, conferred in 1800 on Fevez-Ghesquier, was a total failure and the scheme was dropped in 1805. Depots at Antwerp and Brussels were opened in 1810 and it was hoped that this would be the turning-point in favour of the *toiles de Jouy*.[30] 'My merchandise, being totally printed with fast colours, is much less attractive than those of other manufacturers who print without mordants, or others that are not made with good dyestuffs. With the common fabrics it will be impossible for me to withstand the rivalry of the Belgian factories, whose production is much cheaper than mine', Oberkampf confessed to a Brussels correspondent in May 1812.[31] However, the Brussels depot, entrusted to Georges Choisy & Cie in November 1812, achieved a degree of success in 1813 thanks to an exceptional discount of between 9 and 11 per cent given by Oberkampf for cash payments.[32] This 'pugnacity of the old entrepreneur', in Bergeron's words, proved to be relatively ineffectual for Choisy was slow to remit the sums of money collected. In September 1815 the Jouy manufacturer twice declined proposals from the substantial Brussels merchants, Tiberghien, to sell goods on sale, return or commission, because he felt 'that they could not hold their own very easily against the competition of foreign prints'.[33] After a visit that Émile made to Brussels in July 1818 several new connections were developed.[34] The company even attempted to establish a final depot, in March 1819, on the insistence of Baert, but the highest sales did not exceed 6,500 *f.* per month. The 'problem of price' continued to limit foreign sales.

The Piedmont and Ligurian market on the other hand, proved to be less disappointing, at least until 1815. The first demands from the Lombardy and Genoan merchants in 1793 could not be met because of the prohibition of exports.[35] After the establishment of the depots at Marseilles, Montpellier and Lyons, Oberkampf recommended them systematically to each of his Italian connections. Then in 1803, after the bankruptcy of Turcase, one of the two Marseillais agents, he decided to send some goods to the Aubert brothers at Turin to start a depot. This functioned in a satisfactory manner until, after the 1814 and 1815 treaties, the competition of the English Swiss printed goods eroded the profit away.[36] To increase the sale of goods Émile authorised a 40 per cent reduction in price in 1816 'as nothing was to be gained from letting them rot in the shops'. A similar experience had resulted from the Genoese depot, which since 1806 had been in possession of Mottet, Roche & Cie, a house recommended to the Jouy manufacturer by Montalivet, the prefect transferred from Genoa to Versailles. 'I was quite satisfied with the sales that these men had achieved, and above all with the precision with which they balanced each sales account,' Oberkampf noted with satisfaction.[37] The success of these depots in northern Italy led to the establishment, in 1809, of a new depot at Milan, under the control of Jean Dewelz & Cie, but this did not meet the expectations of Oberkampf, who does not seem to have profited from a series of permits to export to Italy, granted between 1810 and 1812, following the decree which forbade the import into the Kingdom of non-French cotton goods.[38] Sales were more encouraging in the Kingdom of Naples thanks to Dewelz or his colleague Audra, Oberkampf's agents for the purchase of Castellamare raw cotton, without the obstacle of communications and organised highway-robbery to which his dispatches had sometimes fallen victim.[39]

A summary of the distribution of unsold goods in the various depots on 4 October 1815, the day of Oberkampf's death, can be seen in Figure 9.[40] Five of the 90 depots represented 57 per cent of the total number of pieces by value – those of Duheron at Bordeaux (17.2 per cent and 18.3 per cent respectively), Barbet at Rouen (14.2 and 13.4 per cent), Pont, Gaillard & Cie at Lyons (9.9 per cent), Barrau brothers at Toulouse (8.3 per cent) and the Paris sales room at Rue de Choiseul (7.6 and 8.0 per cent). Right up to the end of Oberkampf's career the market for the goods remained almost entirely internal, limited to a few national distribution centres because of his incapacity to reduce costs of production to the level of his Alsatian, Swiss, Flemish and English competitors. He argued that the superiority of his quality goods justified the relatively high prices and certainly this was responsible for his success in an eighteenth-century society of aristocratic consumption, and with a system of production that was really more craft-oriented than industrial.[41] He was aware of his handicap but doggedly refused to abandon his policy of high quality produce from which had come his reputation and his fortune.

For a long time Oberkampf had believed that he could base his competitiveness on a policy of securing supplies 'at first hand', from the very source of the raw materials, fabrics or dyestuffs. 'Until 1767 when M. Pourtalès sold me my first cotton goods, I had only printed mixed [i.e. linen and cotton], Beaujolais and Rouen goods,' Oberkampf confided in 1790.[42] Like most other contemporary

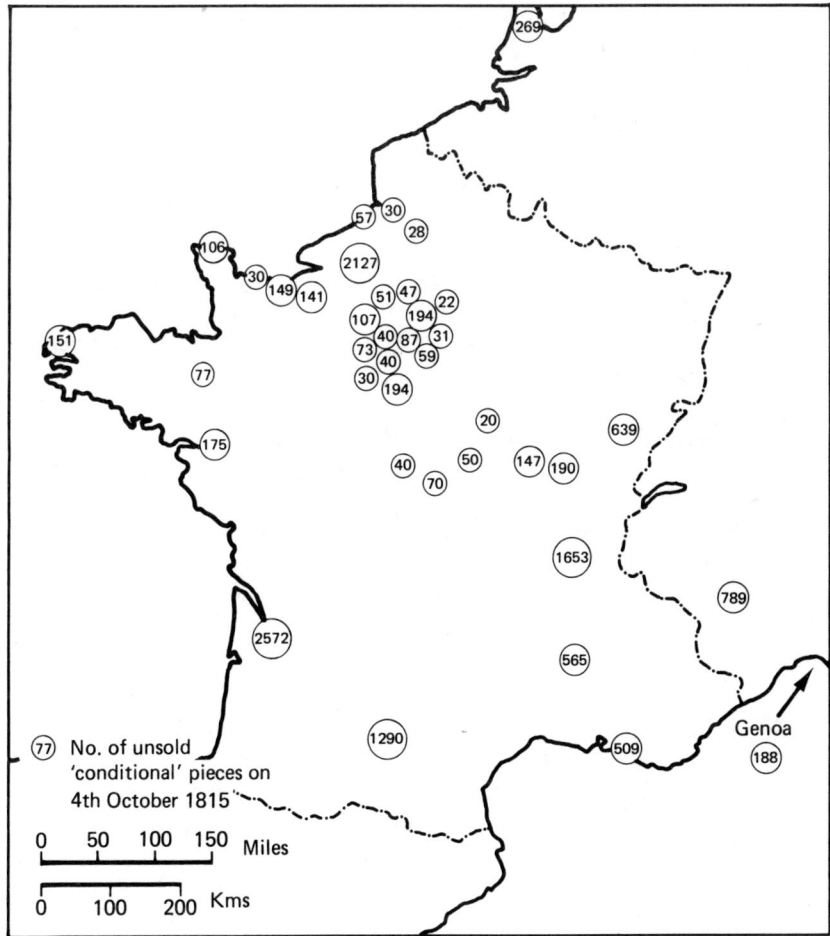

Note: 'Conditional' = sent by Oberkampf under condition of return if unsold 6 months later.

Fig. 9 Distribution of unsold fabrics of Jouy, 4 October 1815

manufacturers at Angers, Sèvres and Orange, Oberkampf at the outset printed exclusively on *siamoises* of French manufacture bought either at the Rouen market through a local agent or from various merchant bleachers of Villefranche or St. Symphorien-de-Lay.[43] After the purchase of Corbeil and the elimination of Levasseur, who had been responsible for commercial connections with the linen-making region of Beaujolais, Oberkampf attempted to diversify his supplies of *toiles blanches*. In 1771 his father canvassed the Toggenbourg region of Herisau and the Canton of Zurich for him, and in one year about 3,500 bleached pieces were supplied from this source. His father, in August 1772, even sent 25 pieces woven to order, a trial of the *verlag* system in Zurich that was not followed up. Doubtless Oberkampf found, in effect, more advantages in the wholly cotton goods imported direct from India than those which were supplied by 'King Pourtalès', a frequent buyer at the London sales of the East India Company. In autumn 1773 Pourtalès persuaded Oberkampf to travel with him. We possess the original pencilled notes of his first trip to London which are rich in information.[44]

In making this journey he expected to learn about the men and the customs of international big business and to familiarise himself with sales by auction and the various qualities of *toiles des Indes* (calico and guinea from Coromandel, senna and baffeta from Bengal). During the nine weeks of his sojourn in London, 3 October 1773 – 5 January 1774, he made enough friendly contacts, thanks to Pourtalès, to assure him from then on of a regular supply to his factory. 'You are perfectly right to say that it is quite essential for us to cross the Channel every year, and that there is nothing like seeing things for oneself', Sarrasin wrote to Oberkampf.[45]

Between sales he visited the warehouses of several Swiss merchants who had set up businesses in London and picked up samples of prints for Rohdorff, his designer. He decided 'to have the larger proportion of the baffeta he bought printed here by copper blocks', persuaded by the excellence of the English cameos. But most important, Pourtalès had obtained entry for him to two of the leading London calico-printing works, those of Robert Jones of Old Ford and John Arbuthnot at Mitcham (Surrey).[46] Several days later he visited two works at Stratford – Pyner & Woodward, and Thomas Preston. 'There is plenty to see here', he wrote later to Sarrasin, 'but I am expecting to see more. I haven't yet come across anything that we haven't got at Jouy'. Two final visits to Vaughn, Fenning & Halfhide at Merton Abbey and to John Munns at Crayford confirmed his conviction. These London printers specialised in the high quality copper plate work in which Oberkampf had won distinction in France.

The return trip via Holland, still in the company of Pourtalès, perfected his knowledge of the intricate workings of European business and printing works. 'I would never have believed that one could make such shoddy work as I saw, and that which is reasonably good fetches ten livres more than ours,' he wrote. At Brussels he made contact with F. Romberg whom he asked to check the forwarding of the cloth he bought in London, and to send it to Paris via Ostende, Brussels and Rheims, a useful route at a time when Anglo-French relations were deteriorating.[47]

On the eve of his departure from London Oberkampf concluded that 'We must devote ourselves to cotton [i.e. cloth of 100 per cent cotton] if we are not intending to make increased use of those from Rouen [i.e. linen and cotton fabrics].' The inability of French producers to respond to increasing demand necessitated increasing resort to the international sources of cotton production, supplied by the East India companies (see Table 26). Consequently, from that time onwards, pure cotton goods provided the whole supply of the factory and the annual purchases finally exceeded 30,000 pieces. The decision to print on pure cotton must have further improved the quality of Oberkampf's prints.

Table 26 The results of the 'internationalisation' of Oberkampf's supplies, 1769–78 (% distribution of supplies of fabrics)

Year	Linen and cotton fabrics	Pure cotton fabrics
1769	51.6	48.4
1770	59	41
1775	30.4	69.6 (London purchases)
1776	51.7	48.2
1777	28.4	75.4 (Lorient purchases)
1778	30.4	69.6

SOURCE: AN: 41 AQ 8–9, Annual Inventories.

During the following 10 years, Oberkampf or his brother Frédéric, if he was kept at home, regularly took two months off each year to go to the London sales or those of Lorient (after 1776). Through his London friends or Robin, a Versailles trader, he was always kept informed of pieces on sale at places that he could not visit. Thus he bought with confidence and knew how to avoid the traps of the Lorient salesmen's tricks. Despite the consequences of the American War of Independence, which drove up the price of the goods, he maintained a high level of purchases (48,000 pieces in 1779) for 'they are the same price for everybody'. 'Now we are well stocked', he remarked after spending 565,400 *l.* at the Lorient sales. 'I have far exceeded the limit that I originally set myself, but I think it will prove to have been a wise move. The next London sale will show whether we are right or wrong. The price of goods can only increase whether there is peace or war.' Through Oberkampf's letters we can follow his intuitive anticipation of shifts in the market; like a seasoned sailor, he knew how to catch the wind and anticipate trouble.

During the voyage to Rotterdam and Antwerp in January 1774 he enquired about the price of madder to compare it with that which he had obtained through his father in Alsace. As the lower price at these ports did not compensate for the difference in quality he maintained his fixed-price contracts, agreeing the price for the next consignment after each collection. From 1778 to 1783 J. Dietrich of Strasburg was his only regular supplier. In case of sudden shortage he could always buy a few tons of the dye from the Paris warehouses of the Alsatian merchant-dyers.

Table 27 Sources of cloth in Oberkampf's stock, 1783–92 (%)

Stock on 31 Dec annually	1783	1784	1785	1786	1787	1788	1789	1790	1791	1792
Toiles from Beaujolais	8.4	7.6	10.6	17.6	19	16.4	16.6	11.3	15.8	15.6
Toiles from Rouen	56	54	42.5	36.7	30.5	43.7	43	48.5	36.5	25.5
Imported *toiles*	35.6	38.4	37.3	45.6	49.8	39.9	40.4	40.2	47.3	58.4
Type of imported cloth:										
Guinées	23.8	20.5	20.5	24.4	28.3	21.5	14.2	15.8	27.7	38.5
Baffetas	10.4	17	16	20.1	20.2	17.3	19.2	15.2	12.4	12.4
Superfines	1.4	0.9	0.8	1.1	1.3	1.1	1.2	2.2	1.8	2.7
Total pieces (000s)	40.2	43.0	40.9	38.4	42.1	38.5	42.3	39.7	41.4	56.5

SOURCE: AN: 41 AQ 8–10. The totals are rounded to the nearest hundred pieces.

In the late 1780s, Oberkampf's stocks were drawn from both the international entrepôts (*toiles des Indes*, indigo, alum and gum sumac) and from the French sources (*siamoises*, madder, metallic oxides and salts used in the manufacture of mordants).[48] Table 27 shows the great importance of the imported *toiles* (i.e. those woven entirely of cotton) compared to the linen and cotton mixtures made in Beaujolais and Rouen. It demonstrates that the Jouy factory was never entirely dependent on the international merchant houses for its supplies.[49] The growth of the business, like those of other well-documented concerns such as the Dantons' factory at Angers and the Wetters' at Orange, took place essentially within a national setting. French calico printing, at least until the decrees of 1785 favouring the import of foreign goods, was more like a successful graft on the roots of the traditional French linen industry than the product of international merchant enterprise.

As early as January 1790 Oberkampf was telling the cloth makers of Amiens 'that it would be necessary to encourage indigenous industry and that the best way of doing this would be to stop importing all Indian textiles'. But he admitted such a step would not succeed unless all the other European importers did the same. The solution, he envisaged, must be found in the perfecting of French products. Consumers' patriotism would come to their aid when it was found not to be such a disadvantage to buy French goods.[50] In these remarks we can recognise Oberkampf's unusual perception of the future industrial development of Western Europe and particularly that of France. It was impossible for him to exploit French productive resources without a general transformation of production and consumption patterns, without a revolution in people's attitudes to work and spending. And such a transformation could not take place in one country alone for smuggling made a mockery of all regulations and prohibitions imposed at national frontiers.

England was the first country to search for ways of imitating Indian textiles to perfection and as early as 1782 Oberkampf sampled Manchester bleached calicoes, bought from Charles Brandt, one of the earliest of the colony of German merchants in the town.[51] This trial produced such good results that he bought several thousand pieces after 1788 and only stopped buying when the collapse of the exchange rate and the growth of the British home market doubled the price in the early part of 1792. However, the price and quality of English calicoes continued to act as Oberkampf's standard and he declined all offers of cloth made in France, whether from Amiens, Paris or Rouen.[52]

The first phase of the Revolution did not alter his buying policy at all. He bought some of the finest Indian fabrics in London in 1790–1 but took the precaution of initiating a connection with a Frankfurt commission agent in case war should break out. However, continuing devaluation of the French currency made him turn to the Lorient sales, where prices were now between 40 and 50 per cent lower than those in London.[53] He bought more than a million pieces there in December 1791, using his young brother-in-law Pétineau as agent. 'Go ahead and don't be afraid to buy anything this year', he advised him.[54] The colossal purchases ensured the continuation of the factory until 1794. His insatiable appetite for cloth was entirely justified while the market held up, as it did throughout 1791. 'Everything that I am producing at present is already spoken for and it will be impossible for me to complete anywhere near all the commissions of the kind you need for a long time', he wrote to a Besançon customer in August. 'I have never seen such keenness', he confided to an old colleague on another occasion. At the end of this quite exceptional year it was confirmed that Oberkampf's business had reached record sales. (The details are set out in Table 24.) His luck turned with the collapse of the *livre* in the inflation of spring 1792 which shot up the cost of his raw materials and prevented his buying any more fine goods in London.

Oberkampf then looked for *guinées* stocked by the Paris agents, but above all he gave full rein to his commission agents at Rouen and at Thizy, in Beaujolais. 'If the goods become scarce', he wrote to the former towards the end of 1791, 'it will prove advantageous to buy today in spite of high prices for we must be well stocked'. Until the Decree of the Maximum (on prices and wages) in October 1793, Oberkampf's orders remained the same: 'buy everything that looks good and reasonably priced', but 'buy only the first rate' and 'without causing a panic'.[56] Although the continuous inflation of prices eroded his determination to keep on buying, he maintained his orders because he had to use his *assignats* (Revolutionary government bills) and because he had no alternative but to keep his workers in employment.[57]

Oberkampf's letters show that the French economy did not begin to seize up until summer 1793. 'There are no more Indian goods in the Paris warehouses', he observed sadly at that time. Some *guinées* that arrived and were put up for sale at Bordeaux reached four times the price of those sold at Lorient the previous January. Moreover the rebellions, whether of Federalists or counter-revolutionaries, disrupted communications and mail. After the Decree of the Maximum, which did not affect bleached or printed fabrics, the price of *siamoises* at the Rouen market remained double that of 1790 while those of Beaujolais 'returned to a reasonable price'. The recovery of sales, which began at the end of 1793, stimulated the revival of the market for raw materials at Rouen, in Beaujolais and shortly afterwards at Lorient, with the support of the Commission for Commerce. But the extraordinary rise in the price of *siamoises* in June 1794 stopped all buying. Once again the warehouse was emptied and work ceased for want of both cloth and chemicals.

The works ceased to do business with many customers but they did not shut down during the Reign of Terror (1793–4).[58] The most difficult time came soon afterwards, in spring 1795, 'when the cost of food absorbed all the available resources. There was no more hope of selling and consequently no hope of buying either.' The supplies from Rouen and Beaujolais resumed in July 1794 and spring 1795 respectively, and regained a 'normal' rhythm after the Peace with Spain in July 1795. From the end of this year the *assignats* went from bad to worse, so Oberkampf re-established his cash prices about 10 per cent above the 1790 level, without discount.[59] Significantly, this hides a more important fact: the tremendous purchases in London made by the intermediary of two Paris-based Swiss traders.[60] Through several Parisian contacts, Oberkampf renewed direct supplies from the London sales of the East India Company, and for 10 years they again supported his business.

His Genevan friends in London sent his bales of cloth to Genevan colleagues in Altona or Hamburg, who then dispatched them by neutral ships, through the account of M. Théodore Rivier of Geneva, to Rouen or Le Havre. Despite the hold-ups and expenses encountered, and despite Oberkampf's distaste for using false certificates of origin, his need of bleached cloth dictated such an indirect route. From January 1797 Hamburg became the centre of trade between England and Jouy. A symbol of this maritime, Protestant connection was the marriage in April 1797 of Oberkampf's elder daughter and the youngest son of the Le Havre shipowner J. B. Feray, former agent of the Hamburg merchant Chapeaurouge.[61]

Chapter 12

The Extension to Spinning and Weaving, 1805-20

The French Revolution severed many of the normal channels of trade and made it more difficult for Oberkampf to obtain supplies of Indian calicoes for printing, but he was never entirely cut off from his sources of supply. Accordingly, in November 1799, we find him expressing the hope that 'from recent changes in government [Bonaparte's *coup d'état*] general happiness and peace will soon come'.[1] The *coup* in fact took place, as Oberkampf recorded, 'when business is at a standstill, and collecting [debts] more and more difficult'.[2] Nevertheless, East India Company calicoes from London continued to reach him through Chapeaurouge's, the Huguenot house at Hamburg.[3] The Peace of Amiens (25 March 1802) allowed him to reopen commercial relations with Charles-Friederich Brandt of Manchester after a break of 10 years. But sadly Oberkampf discovered 'that the prices quoted are not so good as I had from London', and when four bales arrived in the spring he was surprised at the high cost of carriage from Manchester to London. Evidently he had not anticipated the British inflation of the war years. In July 1803, two months after the resumption of war, Oberkampf met Wiss of Ripley & Riviers of London, another Huguenot firm, and it was agreed to supply Jouy via Rotterdam or Hamburg.[4]

The Consulate government inaugurated a new policy on customs duties, and by the Decree of 24 frimaire XI (1802) duties were increased tenfold, up to 1,000 $f.$ per cwt upon imported white fabrics, other than prohibited British goods, and up to 800 $f.$ on untreated cloth. In spring 1803 the 'pedigree' of imported cloth had to be demonstrated, and then it was only allowed to enter French harbours in licenced ships from neutral countries. In the following July Feray's son-in-law was a member of the Paris trade deputation to the First Consul in Brussels which appealed against the seizure of imports that had come through other channels.[7] 'I foresee an immediate scarcity of raw materials to supply my factory', Oberkampf was forced to conclude. In October he learned that 'a new tariff is being prepared, much higher than the last'.[8] In the event the Decree of 6 brumaire XII (1803) imposed a uniform duty of five centimes a metre (roughly 5d. a yard) for every second pound (lb.). The Decree was of course unfavourable to the finer, light weight fabrics. Could the new tariff help French weavers to compete with Indian imports? Oberkampf, at any rate, did not believe so. For 10 years he had told every French merchant or manufacturer who offered him samples that 'your pieces will only suit me insofar as they imitate English calicoes, but I doubt whether you will achieve the standard without competition'.[9]

However, when a Genevan printer urged him to protest against the tariff, Oberkampf replied, 'I am determined to make no more protests as they never come to anything. Moreover I do not completely object to the measures you complain of. They are not favourable to printing factories, but spinning and weaving concerns will benefit a great deal, and although I would have preferred a lower duty I cannot say I find it exorbitant'.[10] This unprecedented response, made precisely on the day following the Decree of 22 ventore XII, which confirmed all the previous decisions on customs, is better understood when it is realised that Oberkampf had just decided to embark on spinning and weaving.[11] Long before he announced it to his numerous correspondents he had made up his mind to profit from 'a good customs system' by 'establishing spinning and weaving as well'.[12] He bought the Chantemerle estate at Essonnes, close to his Bordes printing works, for 192,000 ƒ. At the time it consisted of a dwelling house, two tanning mills and 14 acres of land.[13] In August 1805 the Scots millwright William Aitkins overhauled the Chantemerle waterfall, estimating its power at 17 hp[14]. A few days later Johann-Philipp Widmer, now head of Oberkampf's printing works, petitioned the Vice-Prefect of Corbeil to be allowed 'to change the shape and form of the mill wheels and head races' and to 'convert them to other uses'. The opposition of the owner of the next mill, a fuller, delayed the necessary permission for nine months, and it was only then given after an angry letter to the Prefect of Versailles by Louis Feray. His letter recalled 'the philanthropic principles which have always motivated Mons Oberkampf' and the harmful effects of the delay. As a result of these he had to pay:

> overheads and taxes as if his mills were working, with idle workers

to pay, while he was unable to predict the outcome of such cruel indecision, nor where to look to supply his Jouy work with raw materials that the foreign trade supplied him with before the prohibitive laws which aimed to permanently establish this industrial development in France and to deliver us from a burdensome tribute.[15]

The ageing Oberkampf felt vindicated by the new customs edict of the Bonapartist régime: double duties on all cotton woven goods in September 1805 followed by complete prohibition of all imports on 22 February 1806.[17]

As early as 28 February he offered Samuel Joly 'a contract for a thousand pieces a month at 50 $f.$ each, unbleached, 25 yards long, of consistent quality, with two months notice'.[18] He contracted in much the same way with other manufacturers in Picardy and Hainaut.[19] By the end of May he was asking a former connection, Louis-David Feret of Cormeilles (Eure), 'whether you could distribute on my account all the [spun] cottons to be woven. I'd pay you well for good quality fabrics.... It should be regular work'. A similar enquiry was sent the following month to the Parisian trader Dufrayer, owner of the former Vaucelles Abbey, near Cambrai, where he was setting up a spinning mill.[20] At the same time he asked two leading Lisbon merchants, recommended to him by the Mallet bank, for their terms for supplying Pernambouco cotton of the first quality. 'To initiate our correspondence', he entreated them to buy 300 bales for him to be consigned, 50 every week, to Nantes factors. He also invited his correspondent in Hamburg, Chapeaurouge, 'to find me someone in the States ... who may consider me as a first hand buyer of Georgian cottons, which from now on must be a branch of my works'.[21]

His first purchases of cotton turned out to be more speculations than supplies since the Chantemerle spinning works did not begin to operate until the end of 1810. The purchases proved problematic indeed, interrupted by troubles in Spain and Portugal and ended by a loss of some 1,822,000 $f.$, with 1,320 lost bales out of 4,000 purchased in Lisbon in spring 1807.[22] 'To fill the deficit the Spanish affairs left in our raw cotton account and to assure the supply of your spinning mill with common cottons as soon as possible', Feray proposed to his father-in-law in March 1810 that he should tender with three other firms for the cargos of American ships sequestrated at San Sebastian. This amounted to 4,000 bales worth 4,200,000 $f.$[23]

Political circumstances therefore impelled Oberkampf to seek elsewhere, in Naples and in the Levant, for the necessary cottons when the building of his spinning factory was completed.[24] Building lasted for nearly four years, supervised by the architect Navier, and finally cost more than 400,000 f.[25] In July 1808 the waterwheel made by William Booth from Aitkin's plans and the mill-races were ready, but the building itself and the spinning frames were still being erected; 211 men were working on the former and 70 artisans – blacksmiths, founders, and joiners – on the machinery, directed by an English foreman called John Bland.[26]

Table 28 The 'take-off' of the French cotton industry, c. 1760–1805

Factories (type)	No. of factories in 1805	Total known to be set up (c.1760–1805)	Before 1780 (%)	1780–9 (%)	1790–9 (%)	1800–3 (%)	1804–5 (%)	Combined 1800–5 (%)
Spinning	1,037	402	4.6	10.9	20.5	24.5	39.5	64
Weaving	2,249	222	14.8	8.8	20.4	33.5	22.5	56
Printing	186	123	24.8	16.3	32.4	14.4	12.1	26.5

SOURCE: AN: F12/1562–4.

Table 29 Origin of French raw cotton imports during the Empire, 1800–09

Year	Aggregate raw cotton imports (f.)	% of all French imports	From Portugal (%)	From USA (%)
1800	1,601,900	22.9	5.7	n.d.
1801	51,809,000	86.9	15.4	6.7
1802	39,079,000	21.9	35.3	11.3
1803	40,736,300	32.2	23.3	30.3
1804	46,665,500	28.2	34	32
1805	59,168,200	21.7	35	21
1806	63,395,100	26.9	27.2	21.8
1807	62,802,100	30.5	n.d.	30
1808	65,569,200	46.1	n.d.	4.6
1809	72,248,800	65.4	n.d.	n.d.

SOURCE: AN: AF IV1060–61.

Table 30 Size of the French cotton industry (spinning and weaving sectors), 1811

Factory department	Spindles mules	Spindles throstles	Output (yarn kg)	Looms	Output (calicoes)	Workers spinners	Workers weavers
Oberkampf, Chantemerle	7,392	3,846	76,316	134	6,569	53	134
Lehoult, Versailles	17,076	100	18,424	0	0	50	0
Seine-et-Oise	54,288	16,300	219,794	560	17,000	500	520
Aisne	53,950	5,840	206,672	10,459	103,870	1,360	9,072
Somme	56,201	7,808	218,199	4,274	85,055	5,000	4,635
Seine-Inférieure	c.50,000	c.23,000	223,188	18,000	289,645	6,000	18,600
Nord	96,000	5,276	4,752,017	9,500	247,070	2,555	9,500
Pas-de-Calais	18,870	16,000	95,540	788	6,260	490	663
Aube	52,775	704	194,600	2,855	162,200	5,350	1,849
France: total (estimate)	645,420	140,000	c.8,220,000	c.88,500	c.1,600,000	c.115,000	c.75,000

SOURCE: AN: F12/1570–82.
NOTE: No information for plants in Paris has survived.

The Extension to Spinning and Weaving, 1805–20

The Chantemerle factory, unlike Oberkampf's previous enterprises, was both centralised and dispersed. The spinning and preparatory processes were concentrated in the mill while the weaving was dispersed in small workshops in or about the workers' homes. In October 1812 the mill employed 731 people within its walls and more than 1,400 others outside the works, some 600 in Paris and 800 others in Normandy.[27] Raw cotton cleaning and picking was done at Essonnes, Jouy, or in Paris in several workshops in the Rue Saint-Victor under a supervising *commis*, G. Midol.[28] Oberkampf, or in practice his son-in-law Feray, demanded a 'perfectly picked and cleaned cotton, without any seeds or burrs, a well-opened fibre, neither ropy nor broken ... If the cotton is not sufficiently clean on its arrival it must be done again' and charged to the tendering workshop master. Each contract to purchase cotton wool was renewable every fortnight so that the female cleaners could be kept on or laid off at will. Comparison of output between the Chantemerle or Jouy workshops and outside contractors provided a standard by which to judge the efficiency of the latter in terms of output and allowance for waste.

At Chantemerle both the carding and spinning workshops were controlled by overlookers, the oldest of whom generally earned 80 *f.* a month and the others 60 *f.* The works were directed by a supervisor from the office where orders for yarns were received. Feray explained that:

> This supervisor has no fixed wages; his profit was derived, first, from a commission of 2.50 francs for every 100 kg of cotton spun (commonly in 36s grade), and second, to ensure a perfect yarn by fines and deductions according to mistakes or flaws in the yarns produced, whether these shortcomings emanated from the spinners or from bad dressing.... Apart from this commission, which is expected to produce 18,000 francs a year, my supervisor is liable to provide oil for the frames, ropes and belts, and all accessories used for the frames and in the workshops at a cost of 0.25 francs a kg spun, and reeling, which is done in a separate workshop, at 0.12 francs kg, so that altogether he gets 0.55 francs to every kg spun.... This is how the high cost of labour at Essonnes persuaded me to introduce the system to economise in the mill committed to my charge.[29]

Some years later the bankruptcy of the other mill owner at Essonnes, F. A. Rolland, helped Feray to improve his firm's position. 'I thought you'd find it in your interest to bargain for the worn-out frames and break them up, selling the materials for scrap, so preventing competition from that firm, whose workers have sought employment here. He employed 200–50 workers; if he were to continue the price of labour would be forced to rise', Feray wrote to Oberkampf. He calculated the cost of Rolland's 6,398 spindles and bought him out.

A small part of Oberkampf's yarns were sold on the general market but, as he explained, 'only ill-matched counts unlikely to be of use in my weaving concerns'.[31] Another part was consigned on special terms to traders living in the weaving *départements* – Dubois-Moreau, Preval or Soyer in Rouen, Gaillard-Pont & Cie at Lyons, Merle at Roanne, Sebastian Mulsant at Thizy and Goullioud Frères at St Symphorien-de-Lay.[30] Feray advised these middlemen of the price of his warps and wefts, allowing them a four per cent commission and six per cent discount with payment at the end of every month by bills on Paris. If he was short of woven calicoes Oberkampf could ask these local traders to act as manufacturers by putting out yarns to be woven, a practice which served to strengthen his control over them.

Feray considered the possibility of undertaking weaving on the Chantemerle site but was daunted by the trouble and expense. To begin with, it would require a *commis*, 'well-trained in his job, with good sense and regular behaviour, and a good hand [writing], very methodic and clear in his records'.[33] Then it would require the purchase of looms, with shuttles and spools, and the recruitment of weavers able to work them 'without spoiling or stealing anything'. Such standards called for trustworthy supervisors and numerous apprentices, 'from the country as far as possible as they are the only people you can rely on'.[34] Every autumn the Jouy works defined its monthly needs for the following year by reference to different targets and Feray had to calculate how many looms and how much yarn was necessary to reach them. So it proved much easier to sub-contract to rural workshop masters, consigning to them boxes of mounted yarns and of barrelled wefts every month. The masters were required to maintain exact accounts of the warps and wefts received and were held responsible for all the pieces they produced that were considered too light or badly woven. The supply of completed goods was ensured by the mortgage of the masters' property to Oberkampf.[35]

In autumn 1806 a new system of sub-contracting was launched which aimed at avoiding any social unrest among the weavers. The earliest to benefit from it lived in the Aisne, Eure or Nord *départements*. Until his mill came into full production Oberkampf supplied

Table 31 Factories and dispersed workshops in a rival enterprise: Richard-Lenoir, 1810

Location	Spindles	Weaving looms
Paris (two spinning workshops)	26,353	120
Chantilly (Oise)	7,644	270
Verneuil (Eure)	0	150
Mortagne (Orne)	0	250
Alençon (Orne)	0	800
Mamers (Sarthe)	0	117
Fresnay (Sarthe)	0	70
Ecouché (Orne)	0	150
Argentan (Orne)	0	100
Sées (Orne)	22,680	220
Athis (Orne)	0	180
Caen (Calvados)	18,144	43
Aunay (Calvados)	17,702	147
Laigle (Orne)	16,680	0
Picardy (34 workshops)	0	4,000
Total	**109,203**	**6,617**
Workers employed	*2,600*	*8,822*

SOURCE: AN: F12/1559.

them from outside contractors from time to time. After 1810 there was also one firm at Abbeville, another at Rouen, Joly at St. Quentin, a workshop master at Harcourt (Eure), 10 or more agents in Corbeil and at least as many in the neighbouring Hurepoix, from Dourdan to Fontainebleau, with an outlying agent, Isaac Koechlin, as far away as Willer (Haut-Rhin).[37] 'My proposals will probably leave you little profit', Feray shamelessly wrote to one agent, 'but at least by linking yourself to me, you may be certain that, if you satisfy me, we shall progress together, and you may have work as long as you like.'[38] If an agent's work did not reach Oberkampf's standards he was of course admonished: 'it is only by your excessive leniency that workers could be so careless, for undoubtedly they are clever enough and can do well when they want', Feray wrote once.[39] Quite possibly 'outside fabrics', he confessed, 'are never so fine and carefully made because the workshops [around Chantemerle] are not always so convenient and supervision not so complete [as inside the factory]. But this is a sacrifice that has to be made in order to create a population of skilled weavers like those in the Picardy and Normandy weaving areas'.[40]

The growth of manufacture in domestic workshops was the characteristic path of industrialisation in Normandy and the country around Paris. Workshop owners needed very little fixed capital, for workers traditionally provided their own looms and tools, and no significant concentration of labour. Accordingly, 'weavers who were so foolish as to raise their prices' quickly found themselves out of line with the rate for the job. Workshop masters soon became accustomed to the idea of a fixed price for the job, in effect a kind of wage. Though work continued to be done in the country people's homes, or in small workshops nearby where wives and children could be employed – the former as jenny or mule spinners, the latter as dressers and trimmers – the country people were gradually, without realising it, becoming proletarians. The workshop owners preserved a nominal independence in that they could compete for better contracts from the suppliers, but by providing mortgage bonds for the small fixed capital needed by weavers, the spinners could fix it so that all looms worked exclusively for them, with the result that the weaver even lost the freedom to leave one master for another. The wide geographical dispersion of the biggest spinning and weaving firm of the period of the French Empire (1799–1815), that of Richard-Lenoir, is illustrated in Table 31.[41] The large circulating capital required for distribution was, in other words, the ultimate factor in converting the rural industrial population into proletarians, a process that took place, presided over by men like Richard and Oberkampf, without rural migration or exodus.

Chapter 13

Labour Recruitment and Relations[1]

With nearly 1,000 employees, Oberkampf's Jouy works constituted one of the most important concentrations of French workers during the early period of French industrialisation.[2] It was consequently one of the major centres of the development of the new industrial order, more especially as it formed an isolated industrial community within the rural countryside of the vale of Bièvre.[3] But unlike, for example, the archives of the Cortaillod printworks,[4] Oberkampf's surviving records do not contain any lists of workers, an indispensable source for the study of the size of the labour force and its seasonal fluctuations, of wages and other sources of income, and the ways in which the employers maintained order and discipline. It has been necessary to look for evidence outside the business records, and fortunately sources exist which can show the geographical and social origins of the workforce, the organisation of the business, and something of the quality of the workers' lives, both in their standard of living (housing, food and furniture) and social activities (family life, literacy and political consciousness).

Two types of sources are available for this, but both have the drawback of showing only aspects of the workers' lives outside the factory gates. The census of the early nineteenth-century and the *état-civil* registers (registers of the Catholic Church down to 1792 followed by the civil registers), together with a complete series of local notaries' registers, allow us to list and analyse three-quarters of the workers living in the parish of Jouy at the beginning of the nineteenth century, but the 600 or so individuals recorded in these sources cannot pretend to be representative of the total workforce of the enterprise. Women and children seldom appear in the records (children being minors in the Civil Code), while the ordinary labourers who were too poor to have frequent recourse to law are also severely under-represented. Although not a sample in the strict statistical sense this set of data nevertheless offers valuable evidence on some of the more important sections of the labour force, notably the skilled and male groups.

The workers at calico printing factories were evidently distinguished from other workers of the period by two characteristics. The factory workers were always described by the recorder, be he priest, registrar or notary, as *ouvrier* (or *imprimeur*, or *commis*) *de la manufacture de toiles peintes établie en ce lieu*. The factory, enclosed within walls which separated and protected it from the outside world, clearly identified and defined its skilled workers. The description *ouvrier* was never left unqualified. Whether designer or drawer, colourist or painter, printer, folder or *auneur* (measurer), the variety of specialised occupations described reflects the social and technical divisions of the workforce. This hierarchy of occupations and social status was representative of the spectrum of skills in proto-industrial enterprises. The techniques of calico printing, even after the invention of the roller printing machine, reached the highest levels of skill that could be attained by manual dexterity, and the product was often indistinguishable from the invariable accuracy of machine production.[5] The slightest mistake, whether through ignorance or lack of concentration, jeopardised the perfection of the prints, so inspectors, supervisors and foremen were appointed to make a continuous and close scrutiny of all the workshops and of the tenter fields in case of inclement weather.

When he moved into the house at *Pont-de-pierre* in April 1760, Christoff-Philipp Oberkampf was assisted in his work by his young brother Frédéric and his countryman Henri Haffner who had followed him from Cottin's works to Jouy. According to his partner Sarrasin the various branches of the manufacture employed some 900 people 20 years later.[6] The total wage bill rose from an index of 100 in 1762 (14,500 *l.*) to 206 in 1764, 315 in 1766, 540 in 1769, 770 in 1773, 912 in 1774, 1,217 in 1778, and to 2,026 in 1790. At the end of the 1760s, after the first factory buildings had been established, and also after the failure of the neighbouring printing factory at Sèvres, the decisive rise in production and employment began. From then on the effective workforce remained stable until the beginning of the Empire. When Napoleon visited the works in June 1806 there were 1,021 employees, in addition to 306 at Essonnes.[7] The crisis of 1806–8 involved the dismissal of one-third of the workforce which thus fell to 714 (plus 189 at Essonnes). It rose to over 800 in 1810–12 but thereafter declined to 672 in 1813, 286 in

Labour Recruitment and Relations 173

Table 32 Occupational distribution of the Jouy workforce, according to the Censuses of the early nineteenth century, 1791–1836

	1791	1805	1806	1810	1811	1812	1817	1836
1. Skilled								
Designer	2	3	1	3	2	1	3	5
Engraver	14	45	24	29	32	36	16	12
'Pickers' (pin work)		30						
Colourist	1	6					1	2
Dyer		36						
Printer	64	185	61	56	58	76	64	52
'Rentreurs'		190						
'Roller'		6						2
Clerk	12	15	32	30	30	22	18	3
Foreman					2	1		3
'Ouvrier d'état'	2	14						
Total	**95**	**360**	**118**	**120**	**122**	**136**	**102**	**79**
% of total enumerated workforce	*51*	*27.3*	*15.4*	*13.8*	*24.5*	*24.9*	*?*	*?*
2. Unskilled								
Painters (female)		570						
Labourers (male)	78	125	246	264	203	211	?	?
Labourers (female)		10	398	481	167	194	?	?
'Children'		72						
Total workforce enumerated in Census	**185**	**1318**	**763**	**866**	**497**	**546**		
% of total known workforce		*100*	*75*	*100*	*57*	*67*		

SOURCES: 1791: AD, Yvelines: 1 Lm 445, electoral lists of *Chefs de ménage*, 31 Dec. 1791.
1805: AN: 41 AQ5, information delivered to the Prefect.
1806 to 1812: Archives Communales, Jouy: annual Census.
1817, 1836: AD, Yvelines: 9M 626, enumeration lists.

1814, and 435 in 1815. The lowest employment figures were reached in January and February 1814 with 119 wage earners, when the recovery of the enterprise seemed impossible. The owner, however, preferred to carry on paying wages, even without work to do, rather than abandon the enterprise.

Table 32 shows the predominance of unskilled workers at the beginning of the nineteenth century. The skilled workers, upon whom the sources rightly concentrated, formed at most a quarter of the total workforce.[8] Nevertheless, however high or low their status in the process of production, all the workers in the business were assembled within the factory enclosure each day and passed through the large gate which was opened during the period of the striking of the clock.[9] This concentration of the workers inside the factory walls, within an area of 14 ha (58 acres), gave Oberkampf's works, and calico printing establishments in general, a specific industrial character which other contemporary textile works did not possess. (Other factories of the period were invariably housed in converted buildings or in dispersed premises, or nebulously arranged around the warehouses.)[10] Through sheer numbers of workers and their concentration, Oberkampf's enterprise placed itself among the leaders of contemporary European calico printing works (Table 33).

The technical division of work within the factory necessitated a substantial workforce and the imposition of strict discipline. It was enforced by the most regular, exact and obedient artisans, who were rewarded with a special title and status, that of *commis*, an appointment that brought security of employment and an annual salary, while most workers were paid monthly or even daily.

The employment of juveniles at Jouy and Essonnes presents some problems to the historian. Although in his request to the King for the title of 'Royal Manufacture' in 1784 Oberkampf affirmed that he had in his employ workers of five or six years of age, in the censuses of the Napoleanic era there is not the slightest evidence of the employment of children under the age of eight and only one example, in 1802, of a child worker of eight years. As Oberkampf did not employ children as *tireurs* it is difficult to say how he used them productively in his factory.[11] The minimum age of apprentices engaged by contract between the years 1768 and 1774 was 12, and the average age 14 years, so if the young children did regularly work in the factory, it was to acclimatise them to the discipline rather than to expect any production from them.[12] Oberkampf was concerned to train the children from an early age in the rhythm of work and in the discipline of the manufacture. By watching their parents or the older

Table 33 The concentration of workers in some leading cotton works in France, Alsace, Switzerland and the Low Countries, 1765–1806

	Printing	Spinning	Weaving
1. France			
1765 Wetter brothers & Cie, Orange	600		
1766 Danton, Moreau & Cie, Angers	240		
1779 J. Mainville, Orléans	200		
1781 Garnier, Danse & Thèvard, Beauvais	800		
1785 Lesage & Cie, Bourges	361		
1794 Dupasquier & Cie, Cortaillod	714		
Responses to the Napoleonic Enquête, 1st Jan. 1806			
Gros, Roman & Davilliers, Wesserling	543	185	392
Dollfus, Mieg & Cie, Mulhouse	715		
Verdan, Bienne	425		
Soehnée & Cie, Munster	600		
Average of 186 establishments	79		
2. Belgium			
Schavye & Sons, Anderlecht	320		
Legrelle, Dambrugge	276		
De Vos, Ghent	200	400	
Lousbergh, Ghent	150		270
Tillen, Louvain	250		
Average of 55 establishments	61		
3. Switzerland			
Labarthe & Cie, Geneva	420		
Petit & Senn, Geneva	350		
Various spinning enterprises			
Tiberghien & Bardel, St. Denis (Belgium)		820	
Duport & Cie, Annecy (Savoy)		650	
Foxlow & Bazin, Orléans		480	
Baroud & Cie, Neuville		600	
Richard & Lenoir, Paris		467	
Lehoult, Versailles		445	

SOURCE: 1806 data from AN: F12/1562–4; Cf. S. Chassagne, 'L'enquête, dite de Champagny', *R.H.E.S.*, LIV (1976), pp. 358–68. The first five figures are from S. Chassagne, *Tournemine*, pp. 242–3, the sixth from P. Caspard, *op. cit.*

workers, and occasionally carrying out some minor tasks, they became familiar with the essential features of factory life and would find nothing strange about it when employed as adults.

As we have already noticed, the number of children is difficult to assess.[13] According to the census taken in autumn 1804, the male workers included only 11 per cent of boys between eight and 16 years. Of the remaining 89 per cent, 31 per cent were aged between 16 and 25, 32.5 per cent in the 25–45 age group, and 25 per cent were over 45. Even if the population projection after 10 years of wars is explained, this equilibrium among the age groups calls to mind the workers' career patterns: a short time for initial training, a longer period in the exercise of their trade, whether skilled or unskilled, and a variable length of time for promotion and before retirement.[14] Division of the men's work in the factory was simply between hard physical work (washing the cloths, carrying, stretching and folding them) and precision work (designing, engraving the blocks and the rollers, and printing the fabrics). The women and children were subordinated to the ancilliary group (putting pins in the blocks, printing with blocks, pencilling the cloths in blue, tentering and watering the cloths in the field, and keeping an eye on the dyevats). Under the Empire, because of the relative scarcity of men, a greater number of women were employed. Their proportion increased from 30 per cent (in 1804–6) to 43 per cent (in 1811–12) of the total workforce of the factory. With the exception of two engravers who had acquired their skill before they came to Jouy, all the women were subordinated to male supervision as a matter of company policy.[15] Foremen were in charge of pin 'pickers', engravers, drawers, printers and large numbers of other female workers.[16] As 58 per cent of women workers enumerated in 1804 were over 25 years of age, compared with only 30 per cent between 16 and 25 and 11 per cent under 16, it seems probable that many entered the factory after marriage. (Between 1793 and 1843 the modal age of women at marriage was 25 years and six months.)[17] This practice marked the beginning of the household with two or more wage packets.

Clearly Oberkampf could not personally supervise the entire production process of such a large concern, and to make delegation more effective he dispersed the different processes into separate buildings within the factory enclosure (see Fig. 9). The management of these different buildings was entrusted to clerks and foremen. The whole of this supervisory grade enjoyed Oberkampf's complete confidence, whether he had known them for a long time as relatives, personal friends or German-speaking émigrés quickly promoted to positions of responsibility,[18] or whether he had picked them out for outstanding abilities.[19] They included his brothers-in-law, the two Pétineaus, his Widmer nephews, his relatives Minot and Boecking, his countrymen Bossert, Rordorff and Schramm from Switzerland, and men promoted from the ranks like Boussard the cashier (son of a gardener) and the Champs brothers (sons of a local vine grower), a mixed assembly of talent united by their common loyalty to Oberkampf. All of these trusted men were primarily involved in monitoring the punctuality and industriousness of the rest of the workforce, noting, for instance, 'the worker who left his bench before time to get ready to leave' who received only two thirds of the wage paid for the day as a result. They also accepted responsibility for preventing the theft of raw materials, tools or patterns. The doorkeeper was instructed to prevent anyone leaving the enclosure without a permit and, in the same way, no unauthorised persons were to be admitted. But that was not all. Even the night-watchmen[20], installed since 1772 in the *maison des Suisses* which was built in the middle of the tenter fields, could not prevent all thefts of cloth being tentered in the fields, which were rather a long way from the factory.[21] Consequently, watchfulness and zeal on the part of everyone was necessary to bring the attention of a *commis* to any suspicious behaviour and so prevent thefts or malicious damage to goods or property.[22] Through a system of constant surveillance – e.g. there was one supervisor for every 27 workers in 1810 – and a permanent guard inside the enclosure, through punishing the undisciplined and rewarding the 'good' workers, through the dismissal of the unscrupulous or unruly workers and sending the thieves to be dealt with by a court of law inside the factory, Oberkampf's workforce gradually became accustomed to the constraints of an industrial economy.

Before 1759, except in Marseilles and in several 'privileged' places in Paris, there were no workers in France skilled in calico printing, and up to the end of the eighteenth century the skilled printer or engraver remained a scarce asset competed for by the manufacturers.[23] This was why Oberkampf's social policy, like that of other manufacturers, had the primary aim of retaining the workforce which he had gradually recruited and assembled.

This policy of retaining skilled manpower was all the more firmly established as the part of local recruitment became more important (Table 34). On the other hand, a labour supply of local origins and predominantly rural background greatly contributed to the cultural homogeneity of the wage-earners, and this facilitated the integration of 'outsiders' and foreigners.[24] In the case of Jouy and of Wesserling it also justified the original choice of industrial location as they were capable of attracting the surplus local population and even of

Table 34. Geographical origins of workers in several French calico printing centres and in Cortaillod

Centre and period researched	No. of cases	Local (under 5 km) (%)	Regional (5–10 km) (%)	Nation-wide (over 100 km) (%)	Abroad (%)
Jouy 1760–92	203	65.0	15.7	9.8	9.3
1793–1822	389	68.8	16.7	9.8	4.6
Essonnes 1760–1820	61	59.0	22.2	1.6	16.3
1820–1850	125	8.8	8.0	64.8	15.2
Angers 1760–1820	100	26.0	29.0	30.0	15.0
Nantes 1760–1820	313	38.3	20.1	15.0	26.0
Troyes 1760–1830	132	26.0	9.8	21.2	42.5
Vizille 1776–1865	251	55.0	11.5	21.1	12.3
Jallieu 1788–1862	194	34.7	8.8	7.2	49.2
Wesserling 1800–60	1090	91.2	5.2	0.4	3.0
Cortaillod 1754	86	84.7	7.0	3.5	0
1819	451	54.6	31.0	6.3	2.2

SOURCES: Civil Registers of Jouy, Corbeil, Essonnes, Angers, Nantes, Vizille, Jallieu and around Wesserling, extracted by S. Chassagne; data for Troyes from L. Morin, *Mém. Soc. Acad. Aube* (1913), pp. 99–200; data for Cortaillod from P. Caspard, 'La fabrique au Village', *MS*, XCVII (1976), and *idem*, *La Fabrique-Neuve de Cortaillod 1752–1854* (Paris, 1979). p. 185.

Table 35 Duration of employment of male workers in several calico printing centres

Centre and period researched	No. of cases	less than 1 yr. (%)	1–2 yrs. (%)	3–5 yrs. (%)	6–10 yrs. (%)	11–15 yrs. (%)	16–20 yrs. (%)	21–30 yrs. (%)	31–40 yrs. (%)	more than 41 yrs. (%)
Jouy 1760–1820	364	8.2	4.3	12	28.8	18.9	10.9	13.1	7.4	1.9
Essonnes 1760–1820	80	24.1	12.1	15.6	14.4	15.1	4.6	4.2	6.5	3.0
1820–1850	202	40.5	13.3	19.3	19.8	6.9	0.4	0.4	0	0
Vizille 1776–1865	343	32.1	12.8	10.8	12.2	11.0	6.1	8.2	5.8	0.9
Jallieu 1788–1862	226	22.1	9.7	22.1	16.4	8.8	5.3	9.3	3.5	2.6
Wesserling 1800–1860	348	10.9	6.3	16.3	17.8	15.9	7.4	12.3	7.1	3.4

SOURCE: Civil Registers as for Table 34. Bachelors are, of course, less easy to trace.

drawing some foreigners who could found a family.[25] The success of Oberkampf's business explains why another enterprise set up in competition at Bièvres, only a few kilometres from Jouy, functioned there without any serious recruitment problems from 1800 to 1840.[26] However, for the initial formation and supervision of the original workforce, the contribution of the foreign element, especially the Swiss (mainly from Geneva and Neuchatel), remained indispensable, and this was also true even in a region like Alsace where calico printing was well-established.

The effectiveness of Oberkampf's policy for recruiting and retaining his labour force can be measured by the records showing the long period that many remained in his employment (Table 35). Moreover, the Jouy works was particularly successful compared with its rivals. Oberkampf achieved this success less by legal and contractual means than by financial incentives and promotion opportunities.[27] The reconstruction of several dynasties of Jouy workers helps us to understand the significance of establishing the works in a valley where 'before this factory came, misery was rife ... fathers of families were unemployed for three-quarters of the year and were obliged to beg for their food and only found momentary respite at harvest-time and by selling wood'.[28]

Let us take as an example the Perrier family of Jouy which provided 18 workers for the factory in three generations.[28] François-Marc the elder obtained an apprenticeship as an engraver at the age of 14 and may have worked at the factory before this. Five years later, after his marriage to a printer's daughter, he was effectively an engraver and was earning in the region of 700 *l.*, twice as much as his brother-in-law Pierre Gaumont. In 1790 he was promoted to the position of designer – about one-fifth of engravers were promoted to superior positions between 1760 and 1815 – and remained there until the enterprise ceased to be directed by a member of the Oberkampf family in 1822. Afterwards he worked for several years in Paris and then retired to Jouy where he lived a further 12 years. His half-brother, also called François-Marc, learned engraving on wood as well as on copper, but without serving an apprenticeship as the practice was abandoned by Oberkampf after 1774. His career in the Jouy works totalled more than 60 years of continual service and he died an *annuitant* at the age of 76. His three sisters, all of them workers, married workers from the factory. The eldest daughter and the three sons of François-Marc married into the circle of printers, as did the youngest daughter of his brother. All these intermarriages reveal the strong cohesion of the skilled and literate workers recruited from the local propertied peasantry. Marc Perrier, the father, was not without means. At his death in 1791 his property was worth 3,000 *f.* and was divided between his five heirs, a further sum being contributed on their marriages, which took place between 1760 and 1815. By this time the land of the family inheritance had already been broken into to assure the marital status of the children and their settlement in the village.[30] The Perrier family exemplifies the élite workers with a relatively well-to-do ancestry, showing that the movement into the wage-earning group did not necessarilly signify proletarianisation or pauperisation, and that migration from the rural areas did not have to involve downward social mobility.

For the many other Jouy families, even those less affluent, the factory represented an opportunity to rise socially, or at least made sure that there was less insecurity from day to day.[31] The works offered the prospect of a skilled trade, if not to the first generation then at least in the following one, as printer, engraver, dyer, bookkeeper, clerk etc., and a regular income.[32] The consequent inbreeding is proof of this attraction to factory work, apparently more secure and esteemed than the small rural trades or the conditions of the agricultural labourer on the farms of the large Saclay plateau.[33] Moreover, the husband's work at the factory did not prevent the wife earning extra money by providing lodgings for the other workers or by taking in children to nurse. Despite the great pay differentials between the *commis* and the unskilled labourers, 1:10 down to 1770 and from 1:30 until 1805, Oberkampf was never short of labour for his enterprise. He was so successful at making everyone accept the salary scale that the diverse categories pressed for the maintenance of differentials when the master no longer seemed to follow them strictly.[34]

The salary range exactly reflected the social and technical divisions of the works. At the top of the scale were the people in the office who were paid between 2,000 and 3,000 *f. per annum* in 1790, and between 1,200 and 3,600 *f.* in 1805. Next came the engraving and design technicians, the highest salaries of whom never reached the lowest level of the office workers (700 *f.* around 1780 and 1,000 *f.* around 1805). But normally these technicians received payment calculated on a daily basis, 'winter and summer, whatever the state of the work and even during periods of illness'.

The printers and labourers did not benefit so much from this security, for depending on seasonal fluctuations their salary could vary between 15 to 25 per cent.[35] They were among the first to suffer from a business recession or from the competition of female labour, which began in 1796–8. But prior to this they had also experienced a significant growth in their nominal wages (approximately 350 f. in 1770, 450 f. in 1780 and 600 f. in 1790, an increase of 76 per cent in the two decades). The early years of the Napoleonic Empire, coinciding with the height of the prosperity of the French calico printing industry, saw another rise in their wages, to 800–1,000 f.[36] The wages of these skilled male workers, however, remained twice as high as those of their unskilled counterparts (beaters, pencillers, folders etc) and three or four times greater than those of the numerous women painters whose period of employment was also unstable.

These pay differentials show the value that the manufacturer placed on the respective jobs, but in addition various perquisites were given to 'good workers'. These 'perks', granted at the discretion of Oberkampf himself, were paid on 31 December each year to reward 'industriousness, precision and intelligence', and were more often received by the officers and technicians than by the skilled or unskilled workers. They were not productivity bonuses but marks of recognition given to employees whose continued support was deemed indispensable. Another reward for these same prized workers was a bonus of a 5 per cent interest on the compulsory deductions of their wages, which varied between 10 and 20 per cent and which guaranteed the workers' allegiance to the enterprise, at the same time accustoming them to the virtues of saving and deferred consumption.

To those who managed to save out of their earnings the master offered shares with interest, which from the end of the *ancien régime* was a forerunner of the savings banks of the early nineteenth century.[37] The managerial staff were not the only ones who took advantage of this scheme. For example, a man like Rohdorff could leave 126,825 f. in his interest account when he died in 1810, and one can cite the examples of *20 commis* employees who each left 16,200 f., 15 engravers who averaged 5,665 f. each, while 30 workers, both skilled and unskilled, averaged 2,100 f. each.[38]

Finally, in addition to the customary advances in salaries, a trifling 0.6 per cent of the total wage-bill during the Empire, Oberkampf granted agreed advances to certain wage-earners. There were 19 cases between 1760 and 1815: five to clerks, three to engravers and designers, seven to printers and four to workers. These agreements, which were intended to help in the purchase or construction of a house, gave Oberkampf a further opportunity to retain these people in his employment.

The salaries and wages policy underlines the paternalistic strategy.

By never paying workers with 'bad' money or valueless paper, by employing promisory notes only when nothing else was available (beginning of 1791 to spring 1796), supplying bread and meat to the workers during the terrible years of 1792–1801, providing medical care for sick workers, and by supporting their widows if they died, Oberkampf amassed the treasures of gratitude and faithfulness. 'In order to gain the confidence of all the workers', he advised one of his Widmer nephews, 'be frank and honest with them, rather soft than too hard, never hit anyone, excuse little faults, and remember that the greatest punishment is to sack them'. These points were, for Oberkampf, the cardinal points of a good master who produces good workers.

PART FOUR

Conclusion

Conclusion

We began this study by placing textile printing in the setting of eighteenth-century European industrialisation and will now conclude it by returning to this context, assessing the place of our two entrepreneurs in the mainstream of economic development in their period. We are satisfied that we have been able to recover enough information about Sir Robert Peel, Christoff-Philipp Oberkampf and their respective regions, to identify some valid similarities and contrasts, but in order to bring out the significance of our findings we would like to place them against the results of other published research on the early leaders of this industry. Unfortunately there are very real problems in doing this. Most of the eighteenth-century calico printers about whom we have any significant information were wealthy merchants who diverted capital into manufacturing – entrepreneurs of the class of Nash of London, Deneufvilles of Amsterdam, Pourtalès of Neuchâtel and Munster, Senn-Biderman of Zurich and Wesserling, De Wisser of Osnabruck and Antwerp, and others mentioned at various points in our text and fairly well-documented in the literature. But the men whose careers have been examined in this book came of a different stratum of industrial society, the stratum of *verlegers* and master craftsmen who were equally the hereditary leadership of the industry but, taken as a class, were often subordinate to the merchants, at least so far as finance, supplies and marketing were concerned. Obviously direct comparison between our men and such merchants would be pretty artificial. In fact there are only two calico printers whose careers have been researched who offer a basis for realistic comparison with our subjects – Johann Heinrich von Schuele (1720–1811), the famous Augsburg printer, and Johann Joseph Leitenberg (1730–1802), the most successful of the Bohemian printers. Both have been the subject of useful books and recent academic comment but the account of Leitenberg was written towards the end of the last century and the information that can be derived from it is fairly meagre.[1] We shall make what we can of this source but the most informed comparisons will have to be made with Schuele.

Family and Personality

The legend of the 'self-made man' has stimulated much interest in the social origins of entrepreneurs but contributed little to our intellectual grasp of the nature of upward social mobility. None of our entrepreneurs were 'self-made' in the sense that they rose from rags to riches. They all came from a stratum of society in which cherished skills and sometimes small capital descended from one generation to the next, and they found their first marriage partners in the same rank of society. Before the mechanisation of textile processing, it was the broad stratum to which the small independent manufacturers and lesser *verlegers* belonged, and which was by imperceptible degrees fostering the growth of the proto-factory in a multitude of industries.[2] Above them were the hereditary, landowning and titled classes and a few rich merchants; below them the dependent operatives and labouring poor. Families in this stratum of society were linked to the most successful provincial merchants by trading connections, and might aspire to their rank, so that able sons entered on their careers within sight of the apex of urban society. In a period when the economy was expanding they might hope to reach the élite positions of urban corporate government or find places for their sons in this rank of society. The emancipation of calico printing, anticipating an upsurge in the European economy and the mechanisation of complementary branches of textile manufacture (spinning, bleaching), created spectacular opportunities for those with the necessary skills and connections, and young enough to turn change to their advantage.

The entrepreneurs included in this study turned their backs on the local social and economic hierarchy early in their careers but left by different routes, characteristically to acquire as much experience as possible. 'Parsley' Peel was already embarked on his career as a Blackburn *verleger* at the time when his sons were entering the business, and Robert grew up in a fast expanding printing business, without needing to travel far to keep up with new technology or the development of marketing. Similarly young

Oberkampf spent his youth in a home dominated by father's ambitions, although in this case the father lacked the business acumen to launch a profitable business. He had no real education but was apprenticed in textile printing factories in Basle and then worked with his father in various small workshops in Switzerland. Leitenberg spent eight years of his young life (1750–8) gaining experience in Zurich, Basle, Berne, Frankfurt, Nuremberg, and finally in Schuele's workshops in Augsburg before starting business on his own account. Schuele's father's connections included a well-placed Strasburg draper, with whom the youth served his apprenticeship. He took a common ascent by advancing to wholesaler and then to *verleger*. So it can be seen that while all our entrepreneurs spent their early careers in what may be termed the small local leadership of the textile industry, it was a sector already throbbing with ambition for the vast markets that were opening before them, and full of opportunities for artisans and traders willing to leave the groove of conventional methods. Our men could not wait to get ahead – Peel to leave the family fold to start a completely new industrial settlement in Bury, Oberkampf breaking his contracts to launch out in the unpromising virgin site at Jouy (1760), Schuele to use the town gaol as his first workshop (1758). After 10 or 20 years' strenuous and single-minded activity our men emerged at the head of the calico printing industry in their respective countries. In Britain, Peel led the cotton spinners to defeat the monopolising Arkwright (1781–5) and was left as undisputed leader of calico printing after the collapse of Livesey, Hargreaves & Co. (1788). In France, Oberkampf fought to overtake his Alsatian rivals and then to equal the industry in London. By the time of his first visit to the British capital in 1773 he was already confident of being well ahead. Schuele had to fight his main battle through the courts of the Holy Roman Empire; his legal victory and the edict of 1768 signalled that he had the markets of the Empire at his feet.

There was one common element in the success of these men. Each had an easily identifiable but immeasurable quality of drive and ambition far above that of entrepreneurs of the period. Some manufacturers were inhibited by an aversion to the social consequences of technical change but we have not detected any such reserve in our three men.[3] Their almost unlimited ambition is seen most obviously in their economic imperialism – in their erection of vast and complex industrial and mercantile empires with the accompanying social and political trappings. But when we are searching for personality and motivation it is the details of their characteristic responses that are most telling. We can see their characters most clearly in the order and discipline they brought to their respective factories at Bury, Jouy and Augsburg, in their imperious, sometimes militant, attitude to workers, in their selection and ejection of partners, in their political opportunism – Peel's opposition to free trade with Ireland, Oberkampf's support of Jacobinism and then the prohibitive customs policy, and Schuele's supplications to the Duke of Wurtemburg and to the Holy Roman Emperor – and in their opportunism in dealing with other people in the trade, e.g. Peel's exploitation of Hargreaves, Crompton, and other inventors, Oberkampf's dismissal of Maraise, Schuele's contempt for his sons. These are topics to which we shall return; for the moment it will suffice to state that our men exploited their early advantages with a determination that refused to be daunted by conventional restraints, powerful rivals, labour hostility or government attitudes.

Consciousness of belonging to a new social class and contributing to a new social order was evidently in the minds of all of our three men, but it manifested itself in different ways because of personality differences and the varying political contexts of their careers. Schuele, the brashest of the three, did not miss an opportunity to advertise his role in economy and society. In his public statements and in his addresses to the guild-dominated Augsburg Senate he repeatedly stressed the point that future production of goods would take place in factories, and as a manufacturer he claimed he was 'the most important man in the city.' On his visits to Vienna, where he was received by Empress Maria Theresa, Emperor Joseph II and their entourages, he did not stop stressing the point that the industrial entrepreneur would be 'the alpha and omega' of the new economic order which was taking shape. Born into a more democratic society, Peel chose to enter the Establishment rather than rail at it. At the early age of 40 he announced his entry to the governing class by purchasing a large part of the pocket borough of Tamworth and so securing a seat in Parliament. Oberkampf, a member of a minority national and religious group, retained a much lower social profile for many years. Nevertheless, his very survival through the turmoil of the Revolution, and his public recognition by both Louis XVI and Emperor Napoleon, suggests a parallel political adroitness and will to remain at the pinnacle of the social pyramid.

Ever since Max Weber's *Protestant Ethic and the Spirit of Capitalism* was published historians have enquired whether Protestantism generated a set of values conducive to business success. Our entrepreneurs offer a striking variety of religious contrasts. It has often been observed that many eighteenth-century industrialists in England were noncomformists, i.e. dissenters from the Church of England, and although it is by no means proven that noncomformists constituted a majority of this whole group of entrepreneurs, many of the vanguard appear to have been dissenters of one kind or another. However, the Peel family were all orthodox Anglicans, and they appear to have been close to the evangelical wing of the denomination – a very determined kind of orthodoxy. Oberkampf, of course, belonged to the Protestant minority in France and retained the external manifestations of the deep, personal piety of his forebears but there is nothing in his creed or letters to link his religious ideology with his devotion to work (see pp. 116–17). The career of J. J. Leitenberg displays just as much ambition and dedication to business and he came from a village controlled by the Jesuits. Indeed, his brother followed father's wishes and became a Jesuit missionary.[4] The position of Schuele contrasts in yet another way. In central Europe willingness to take unconventional entrepreneurial initiatives, often with the connivance of royalty, is frequently linked with the Jews, but Schuele had no early connections with the religion.[5] His parents struggled to bring up their family to be as 'decent, honest, and pious' as they were themselves, but the opportunism of Schuele's business career suggests that worldly ambition soon overrode these traditional moral values. His self-advertisement suggests anything but the traditional Christian virtue of self-effacement and his lack of scruples, particularly in his behaviour to his first wife and his sons, leaves little doubt that he was primarily an opportunist. So it seems that religion, whether orthodox or dissenting, was not the determining influence in the business careers of the entrepreneurs examined here.

Political Environment

The most striking difference between these entrepreneurs is seen in the political environment in which they worked and the different ways in which they responded to it. Building their enterprises in conditions as different as Habsburg autocracy, the French Revolutionary régime and the British struggle for middle-class representation in Parliament, such contrasts are of course inevitable.

The only political strand common to our three men was that each was born into a period when calico printing was severely restricted in some way, and each contributed to the relaxation or repeal of the law and exploited the advantages that flowed from its reform. The French prohibition was formally lifted in 1759 and the British in 1774, though, as we have seen, the law had been widely evaded in France and generally disregarded in Britain. In the German Empire control was decentralised and there were few prohibitions, except in Prussia, but this often served to encourage the local vested interests, like the Augsburg *Weberhaus*, to become more militant. The struggle with the local interests was inevitably more intense than the more remote and less well-informed government authority, whether of State or Empire. Schuele's main advantage was that he was able to expand his business before legal restrictions were lifted in Britain, France, and, above all, in Prussia.

The repeal of 1774 by no means satisfied the Lancashire manufacturers for printed calicoes were still subject to duties and these were increased in 1785. Moreover, there were, or appeared to be, other threats to their prosperity: the monopolising of warp spinning by Arkwright (1778–85), the rise of free trade ideology and especially the proposed treaty with Ireland (1785) and the early emergence of strong trade unions, especially among the journeymen block printers. There was also the growing jealousy of the landed interests which around the turn of the century began to be expressed as pressure for government control of cotton factories. As the largest and most militant manufacturer, Peel soon appeared at the head of the earlier pressure groups in Lancashire, and when he bought himself into Parliament trade politics became his major preoccupation. His later commitment to the factory reform interest was seen by some contemporaries as evidence of his deviance to the Tory (landowning) interest, but the vital influence was the Manchester intellectual radicals. Suffering a bad conscience over the Radcliffe mill scandal, Peel was readily moved by Dr Percival and his circle of medical reformers.

By contrast, Oberkampf kept out of politics during the early part of his career (1760–90). Although his works were near to the centres of political power in Versailles and Paris, he left Maraise to attempt to maintain contact with the court circles. He was a German and a Protestant, a stranger in an unfamiliar culture, and his social life was largely confined to his own circle of German friends. Instead, he relied on Maraise, a lawyer, for counsel and connections with the establishment. It was only when the Revolution threatened the future of his enterprise, and perhaps even his own life, that he found it necessary to develop the skills of a political manipulator. We may suspect a certain sympathy with Revolutionary ideals, at least from a foreigner's antipathy to the *ancien régime*, and in 1793 he took the pledge against the deposed order. Citizen Oberkampf thrived in the enlarged free trade area of the Empire and reached his greatest eminence then, enjoying the personal recognition of Napoleon himself, a rare honour for a manufacturer. As with Peel, we may suspect that humanitarian ideals had some appeal for him, but it is not easy to disentangle motives even when, as in this case, we have the advantage of private papers.

The strongest contrast between Sir Robert Peel and Oberkampf, however, is to be seen in their very different responses to the opportunity offered to them by success to climb the political ladder. At the relatively early age of 45 Peel invested a large part of his fortune in buying a stake in the pocket borough of Tamworth, and for the remaining 35 years of his life his mind was largely absorbed in political questions, and in socialising in the class into which he had risen so rapidly. By contrast Oberkampf declined to become a member of the French Senate in 1800, notwithstanding that he was proposed by Napoleon. Appointed a member of the *Conseil General* of his *département* (county council) for three years in the same year, Oberkampf never attended a meeting. When Feray became a member of the *Conseil General des Manufactures* in 1810, Oberkampf sent his congratulations but added that it was a waste of time. No doubt these contrasts reflect differing birth and personality rather than their economic policies, but we can note Oberkampf's lifelong dedication to business, and observe how far it differs from the allegations made about French entrepreneurs' lack of interest in business at this period.

Schuele readily emerges from this comparative study as the entrepreneur who devoted the largest part of his time to legal affairs and negotiation with the political powers and who gained most from his endeavours in this sector. His initiatives helped to develop two new legal concepts in the Empire. He asked for and received an Imperial *privilegium* in 1772 which is supposed to be the first attempt to protect industrial designs legally from being pirated. Secondly, in the celebrated court battle Schuele *v.* the Guilds of Augsburg, fought out in the *Reichshofrat* (Supreme Court of the Holy Roman Empire), Emperor Joseph II sided with the entrepreneur against the guilds and long-established legal precedents to produce a landmark decision in favour of capitalist progress. Schuele had a passion for going to court whenever he thought his rights were infringed. He kept a lawyer (*syndicus*) on his payroll and made him a constant companion; the lawyer even participated in family meals sitting next to his employers. In short, Schuele's business lived by political manipulation and the cultivation of imperial patronage.

The Holy Roman Emperor and most of his princes were eager to promote industry within their frontiers, while in France some parts of Colbertist policies survived into the age of Napoleon. Having once surmounted the legal and diplomatic hurdles that had to be crossed by any innovator, Schuele, Leitenberg and Oberkampf benefited from the privileges conferred by official government recognition. The recognition of Jouy as a *manufacture royale* (1783) gave the enterprise special legal status. Schuele's achievement in gaining imperial favour enabled him to override all opposition in Augsburg and to secure a permanent copyright for his printing blocks and fabric designs simply by stamping the initials of his *Fabrik Privilegium* (C.P.S.C.M. I.H.E.v.S.) on them. Leitenberg followed in the path pioneered by Schuele and won an imperial *privilegium* in 1792.[6] The Peels had none of these privileges and, if they were typical of early Lancashire factories, suffered from a high labour turnover and constant piracy of patterns. Evidently the 'free enterprise' of Britain had some drawbacks as well as advantages for the innovating entrepreneur.

Technology

Economic historians have grown accustomed to describing the varying pace of mechanisation in Britain and on the Continent in terms of varying scarcity of labour. Thus Habakkuk writes that:

> In eighteenth-century England ... the increase of industrial investment tended to run up against rising labour costs, and so manufacturers had an inducement to adopt more capital-intensive techniques where these were available, and to invest labour-saving techniques... But had the supply of English labour been abundant the increase in demand would have been met in England, as on the Continent, simply by expanding the domestic system with equipment of the existing type.[7]

This comparison seems right for the early processes of the cotton industry (carding, spinning, weaving, bleaching) but does not fit the experience of calico printing. In this highly-skilled and novel occupation the scarcity of artisans was just as acute in France and Germany as it was in Britain. To be sure, the French scarcity was due to earlier legal restrictions on the industry, but the fact remains

Plate 7 Jouy floral design, with the celebrated inscription of the *Manufacture Royale*, c. 1790–91 (Musée Oberkampf, Jouy)

that British experience in this area was by no means unique. When growth came, the London proto-factory system was simply multiplied in the provinces where labour was cheaper.

The early mechanisation of textile printing in Britain was not so much the product of a unique scarcity of labour as of the unusually precocious development of a trade union élite. It was their restrictive practices that led to the sharp rise in labour costs and subsequent rush to adopt the roller spinning principle, a technique that we have noted as being almost 100 years old at the time. It is worth recalling in passing that some other critical developments in the early history of textile technology, the automatic mule and wool-combing machine, were also induced by restrictive practices. Of course, it is distorting to consider one development in isolation from others, and in this instance it must be conceded that roller spinning quickly gathered momentum from easier and cheaper supplies of cotton and from mechanisation of the early stages of production. Nevertheless, the initial impetus came from a quite separate source. Feeling themselves threatened by trade union pressures, the Peels seized the technical initiative that bankruptcy had wrenched from Livesey, Hargreaves. But this development took place more than a century after the establishment of textile printing in Europe and did little to challenge its traditional structure until the crisis at the end of the French Wars (see pp. 33–57); the careers of the European textile printers ran parallel courses throughout the eighteenth century.

In printing technology as in some other matters the similarity between our entrepreneurs is more striking than the differences. The principal approach was to develop the proto-factory form of organisation to maximise the skills deriving from the division of handicraft labour. Each planted his enterprise in a locality where there was a relative labour surplus and in or near towns where there were traditional textile skills. It was easy to redeploy the workers of the old textile towns of Burton, Bury, Tamworth and Levin, and, after the initial hostility had been overcome, those of Augsburg also. Jouy was a slightly different case but was still near enough to Paris to recruit key workers there, while the Saclay plateau offered a pool of intelligent, hardworking, small property-owning peasants who were willing to divert their talents to a more promising future. All the entrepreneurs organised their respective factories on elementary labour-intensive techniques and devoted a good deal of thought to recruiting, training and disciplining workers to new industrial skills.

The refinement of artisan skills was not restricted to the workers assembled in the proto-factory. The master calico printer's initial problem was to raise the quality of his unprinted fabrics to reach the standards of the oriental imports, and each of our entrepreneurs had to devote themselves to this problem at some point or other in their careers. For reasons that are still obscure the Lancashire weavers took an early lead, and under the leadership of *verlegers* like Samuel Oldknow and Thomas Ainsworth, 'Parsley' Peel's partner, approached the finesse of Indian goods. Ainsworth brought his Bolton weavers under his immediate supervision in a colony known as Bengal Square. As early as 1758 Schuele was pushing his Augsburg weavers to improve the fineness of their cloths so that he could be less dependent on imports, but he never succeeded in attaining the oriental standards. Oberkampf always preferred Indian woven fabrics until the Napoleonic decree of prohibition forced him to resort to Normandy and Picardy *verlegers* and to negotiate for higher standards.

Scarcity of skilled labour also compelled each of our entrepreneurs to look for alternative methods of production on which they could employ teams of low-paid girls. The manufacture of printing blocks by arranging pins and wire in patterns in wooden blocks (*picotage*) was introduced about the middle of the eighteenth century and in due course was taken up by our men, more especially by the Peels. Sir Robert Peel was said to be the earliest to adapt the technique for roller printing. Girls were also trained to 'pencil' indigo designs, a technique that evidently appealed to Oberkampf. Meanwhile, Schuele seems to have saved skilled labour by making himself the master of batiks, i.e. resist dyeing, making patterns by waxing the parts intended to remain white before immersion in the dye vat.

In the eighteenth century much scientific and technological advance took place in the social context of dissenting or rationalist sects or movements, but it cannot be said that any of the leading European textile printers of the age were prominent members of these. In very different ways both Peel and Oberkampf came of families that were outside the mainstream of rational thinking in the localities where their factories were situated. As loyal members of the Church of England the Peels dissociated themselves from the progressive Dissenting tradition of English life. As Thackray explains:

> Such Church-orientated manufacturers as the Peel family chose to stand aloof from the [Manchester Literary & Philosophic] Society in its early days; the first [Sir] Robert Peel joined only in 1799 when the initial radical thrust had been throughly blunted.

It was the physicians and manufacturers congregated at Cross St. Chapel who gave the 'Lit. & Phil' its tone, its energy, and its orientation.[8]

Though a Protestant and a German, Oberkampf was not left out of the most dynamic French societies of his day for Maraise kept him in close contact. However, this did not prevent either entrepreneur from maintaining his position in the vanguard of the rapid technical advances, including management practices, of his lifetime. Each was an opportunist capable of attracting the support of the most eminent men of his day. The role of Sir Robert Peel in scientific research is a little obscure so we cannot be too categorical on the matter, but the influence of Dr Percival on his social ideology shows his readiness to absorb the ideas of the Cross St. group. Oberkampf's drive for perfection in printing led him and his qualified partners to devote much time to laboratory work on dyes, mordants and new mechanical techniques, and they tapped the brains of some of the best chemists of the day. Oberkampf entertained many of the most noted French chemists, Senebier, Gay-Lussac, Chaptal, Fourcroy and Berthollet. The results of this enterprise were certainly rewarding; Berthollet's discovery of the bleaching properties of chlorine was first adapted at Jouy, and Samuel Widmer discovered *vert solide* in the course of his experiments at the factory. However, these successes did not create a science-based industry as Oberkampf's employment of Robert Hendry, the Glasgow artisan, makes clear. Moreover, the Peels were almost as quick off the mark with the new bleaching techniques.

A distinguished twentieth-century dyer and bibliophil has identified 13 'key books' which marked the technical advance of his industry between 1500 and 1856, when Perkin discovered synthetic dyestuffs. Ten of these were originally published by French researchers while the other three were contributed by a Venetian (in 1540), a Scot, and an international adventurer of American birth. This collection of nationalities appears to reflect the French lead in applied science in the eighteenth and early nineteenth centuries. However, it must be added that the earliest book on calico printing, as distinct from dyeing, was entitled *L'art de faire l'indienne à l'instar d'Angleterre* (1770) and reports the success of the London printers in imitating oriental techniques, more especially at the peak of their achievement in the period *c.* 1775–1800.[9]

True to this tradition, Peel and his German rival, Schuele, are more easily recognizable as imitators and pirates than as scientists or originators of ideas. As the London printers stole and imitated the Indian techniques, so these two entrepreneurs helped themselves to the empirical technology of the London industry. When Schuele failed to make headway with copper plate printing in Augsburg, he travelled to London where Nixon had recently arrived from Dublin with his improved gums, and succeeded in inducing two of Nixon's artisans to return to Augsburg with him. Most German cotton printers of the period were content to rely on their colourist, but Schuele, with characteristic energy, took the trouble to teach himself about mordants and colour chemistry, and to make regular visits to printworks in Hamburg and Amsterdam to fill in the gaps in his knowledge. If he achieved greater commercial success than any other eighteenth-century German printer, it was because he raised the quality (fineness) of the Augsburg weavers, and because he recognised the value of a good designer and was prepared to pay the top salary.

The Peels' dependence on the technical and design achievements of the London calico printers was even more immediate than that of Schuele. The elemental techniques with which they started printing and their key artisans came directly or indirectly from London and their simple designs were popular versions of the latest fashions from the metropolis. If they were a few days behind London with their designs it did not greatly matter as they were several days' travelling time nearer the rapidly growing north of England and American markets, and in any case consumers in these regions were not so fashion-conscious as people in London and its environs. In all the later developments – in roller printing, chlorine bleaching, muslin manufacture, the application of steam power, jenny spinning, warp spinning, mule spinning and power loom weaving – the Peels were invariably among the most advanced group of innovators, not primarily as inventors but rather as entrepreneurs with an incredible capacity to close an early deal with the inventor or pioneer.

The most obvious and striking difference between the Peels and their Continental rivals is that the former took an early and active interest in technical developments in the spinning sector of the industry. Leitenberg's firm, one of the earliest in Bohemia to mechanise spinning, did not open a factory until 1797, and Oberkampf not until 1805. It would be easy to say that the Peels were swept along by the tide of events in Lancashire, but the evidence of this book shows that 'Parsley' Peel and his sons led the advance rather than followed it. Economic histories of Britain have found an explanation of the mechanisation of spinning in rising production costs (of power, labour, distribution, etc.) but have not really shown how and why costs were rising. The only relevant data in this book, which unfortunately relates to Oberkampf alone, shows that costs remained fairly steady over the period 1765–1790 (see Table 22). The only comparable data available for Britain is that of the average value of Indian goods sold at auction in London, which were not rising either (see Appendix). Indian fabrics represented a ceiling price for Lancashire, and other, imitations but otherwise tell us nothing of the experience of the industry.

However, there is another possible approach to the problem of the contrasting experience of British and French producers. The most remarkable feature of Table 22 is that some 80 to 90 per cent of Oberkampf's production costs were attributable to *toiles blanches*, and if he was being pressed to make economies this was surely the first place to look for them. We have no comparable data for the Peels, but an attempt to reconstruct English printing costs for the period 1771–90 suggests that the percentage of costs attributable to white calicoes was probably closer to 70 per cent in the popular patterns favoured by Lancashire producers. Why then did the Peels and their local rivals concentrate on producing cheaper fabrics? The only plausible answer must be the fear of Indian competition in 'white goods' which is so prominent in the trade lobbying of the period. Obviously France also imported Oriental piece goods, but the destruction of the French empire in India (1761) focused that trade on London, which was also Lancashire's principal market. The essence of Lancashire's problem, as we remarked in the Introduction, was that in India 'millions of ingenious and industrious manufacturers .... work for one-fifth part of the wages given in England', and the East India Co. had geared their Oriental labour force to the European market. By 1788 the Indian industrial army was in rapid retreat for the Indian producers had to employ 15 operatives for every one in British industry. The rout of the Indian artisans furnished the means and the confidence for onslaughts on a sequence of other markets round the world, beginning in Europe.

Structure of the Enterprises

In his valuable work on *Les banques européenes*, Lévy-Leboyer has advanced an attractive interpretation of the contrasting development of the British and French industries in the later eighteenth century. The British industrial revolution, he writes, started with basic industries making semi-finished goods such as yarns and pig iron and later progressed 'downstream' to the mechanisation of the manufacture of consumption goods such as weaving and calico printing. Continental industry, by contrast, he argues, began with specialised and labour-intensive quality consumption goods and then later on moved 'upstream' towards such processes as mechanised spinning or the primary iron industry.[10] Unfortunately this theory, attractive in its simplicity, is quite inadequate for our purpose for it neglects the indispensable craft base of British industry, whose early success led, by way of steeply rising cost-curves, to mechanisation. In the case of calico printing the industry was nurtured for three generations in London and reached a pinnacle of excellence in *European* markets before the rise of labour costs encouraged the cheaper lines to migrate to Lancashire.

From our point of view the work of Professor Mendels offers a more convenient starting point for understanding the growth of firms. Our three entrepreneurs were all born into what Mendels calls the proto-industrialisation period. Their most important initial asset was the craft-based skills that had been steadily improving in numerous European cities during the past two or three generations.[11] Entering the industry at the point when legal restraints were falling away, they were able to develop the full potential of the proto-factory to produce quality fashion-conscious goods to supply a rapidly rising market. The critical role of the market is underlined by Oberkampf's office in Paris and Leitenberg's warehouse in Prague (1792), by Schuele's early establishment of connections with Frankfurt, Hamburg and Amsterdam, and the early distinction of the Peels as suppliers of the popular market in England, Germany and America. It was the favourable market situation that led, by degrees, from the proto-factory to the fully-evolved (mechanised) factory, for bottlenecks soon appeared in the supply of various inputs, notably in spinning, bleaching, transport and the use of power. The need to pioneer some of these developments led the Peels from a simple Blackburn printing and *verlag* enterprise to the huge vertically integrated concern that appears in their later inventories. Oberkampf also moved into spinning, as did several other leading Continental printers notably Bidermann & Co. at Wesserling, Pelloutier at Nantes, Pourtalès at Munster and Leitenberg at Levin, but none on the scale of the Peels.

Each of the businesses described in this volume stood at the apex of the calico printing industries of the respective countries. In each country the industry consisted of a pinnacle of successful firms surmounting a broad base of numerous 'small to middling' firms, which often had few resources, whether of capital, market connections, or experience, so that there was a high turnover of entrepreneurs. However, in a fashion industry like calico printing the problem of all firms, except commission printers, was essentially the same: to catch the ever-changing shifts in consumer demand. The market, that is to say, favoured enterprises that were structured to make and implement decisions quickly. This was the justification for the way in which the entrepreneurs studied in this book dominated their respective firms. The strong, centralised control of a single, determined mind produces results so much more quickly than a board, a committee, or even a family partnership in which the members compete for power. No doubt the temperaments of the men studied was of a dominating kind, but the point remains that this characteristic was essential and is the prime feature of the systems of organisation studied here.

Strong, central control had to be reconciled with local autonomy in the dispersed, ancillary manufacturing-units, notably spinning mills and weaving workshops. The initial response of our entrepreneurs was to train their sons and other relatives in the business. 'Parsley' Peel was most successful in this in so far as his wife reared five able sons and this unusually large family interest was extended by the marriage of his most able son, Robert, to the daughter of William Yates. 'Parsley' Peel commanded the loyalty of his sons until his death in 1795 and thus held together his concerns while those of several British rivals, like Arkwright and David Dale, were disintegrating.[12] Similarly, Leitenberg's two sons grew up as his energetic lieutenants, in this case expanding the business beyond the father's dreams. Oberkampf was less fortunate, producing only one son of mediocre talent from two marriages, though he had several nephews who were educated as if they were sons. By contrast, Schuele believed that his sons were so incapable of running his concerns that he virtually drove them out of the business, which consequently did not survive his death.

But even in the case of the Peels continued growth of the business soon placed its outposts beyond the immediate control of the new generation. The problem was two-fold: the creation of manageable productive units, and the recruiting, training and retaining of responsible managers for them. Judging from the available inventories the Peels avoided taking too much risk investing in big factories, preferring to duplicate the smaller and more familiar water-powered units. In Sir Robert's words the mills and dispersed printworks were 'put under the direction of a partner or superintendent who has an interest in the success of the business,'[13] and who was appointed as the crowning achievement of a system of promotion by merit. Oberkampf had to face the problem of control of dispersed units as early as 1769 when he started Corbeil, which was first put under his brother's direction and later (1798) under that of a nephew. He also had to control a multi-departmental business at Jouy and developed the important technique of promotion to the salaried and prestigious *commis* grade. His weaving, necessarily done at a distance from Jouy, was in the hands of local contractors tied to Oberkampf by bond. If we knew more about the Peels we should probably recognise a similar system operating from their weavers' warehouses. Once again the achievement is thrown into relief by contrast with Schuele's practice in the more traditional Augsburg setting. His problems were rather different, however, for apart from bleaching he concentrated all his production at his famous Palace Factory in Augsburg, where he gave unremitting attention to every department of the business. But it seems that he never learned to delegate his authority, and so lost a sequence of capable managers, not least from among members of his own family. In this respect, we can see how far the Peels, and to a lesser extent Oberkampf, advanced beyond the simple autocratic kind of business that was still fairly representative in the eighteenth and nineteenth centuries. The ability to delegate was clearly one of the outstanding achievements of their management and the one that permitted them to grow so much bigger than their competitors in the calico printing industry.

Capital

The evidence collected in this book confirms that the fixed capital requirements of the proto-factories was modest compared with the later fully-mechanised factories. More capital was required than that employed by *verlegers* and the largest calico printing proto-factories represented an investment as large as the early Arkwright-type factories, but the major requirement of the calico printer was still for working rather than fixed capital. A collection of small buildings which could be converted from some other use, or made of wood or other cheap materials, was the main requirement apart from a few acres of land for bleaching and drying by sunlight. Water power was a valuable additional asset, but horse wheels could serve a similar purpose in small enterprises and steam engines in larger, so it was possible to function on a site without running water. The cost of printing tables, brushes and other utensils was evidently modest. The only expensive item was the engraved copper plates, and many manufacturers, including our men, found a cheap substitute for them by *picotage*, i.e. making printing blocks with numerous small pins tapped into patterns by low-paid girls.

Schuele spent most extravagantly on factory buildings, but his famous Palace Factory at Augsburg, built as early as 1771, was not unlike the cloth factories of Van Robais at Abbeville (1716) or Dijonval in Sedan (1775). It was clearly intended as a show piece of the new industrial age and industrial entrepreneur, and in this it amply succeeded; but although manufacturing needs as such did not require such ostentation, the building nevertheless was an integral part of Schuele's prestige marketing policy and heralded a new scale of manufacturing. In this respect Schuele is to be compared to Arkwright rather than to the Peels or Oberkampf, for Cromford too was developed to create a spectacle, and was only followed by other entrepreneurs who were exhibitionists, like Robert Owen at New Lanark, the Ashworth Brothers at Turton, Pouyer-Quertier at La Foudre (Rouen), Titus Salt at Saltaire and other builders of mighty monuments. While aristocratic owners were converting their unwanted palaces to industrial uses Schuele signalled his entry to their ranks by building his own industrial palace. In other words, expensive building was a product of personal ambition and politics rather than economic necessity, but had important economic advantages.

Reading the various textbooks available on European industrialisation, the student could easily be persuaded that all the biggest factories were in the north of England and Scotland in the late eighteenth century, but the evidence assembled in this book shows that this impression is little more than a caricature of the true situation. When we focus on the leaders of the industry it soon becomes clear that there was nothing in England to match Schuele's celebrated Palace factory, while Oberkampf's 1793 building was nearly three times as long and twice as wide as the larger Arkwright-type mills being erected by Peel and other British cotton spinners at the time. Strutt's famous iron-framed North Mill at Belper, built in 1803–4 and featured in a much-quoted article in Abraham Rees's *Cyclopaedia* in 1812, was taller than the Oberkampf building but no longer or wider than the earlier Arkwright-type mills.

Our entrepreneurs all found it necessary to find partners with capital in their early years in business. Schuele relied on the merchant and banker Reichsgraf Johann von Fries for a vital dozen years of his career (1770–82), afterwards turning to Goldschmidts and Bethmanns (Frankfurt merchants) for support, while Oberkampf leaned on the experience and connections of the lawyer Maraise for some 30 years (1762–90), as well as drawing financial support from him, particularly in the years 1760–4 when Jouy was being launched. Leitenberg drew on Dollfack, the Leipzig merchant, to build his 1773 factory. Sir Robert Peel found a sequence of partners to introduce him to new technology and new manufacturing locations, notably Yates in Bury, Ainsworth in Bolton, Tipping in Manchester, and Wilkes in Tamworth, and these men evidently injected capital as well as know-how and local expertise into the Peel empire. In other words, all leaned heavily on established mercantile wealth and experience.

Of course, the main source of capital in this period was profits retained in the business. We have assembled evidence to indicate that the profit levels of several textile printers of the period were abnormally high, even by eighteenth-century standards, and Monsieur Caspard has reached a similar conclusion.[14] Sir Robert Peel's accounts have perished but we know that his profits were running at £70,000 a year in the early 1790s, a figure that was greater than the total insured capital of all but one of his British competitors. The balance sheets of Oberkampf, which fortunately have survived, show profits fluctuating widely but exceeding 30 per cent in the best years (see Table 21). Schuele's profits averaged 200,000 florins (about £20,000) a year during the 12 years after 1770 when he was in partnership with von Fries. This represented about 30 per cent profit on the capital invested in the partnership, a profit level very close to that achieved by Dupasquier of Neuchatel over the period 1754–1815. The main financial problem, as Peel once recorded, was therefore the initial one of launching the business, or in starting a completely new branch, for thereafter the enterprise generated more than enough profit to meet all fixed capital requirements. However, recurrent commercial crises could threaten the solvency of even the most stable business, as Peel learned through his unsuccessful bank in the early 1790s, and as Oberkampf found following a collapse in profits in the years 1793–6. It was perhaps because of the omnipresent threat of a run on working capital that our English and French entrepreneurs retained wealthy partners for most of their business careers, while Dupasquier worked on commission for merchant houses to which he was closely tied.

Supplies and Marketing

For most of the eighteenth century, printed calicoes were something more than a passing fashion. They were a rage that seized large sectors of the population of Europe and North America. As we have already seen, this passion was not limited to the more industrialised countries of the Atlantic seaboard, England, France and the Low Countries, for the extraordinary demand spread eastwards and found a response in Bohemia, Saxony, East Prussia and other countries of central Europe. The problem of the textile printer, therefore, was not to create demand, for that already existed in abundance, but to reach oriental standards at prices which the middle and lower ranges of consumers could afford. The high turnover of small printers was undoubtedly related to the inferior quality of much of their work.[15]

The success of our entrepreneurs in meeting this challenge was evidently spectacular. We have eyewitness accounts of country drapers scrambling to buy prints at the Manchester warehouses, and of buyers flocking out to meet Schuele's carts on the road to the Frankfurt fairs, while his prints in the Amsterdam warehouse were sold out soon after arrival. For much of his career Oberkampf could sell as much as he could produce in France by showing the Jouy label. Once a manufacturer had achieved a reputation it was easy to sell. The evidence shows that our entrepreneurs took different routes to marketing success. In European terms, Peel led in price while Oberkampf, Schuele and Leitenberg won their celebrity with quality, but it is possible to demonstrate that these are only differences of approach for all were striving in different ways to reach the popular end of the market.

Most writers on textile printing have failed to recognise the importance of the popular market because nearly all of them have been essentially historians of design, entranced by the 'classic' copper prints of the period, more particularly J.-B. Huet's designs depicting rural, topical, oriental, legendary, sporting, biblical and other scenes, as well as more abstract floral designs. To judge from fragments of evidence these fine prints were not so expensive to produce as has been supposed, and generally within the upper range of the popular British price bracket, i.e. retailing at less than 2s. 6d. a yard (see Table 16).[16] They were especially popular for wall hangings, bed sets, curtains and upholstery, and to the factory they served as advertisements for the smaller and cheaper patterns produced for women's dresses and sold in large quantities, reaching, it was claimed, the servant class before the end of the century. In central Europe the widespread popularity of printed textiles destroyed the remnants of the *Kleiderordnung* and evaporated pride in traditional peasant costume.

The sales record of both Peel and Oberkampf is incomplete, but it is possible to identify some comparable strands. It seems that the Peels began with the most simple and popular designs for their unsophisticated regional market but in the course of a generation evolved into producers of goods for what we may term the upper end of the popular price bracket. By contrast, Oberkampf concentrated his early attention on the upper end of the market as his Parisian and London rivals were doing, but by the turn of the century was producing at least half his output for the popular market. However, the contrast here is more between a metropolitan and a provincial producer than a French and a British one. Despite the French Revolution, French society continued to be more polarised than the British, so it seems that Oberkampf sold to two social classes, upper and lower, while the Peels evidently found that they optimised their returns in selling the merging 'middling' and lower classes in Britain and North America. Oberkampf never sold anything in the USA himself leaving his Nantes rivals, notably Petitpierre and Gorgerat, to exploit the trans-Atlantic market. A recent exhibition of the work of the Nantes printers demonstrated that they produced a wide variety of good quality designs much like those of Oberkampf, so it seems fair to surmise that the latter might have become an American exporter if his base had not made the domestic market more enticing.[17]

The cost of commissioning the more fashionable designs have been exaggerated, particularly in the journalism of Dingler of Augsburg.[18] Oberkampf paid his most famous designer, J.-B. Huet, a standard price of only 200 *f*. (£8) for each design, and we have seen that French designs were available cheaply in Manchester, at any rate after the Napoleonic Wars. The Peels never employed a designer in the way that Oberkampf commissioned Huet and Schuele Mme Friederichs, for they did not find it necessary to go to such expense. Instead, they were happy to see the leading London printers represent *haute couture* while they produced more popular imitations in the north of England. The short period of copyright in designs, two months in 1787, extended to three months in 1794, did little to restrain this plagiarism because it took months for new patterns to

Plate 8 One of J.-B. Huet's famous designs, *Les Travaux de la Manufacture* (1783), showing the sequence of processes in calico printing (Musée Oberkampf, Jouy)

permeate down to the servant's hall and perhaps years to reach the peasants and colonists, by which time the Lancashire and Glasgow producers had their imitations on sale everywhere.[19]

If the ultimate aim of our entrepreneurs was the same, there were considerable variations in success in serving markets, more especially the foreign ones. Oberkampf made serious attempts to sell in London (1790–2), and after 1800 in the German fairs, Flanders and parts of the north of Italy, but he was unable to reduce his costs to the level of his foreign competitors, more especially the low-cost producers like the Peels. He justified the price differential by concentrating on quality *toiles* and designs to retain the domestic market, where his name and reputation continued to be a means of ready sales.

Supply of materials presented our entrepreneurs with few problems for each of them inherited a well-established system in his own country. Even during wartime they benefited from a system of supply of oriental fabrics through the English, Danish and French East India Companies. At the end of the eighteenth century only the Manchester region was able to approach the perfection of Indian cottons, so that London, Amsterdam and Lorient continued to be the most important distribution centres. Similarly, on the marketing side, printers benefited in varying degrees from the network of the 'international houses' (the Dutch, Huguenot, and German Jewish trading dynasties that were dispersing across Europe), from the great international fairs at Beaucaire, Frankfurt, Leipzig and other traditional centres, and, in the Peels' case, from the growing colonial trade, with its easy markets in America and the West Indies. Working through an established system our entrepreneurs pursued similar selling techniques, doing their main trade from their own warehouses.

Looking at the supply and distributions process in a little more detail, we can identify variations in emphasis. Industrial location conferred advantages on Peel and Schuele for supply, but on Oberkampf for marketing. The Peels were able to rely on the quality of fabrics woven in their own part of Lancashire, the Blackburn area, and in this respect they may be compared with Schuele who had the advantage of the traditional skills of his native town of Augsburg for all the weaves but the very fine ones. Contrariwise, Jouy was convenient to Oberkampf's principal market in Paris but distant from the Norman and Picard weavers he employed. A rival manufacturer insisted that Jouy sold considerable quantities to Parisian traders in the early years simply because the factory was only 10 miles from the capital. It was said that a mercer who only wanted a few pieces did not mind paying a little more if he could buy them and return home the same morning.[20] Moreover, in later years Oberkampf was absolved from the expense of employing travellers as the Peels did.

At first sight, design and taste seem to separate our men more than any other single topic, but here again historical perspective has been distorted by the particular interests of the art historians. According to the widely-received account Schuele drew many of his own patterns which showed great skill and design sense, but employed the famous designer Mme Friedrich, while Oberkampf commissioned J.-B. Huet and other well-known artists. Meanwhile Peel, remote from London and the international centres of fashion, preferred his own judgement of popular demand and employed a single drawer to copy designs brought post-haste from the capital. It seems to us that this misses an essential point. In considering the Peels' marketing policies we have laid emphasis on the simple cheap designs that formed the staple diet of British and colonial consumers in the early years of the Lancashire printers' success. Over 100 of these simple motifs, as we remarked in the Introduction, are illustrated in the frontispiece of O'Brien's pioneer textbook of 1790. However, strikingly similar designs – monochrome circles, squares, lines, flower patterns, etc. – can also be seen in four books of samples used by one of Jouy's most important customers, Guerbette of Versailles, towards the end of the eighteenth century, and other examples are known which date from the years 1775–80.[21] Of course, we do not know how much of these qualities were produced by either manufacturer, but it is clear that both entrepreneurs had a major commitment to the popular market, a strategy shared by other European leaders of the industry. Du Pasquier's Cortaillod works concentrated on the higher quality work but this was because the owner was heavily involved in the smuggling of cheaper English prints into France. Schuele's goods were sold throughout the German Empire, Holland and France, but a large part went to the more simple peoples of Poland, Russia, Spain, Portugal and Italy. Surviving Schuele prints in museums in Krefeld and Mulhouse show very simple floral motifs produced for mass consumption.[22] The evidence on this point coincides with that on price, cited above. It seems that Oberkampf, like the German printer Schuele, who entertained royalty and the nobility at his 'Palace Factory' in Augsburg, secured a ready market for his goods by the social cachet he won for them, while the Lancashire producers, remote from court and noble patronage, had to reach the popular market on the elementary merit of price and quality.

Labour and Management

The subject of industrial relations brings Sir Robert Peel and Oberkampf closer together than almost any other. Both were martinets who used their considerable organising powers in rural areas to create a corps of disciplined and loyal workers, officers, NCOs, men, women and juveniles, all inured to the system. Contemporaries like Arkwright, Wedgwood and Marshall in England, and Richard-Lenoir, Koechlin and Perier in France, may have had an equal reputation, but none ruled with greater personal authority. It seems that Oberkampf did not even encourage the more constructive forms of self-help like friendly societies, but Peel realised their value in propagating capitalist values. When the real challenge to their power came in the 1790s it is surprising to find that the Peels gave more ground than Oberkampf, and it is important to ask why. One would have expected the democratic movement to have gripped French workers much more powerfully than the English proletariat, but evidently the Peels faced much more determined opposition. Jouy was by no means isolated from price and wage inflation or Revolutionary ideals, so the answer probably lies in two directions; Oberkampf's adroitness in identifying himself with the ideals of the Revolution, while the Peels stood at the head of the militant opposition to the printers' trade union; and the greater concentration of skilled labour in Lancashire, which gave the union movement more leverage. Interestingly enough, Sir Robert Peel later identified himself with the Tory interests that were critical of the cotton mill system, but this was not until after the turn of the century when he had been in Parliament for more than a decade and had largely divorced himself from his executive responsibilities in industry.

Nevertheless, both Peel and Oberkampf combined their authority with a real sense of paternalism for the 'family' in their care. Their attitude may be contrasted with Schuele who simply regarded his workforce as the instruments of his production system and took no interest, so far as we can discover, in their welfare. This situation may be explained partly by the absence in his background of any family tradition of leadership in the textile industry, partly by his all-consuming ambition to make himself into a manufacturing prince, assuming what he took to be the unbridled power of noble birth, but above all by the location of his factory in a town long dominated by the guild system. By contrast, the memories of the Bury workers were unequivocal on Sir Robert's attitude. 'Though he scarcely appeared to notice many of the people in his employment .... He was deeply conscious of his situation as a master, controlling the livelihood and comfort of a number of persons greater than had hitherto been brought together as the work people of one firm'.[23] Oberkampf kept his ideals more to himself until the 1790s, but at Jouy there was a parallel sense of building up a community in which reciprocal responsibilities existed, and the master felt it his duty to be 'unceasingly occupied' with his workers' interests.

Each of our entrepreneurs faced the opposition of organised labour at one time or another but Schuele had the most persistent difficulty for the Augsburg guilds turned out to be implacable, even by central European standards, in maintaining their restrictions on innovations when they posed a threat to employment. In Britain, France and Prussia the weavers' campaigns against imported textiles, especially printed calicoes, resulted in legislation restricting their manufacture, but in the *Freireichstadt* of Augsburg there was no general restriction or ban. Consequently, Schuele spent a large part of his business career involved in a running legal battle with the weavers over his foreign imports, a battle that occasionally erupted into riots, notably those at the *Rathaus* in 1768. His struggle with the guilds finally reached the *Reichshofrat* (supreme court of the Holy Roman Emperor in Vienna) where it dragged on for at least 20 years (1766–86). Schuele was pressed to accept various restrictions on foreign imports, but it was widely suspected that he was exceeding his quotas and trouble rumbled on.[24]

By contrast, the only powerful opposition to Sir Robert Peel, from the Block Printers' Union, did not come to a head until 1790 when the family business had been established for more than a generation and was already the most successful textile printing business in Britain, if not in Europe. In this book it has been argued that the Peel family's response, the dispersion to peripheral locations at Tamworth and Accrington and mechanisation, must have contributed to the later decline of the business. Moreover, the long struggle of 1790 by no means destroyed the Union, and the Lancashire printers faced regular challenges from this well-organised body of workmen. Oberkampf was least troubled by labour problems, partly because of the rural location of Jouy and the absence of a traditional calico printing craft in France, and partly, one surmises, from the entrepreneur's skill in habituating his rustic labour force to factory organisation and setting up an administrative hierarchy that effected the most detailed control over the workers. After the Revolution labour organisations were banned, so Oberkampf did not have to fear trade union pressures as such. But he had to show great skill in diverting the workers' revolutionary fervour into channels that were harmless to himself and his business, and in this a measure of sympathy with the ideals of the Revolution and then of the Empire probably helped him. The main ingredient of his continuous reign at Jouy was no doubt the kind of determined opportunism displayed by the Vicar of Bray: that whatsoever king or government would reign, Oberkampf was determined to remain master of Jouy.

The experience of our entrepreneurs, which is in this respect representative of some other leaders of their industry in the three countries, therefore serves to modify the textbook picture of England as the home of unrestricted enterprise, and of Lancashire in particular as the unhampered 'new frontier' of European industrial enterprise. In terms of labour restraints, Oberkampf seems to have had the easiest run and Schuele the most difficult, for he spent most of his career as a calico printer dodging medieval regulations or fighting their exponents. The Peels faced few problems in the vital years of rapid growth (c. 1760–90), but after that they could only free themselves by founding new and more remote rural factory colonies, an expensive operation that could not be maintained when profit margins contracted after the Napoleonic Wars.

Productivity

In their recent work on *Economic Growth in Britain and France 1780–1914*, O'Brien and Keyder assemble and process data purporting to show that the productivity of labour was higher in French industry than in British industry until the end of the nineteenth century. While they concede that Britain took an early lead in cotton spinning and weaving, it is surmised that the French textile industry must have possessed relative advantages in other sectors – 'perhaps, as the figures for 1905–13 indicate, in linen and bleaching and dyeing'.[25] The authors offer no more specific information about where the compensating advantages may have lain, but France's eighteenth-century achievement in textile printing, and the leading role that French economic historians have conferred on it, must make this sector the first to be investigated for any claim of superior productivity. We began this book with a survey of the drive for quality and productivity to equal the oriental standards and it seems fitting to end it by trying to establish which countries and firms were most successful in productivity terms. In other words, is it true, as O'Brien and Keyder's statistical analysis might be taken to imply, that the leading French printworks were more productive than the British? And if so, were other leading Continental works equal to the French? Even where data can be found the answers are difficult to calculate for various reasons. The product was not homogeneous, measures varied and output fluctuated widely from year to year.[26] Moreover, the manufacture followed a seasonal cycle and the labour force varied accordingly; the earlier the data the more this factor is likely to distort any attempt at comparisons. We have ventured to obviate these problems by representing numbers of firms and where possible groups of years. A further positive factor to be noticed is that in the case of Peel and Oberkampf the types of work were more similar than has been supposed, and in the case of other firms the division of labour seems remarkably similar. We realise that our calculated data is crude but trust it is adequate to bear the limited conclusions we draw from it.

Our results are set out in Table 39. Although some allowance must obviously be made for the fact that Lancashire inclined towards the more popular products, the conclusion seems irresistible that the Peels' productivity was quite significantly above that of Oberkampf and their earlier Continental rivals. The data dramatically demonstrate the results of the Peels' drive for 'long runs', economy of labour and perhaps the beginning of mechanisation (roller printing). The evidence that we have assembled is not sufficient to define precisely the differences between British and French printers, though in this conclusion we have already eliminated several possibilities for our two entrepreneurs, notably significant differences in entrepreneurial drive, religious and social background, management style, labour opposition, technological knowledge and capital investment. Political context and market opportunity were obviously different but not so much before the French Revolution as to produce large differences in productivity. If the Lancashire printers characteristically opted for quantity and the Parisian for quality, it was a regional rather than a national response to market opportunity. If we had more data we could no doubt demonstrate that productivity in Alsace steadily overtook that in London in much the same period as Manchester outpaced Paris. We can only conclude, therefore, that such advantages as were accumulated by the Peels in textile printing were in that tradition of 'industriousness and plodding patience' that,

Conclusion 213

Table 39 The productivity of some leading European calico printing works in the eighteenth century

Works	Year	Output Pieces	Workforce Year	Workforce Total	Output per worker p.a.
Peel, Bury	c. 1785–90	50–60,000 (=75–90,000)	1785	800	62.5 to 75.0 (=93–110)
	c. 1792	70,000 (=100,000)	1785	800	87.5 (=130)
Oberkampf, Jouy Essonnes	1795–1804 (average)	53,532	1806	1021 306	
				1327	40.3
Du Pasquier,	1764–8	19,821	1764–8	426	46.5
Neuchâtel	1793–7	37,729	1793–7	578	65.3
De Wisser, Antwerp	1767–71	63.480	1769	576	110.2
Wetter, Orange	1764/5	30,000	1764	530	56.6
Waldner, Mulhouse	1772	20–22,000	1772	293	68.3–75.1
Senn-Bidermann, Wesserling	1785	c. 40,000	1785	900	44.4
Baron, Beauvais	1785	20,000	1785	800	25.0
Lesage, Bourges	1785	4,000?	1785	246	18.5
Haussmann, Logelbach	1786	c. 30,000	1786	800	37.5
Hartmann-Riégé, Munster	1786	c. 10,000	1786	400	25.0

SOURCES: Peel: *supra*, Chapter 5. Oberkampf: *supra*, Chapter 10. Du Pasquier: P. Caspard, *La Fabrique-Neuve*, pp. 186–7, 195. De Wisser: A. K. L. Thijs, *op. cit.*, pp. 175, 185. Wetter: H. Chobaut, *op. cit.*, pp. 19, 20. Waldner: E. Albrecht-Mathey, *The Fabrics of Mulhouse and Alsace 1750–1800* (Leigh-on-Sea, 1968), p. 15. Senn-Bidermann, Hartmann, Haussmann: J. M. Schmitt, *Aux origines de la Revolution industrielle en Alsace* (thesis, III[e] cycle, Strasbourg, 1979). Baron, Lesage: AN: F12/1405A, 1404.

CALCULATIONS: French equivalents of English measures in brackets. The English piece measured 28 yards long in the lower price brackets (60% of output) and 30 yards in the higher price ranges; averages 28.8 yards. The Continental piece averaged 20 aunes = 24m. = 26.3 yds.

quoting Ryhiner of Basle, we remarked on in the Introduction. 'They employ the same dyestuffs and the same methods and they use the same tools [as we do], but everything is done with more precision, exactness and order', Ryhiner noted, and though his remark was made as early as 1766, it cannot be bettered, even for the period of roller printing, when British persistence profited from an elementary principle known on the Continent at least a century earlier.[27]

Fifty years later Andelle picked up the same theme, emphasising in his report on Lancashire that in general 'the English are remarkable for the simple and methodical administration of their businesses', with consequent economies of manpower and materials and cost reductions.[28] The only difficulty about this so far as direct comparisons between Sir Robert Peel and Oberkampf are concerned is that we only have intimate knowledge of their buildings, not the efficiency of their plant and labour, and the Peels' processes were dispersed around various buildings while in 1793 Oberkampf's were rationalised in one central carefully supervised concern. Although few, if any, French printers followed his lead, this concentration was no great novelty in European terms for Schuele had opened his 'Palace Factory' at Augsburg 20 years earlier. This prompts us to believe that the superior productivity of Lancashire was more connected with 'long runs' of simple designs at low prices than impeccable organisation. In other words, it seems probable that several distinguished French and German producers of the age were no less efficient than their best-known English rival, and differences in productivity must be attributed to the structure of the domestic and overseas, principally North American, market.

Earlier in this Conclusion evidence was produced which suggested that the most fundamental and far-reaching difference between the Peels and their Continental rivals was the strong initiative taken by the English firm in the various branches of mechanised spinning, and we linked this with the pressure of Indian competition. A similar view has been ventured by Dr Chaudhuri in his monumental work.[29] This view of the root cause of change must now be set alongside that just made about 'long runs' created by the combined effects of the growing domestic and American markets. The evidence assembled in this book persuades us that such differences as existed between Sir Robert Peel and Oberkampf, and perhaps British and Continental cotton printers generally in the eighteenth century, were more to do with international trade opportunities than the range of endogenous factors, from attributes of entrepreneurs to availability of capital and the alleged rising costs of production. In other words, we believe it is much too simplistic to conclude as Kindleberger has done that 'Trade thus grew with the industrial revolution rather than starting it.'[30] On the contrary, trade with the Orient and in oriental goods within Europe was the vital initial stimulus, and trans-Atlantic markets an important sustaining force in the growth of British textile printing and then in mechanised spinning for, as we have observed in earlier sections, calico printing gave the initial impetus to the mechanisation of spinning and was still absorbing 60 per cent of the white cotton fabrics produced in Britain in the early 1790s.

The sharp increases in productivity are of course crucial to the far-reaching economic changes of the period. On the 'new frontier' of industrial Europe, uninhibited by any traditional restraints but in continuous contact with the latest technology in London, and with the best-quality fabrics produced on their doorstep, the Peels raised labour productivity to the highest levels known in the protofactory. It was this achievement that provided the opportunity and incentive for transition to the fully-evolved factory system. In Britain, as in France, calico printing represents the missing link between proto-industrial and the modern industrial system in the textile industries, and in the careers of the Peels and Oberkampf we may exactly trace the evolution from the one to the other.

Appendices to Conclusion

Appendix A Estimated costs of calicoes printed in Britain 1771–90

Year	Indian pieces sold (£000s)	Value (£000s)	Value per piece (£)	+ Printing costs (£0.7–1.98)	Pieces as % of total cost
1771	868	1,435	1.65	2.35–3.61	70–46
1772	1,067	1,654	1.55	2.25–3.53	69–44
1773	964	1,798	1.87	2.57–3.85	73–49
1774	874	1,815	2.08	2.78–4.06	75–51
1775	752	1,610	2.14	2.84–4.12	75–52
1776	842	1,622	1.93	2.63–3.91	73–49
1777	873	1,661	1.71	2.41–3.69	71–46
1778	1,177	1,663	1.41	2.11–3.39	67–42
1779	457	747	1.63	2.33–3.61	70–45
1780	608	1,258	2.07	2.77–4.05	75–51
1781	445	851	1.91	2.61–4.59	73–42
1782	580	1,287	2.17	2.87–4.85	76–45
1783	549	1,143	2.08	2.78–4.76	75–44
1784	611	1,056	1.73	2.43–4.41	71–39
1785	840	1,561	1.86	2.56–4.54	73–41
1786	845	1,570	1.86	2.56–4.54	73–41
1787	852	1,439	1.69	2.39–4.37	71–39
1788	746	1,203	1.61	2.31–4.29	70–37
1789	820	1,229	1.50	2.20–4.18	68–36
1790	1,055	1,752	1.66	2.36–4.34	70–38

SOURCES: Unfortunately there is no statistical series of costs or prices related to calico printing in Britain for the critical period 1760–90, but the data reproduced here should approximate to the position. Columns 2 and 3 are data from the East India Co.'s files assembled in *Report of the SC of the Court of Directors of the East India Co.*

Appendices to Conclusion 217

upon... *the Cotton Manufacture of this Country* (1793), p. 2. These were the fabrics that were ornamented by calico printers in this country, though they included some 'coloured piece goods' so the average price stated is probably high rather than low. Such quality fabrics set the standard and price for British calico manufacturers for many years. Column 4 is calculated from the first two columns. Column 5 is the shakiest part of this calculated evidence. The printing costs represented are those of Manchester commission printers in 1803, taken from the Rothschild Mss. (see S. D. Chapman, 'The Foundation of the English Rothschilds', *TH*, VIII (1977), p. 106) and cover the whole range of processes and charges. The highest and lowest prices are cited here, but the great part of Lancashire output would be at the lower end. Apart from the introduction of roller printing, the numerous labour-intensive processes appear to have been much the same in 1803 as in 1771–90. Roller printing may have begun to lower costs by 1803, but if production costs were higher from 1771–90, pieces must have been proportionately lower, say 60 per cent at the cheap end of the range. In other words, the data and calculations presented here represent a limiting case: white calicoes were at all events a smaller proportion of total costs than were *toiles blanches* in Oberkampf's experience.

Appendix B Valuation of Peel, Yates, Halliwell & Warren's works in 1795 (see p. 59)

Location and item	Fixed capital	'Stock, Utensils and Goods'
Bury Centre (9 miles north of Manchester)		
Elton print works		
Water corn mills [original buildings on the site]	200	600
Printing and Colour Shops adjoining	300	700
Double Printing Shop	300	700
Large Double Printing Shop, Drawing and Cutting Rooms	200	800
Iron Liquor and White Rooms	200	3,000
Block Shop and Iron Liquor Shop	80	920
Old and New Calender Houses	70	800
Colour Shop and Cooking oven Room	40	500
Blue Dyehouse and Printing Shop	200	4,000
Madder Mill, Block and Printing Shops	200	800
Blacksmith's Shop	60	100

continued overleaf

Appendix B continued

Location and item	Fixed capital	'Stock, Utensils and Goods'
Stove Warehouse	50	950
Stables and Blockshops	100	100
Drying Stove	80	900
Cotton Drying Stove and Warehouse	80	400
Piece Room	40	300
Printing Shop and Copper Plate Rooms with Carding Room	1,300	500
Shippon and Pencilling Rooms	300	1,500
Machine Room	50	400
Madderhouse and Printing Room	200	800
Stove Room and Room over	40	500
New Store Warehouse	300	5,000
Printing Shop	300	700
Counting and Warehouse	100	1,000
Iron Liquor House	50	200
Drying Room	20	50
Printing Shop and Pencilling Shop	200	800
Twenty cottages in tenure of servants	600	
Total	**5,660**	**27,020**
Cotton mills		
Butcher's Lane, Bury	800	200
Two mills at Burrs	2,400	600
Heywood	1,400	500
Ratcliffe	3,200	800
Summerseat I	1,500	400
Summerseat II	1,200	200
Summerseat III	1,800	500
Hinds	1,900	500
Thirteen cottages	520	
Total (nine mills)	**14,720**	**3,700**
Hinds dye works		
Store Rooms	340	2,200
Fancy Dyehouse and Drying Rooms	300	1,500
Store Rooms and Singing Rooms	100	600
Bowkhouse	40	600
Scowering House and Shed and Drying Stove	70	1,200
Total	**850**	**6,100**

Appendix B continued

Ramsbottom Centre (4 miles north of Bury)		
Printing Shop, Drawing Room and Cutting Shop	100	800
Cutting Shop, Stove Room and Blockmakers' Shop	50	500
Warehouse, Colour House and Printing Shop	200	700
Iron Liquor Room, Stove Room, Pin Roller Rooms and three cottages all communicating	200	800
Printing House and Dryhouse	200	1,500
Calender House and Whiting Room	50	500
Factory Building used as a Store and Printing Shop	300	1,500
Building called Candry Mill with Timber Dyehouses	50	300
New Store Room	10	90
Double Printing Shop and Pencilling Shop	200	600
Building used as Store and Printing Shop	200	500
Barns, Stables and Shippens	25	25
Stove and Singeing Rooms	50	300
New Printing Shop	300	950
White Room and Liquor Room	200	3,000
New Building used as a Pencilling Shop	100	800
New Store House	300	2,000
Total	**2,545**	**14,865**
Warehouses at Manchester and Rochdale		
Warehouse in Peel St., Manchester	1,500	15,000
Warehouse in Yorkshire St., Rochdale	100	800
Total	**1,600**	**15,800**

SOURCES: Sun N S: Vol. 7, policy nos. 640035, 640037, 26 Mar. 1795.

Notes and References

Abbreviations

LOCATION OF MANUSCRIPTS

AD	*Archives Départementales*
AN	*Archives Nationales*, Paris
BM	British Museum Library (now called British Library)
BRL	Birmingham Reference Library
CRO	County Records Office
IOR	India Office Records
RO	Record Office
PL	Public Library
PRO	Public Record Office, London

JOURNALS AND NEWSPAPERS

BH	Business History
BHR	Business History Review
EcHR	Economic History Review
EEH	Explorations in Economic History
JEEcH	Journal of European Economic History
ME	Manchester Examiner and Times Supplement
MM	Manchester Mercury
MS	*Mouvement Social*
RHES	*Revue d'Histoire Economique et Sociale*
TH	Textile History

GOVERNMENT PUBLICATIONS

PP	Parliamentary Papers
SC	Select Committee (reports)

The place of publication of books is London unless otherwise stated.

Introduction

1. For a summary of the British literature, see S. D. Chapman, *The Cotton Industry in the Industrial Revolution* (1974).
2. S. D. Chapman, 'The Peels in the Early English Cotton Industry', *BH*, XI (1969); R. S. Fitton and A. P. Wadsworth, *The Strutts and the Arkwrights* (Manchester, 1958), Ch. IV (2). Since the publication of this book a new collection of Belper Estate maps has been found, including Strutts' 'Survey of the Homestead' (*c.* 1792), showing a large printing mill next to the Arkwright-type spinning mill. Guildhall Library (London), Sun Fire Office Registers, Old Series: 376/58236 (1791) for Oldknow's printworks (subsequently cited as 'Sun OS'). (The later 'Country Series' is abbreviated 'Sun CS', and the 'New Series' is cited as 'Sun NS'.)
3. S. D. Chapman, 'The Foundation of the English Rothschilds', *TH*, VIII (1977), p. 106. (Subsequently cited as 'Rothschilds'.)
4. Nat. Lib. Scotland: Melville Mss. 1064, fo. 60.
5. M. Lévy-Leboyer, *Les banques européennes et l'industrialisation internationale* (Paris, 1964). (Subsequently cited *Les banques*.)
6. H. Lüthy, *La banque protestante en France*, II: *1730–1794* (Paris, 1961), pp. 104–5, 318–9, 326–8, 718–21 etc.
7. S. Chassagne, *La manufacture de toiles imprimées de Tournemine-lès-Angers* (Paris, 1971). pp. 45–6. (Subsequently cited as Tournemine.).
8. M. Lévy-Leboyer, *Les banques*, p. 419.
9. L. Bergeron, *Banquiers, Négociants et Manufacturiers Parisiens du Directoire à l'Empire* (Paris, 1978), p. 78
10. A. Dietz, *Frankfurter Handelsgeschichte*, IV (Frankfurt, 1925), pp. 309–20.
11. S. D. Chapman, 'The International Houses: The Continental Contribution to British Commerce 1800–1860', *JEEcH*, VI (1977).
12. S. D. Chapman, 'Rothschilds'.
13. S. Chassagne, *Tournemine*, Ch. I. H. Freudenberger, 'Fashion, Sumptuary Laws, and Business', *BHR*, XXXVII (1963).
14. J.Irwin and K. Brett, *Origins of Chintz* (1970), pp. 3–6.
15. A. P. Wadsworth and J. de L. Mann, *The Cotton Trade and Industrial Lancashire* (Manchester, 1931), pp. 130–1. (Subsequently cited as *Cotton Trade*.) See S. D. Chapman, 'The Textile Factory before Arkwright: a Typology of Factory Development' *BHR*, XLVIII (1974) for the early London factories. Amsterdam, Notarial Archives: 3887 fo. Not. 2006/937–942. P.-R. Schwarz, in M. Daumas (ed.), *Histoire Générale des Techniques* (Paris, 1968), p. 722.
16. Amsterdam, Marriage Registers, record 161 *katoendrukers* 1672–1700. D. Dollfus-Ausset, *Materiaux pour coloration des étoffes*, quoting Ms. by J. H. Ryhiner of 1766. (Subsequently cited as *Materiaux*.)
17. S. Chassagne, *Tournemine*, pp. 45–6. At least 15 Huguenot calico printers are known to have fled France.
18. D. Dollfus-Ausset, *Materiaux*, p. 74. A. K. L. Thijs, 'Ontwikkeling der Katoendrukkerij te Antwerpen 1753–1813', *Bijdragen tot de Geschiedenis*, LIII (1970). Information from E. Oxenbøll, Institute of Economic History, Copenhagen, and from Dr Ingegard Henschen, Nordiska Museum, Stockholm.
19. H. Hassinger, 'Der Stand der Manufackturen ...', in F. Lütge (ed.), *Die wirtschaftliche Situation in Deutschland u. Österreich um die Wende 18.–19. Jh.* (Stuttgart, 1964), p. 135. O. Reuter, *Die Manufaktur im Frankischen Raum* (Stuttgart, 1961), pp. 34–40. G. Slawinger, *Die Manufaktur in Kurbayern... 1740–1833* (Stuttgart, 1966), p. 126. A. K. L. Thijs, *op. cit.* W. H. Blackwell, *The Beginnings of Russian Industrialisation* (Princeton, 1968), pp. 245, 249. R. Forberger, *Die Manufaktur in Sachsen* (Berlin, 1958). J. J. Waitzfelder, *Der*

Augsburger Johann Heinrich von Schuele (Leipzig, 1929). H. Rossovsky, 'The Serf Entrepreneur in Russia', *EEH*, VI (1953–4). A. Klima, 'Industrial Growth and Entrepreneurship in the Early Stages of Industrialisation in the Czech Lands', *JEEcH*, VI (1977). F. W. Carter, 'The Cotton Printing Industry in Prague, 1766–1873', *TH*, VI (1975).

20. E. Hasse, *Geschichte der Leipziger Messen* (Leipzig, 1885), p. 336; M. Freudenthal, *Leipziger Messgäste: Die Judischen Besucher der Leipziger Messen, 1675–1764* (Frankfurt, 1928): S. Chassagne, *Tournemine*, pp. 50–3; M. Lévy-Leboyer, *Les banques*, pp. 52ff.
21. M. Lévy-Leboyer, *Les banques.*, pp. 51–5. S. Chassagne, *Tournemine*, pp. 46, 126, n. 251.
22. C. W. Gerhardt, *Geschichte der Druckverfahren*, II (Stuttgart, 1975), pp. 8, 78; III (1978), pp. 62–5, 68, 78–87, 97, 93–103, 705, 738. W. Gellendien, 'Uralter Zeugdruck III', *Bayer Farben Revue*, No. 3 (1962) has a reproduction of the 1699 engraving. P. C. Floud, 'The Origins of English Calico Printing', 'The English Contribution to the Early History of Indigo Printing', and 'The English Contribution to the Development of Copper Plate Printing', *Journal of the Society of Dyers and Colourists*, LXXVI (1960), pp. 275–80, 344–9, 425–34; S. Parkes, *Chemical Essays* (1815), pp. 528, 540; P.-R. Schwartz, 'La coloration partielle des étoffes', in M. Daumas (ed.), *Histoire Générale des Techniques*, III (1968); L. Gerschel, 'Couleur et teinture ... indo-européens', *Annales E.S.C.*, XXI (1966), p. 628.
23. D. Dollfus-Ausset, *Materiaux*, pp. 4–5.
24. F. M. Montgomery, *Printed Textiles: English and American Cottons and Linens, 1700–1850* (1970), p. 24. The percentage given is approximate based on a total printing of 4 million yards. See T. S. Ashton, *An Economic History of England: the Eighteenth Century* (1955), p. 248.
25. D. Dollfus-Ausset, *Materiaux*, p. 18. M. Lévy-Leboyer, *Les banques*, p. 27.
26. Quoted in A. D. Wadsworth and S. de L. Mann, *Cotton Trade*, p. 137.
27. W. J. Smit, *De Katoendrukkerij in Nederland* (Amsterdam, 1928), pp. 97–8.
28. A.-M. Piuz, 'Note sur l'industrie des indiennes à Genève ...', in P. Léon, F. Crouzet and R. Gascon (eds.), *L'industrialisation en Europe au XIXe siècle* (Lyons, 1972).
29. Dollfus-Ausset, *Materiaux*, pp. 140–1.
30. A. K. Longfield, 'History of the Irish ... Cotton Printing Industry in the Eighteenth Century, *Journ. Royal Soc. Antiquaries Ireland*, LXVII (1937); F. Brunello, *The Art of Dyeing* (Vicenza, 1973), p. 250; A. K. L. Thijs, *op. cit.*, p. 175.
31. D. Dollfus-Ausset, *Materiaux*, pp. 74–5.
32. Sun OS: 112/149713 (1755), 105/140810 (1754). A. P. Wadsworth and S. de L. Mann, *Cotton Trade*, pp. 420ff; S. D. Chapman, *The Devon Cloth Industry in the Eighteenth Century* (Exeter, 1978), *passim*.
33. AN: Minutes Central, XXVIII, 411; see also LXXXVII, 1110. P. Caspard, 'Calico Printing at Neuchâtel ... 1752–1854', *T H*, VIII (1977), p. 156
34. P. C. Floud, *op. cit.*, pp. 425, 427. D. Dollfus-Ausset, *Materiaux*, pp. 74–5.
35. Quoted by Bernard Roy, *Une capitale de l'indiennage: Nantes* (Nantes, 1948), pp. 148–9.
36. D. S. Landes, *Unbound Prometheus* (1969), p. 46.
37. D. E. Robinson, 'The Importance of Fashions to Business History', *B H R*, XXXVII (1963).
38. R. Campbell, *The London Tradesman* (1747), pp. 116–18, 332.
39. *Infra*, Ch. 1.
40. D. Dollfus-Ausset, *Materiaux*, p. 144.
41. See examples in Deutsche Museum (Munich), Victoria and Albert Museum (London), Smithsonian (Washington), etc.
42. The equipment of London calico printers is listed in (a) Sun Fire Office insurance policy registers, calendared in S. D. Chapman, 'The Textile Factory before

Arkwright', *B H R*, XLVIII (1974). (b) PRO: E 144 (Exchequer Extents and Inquisitions), nos. 20 (Dalton of Stratford, 1755), 23 (Asterley of Wandsworth, 1760), and 29 (Read of Fordingbridge, Hants., 1784). Asterleys were using a horse mill, steam engine, alum mill and indigo mill as early as 1760.
43. PRO: E 144/23. Nat. Lib. Scotland: John Rennie's Notebook (1782–4), pp. 23–5 (ms). AN: Minuties Central, XXVIII, 411. F. E. von Seida, *J. H. E. von Schuele* (Leipzig, 1805), p. 112.
44. *Infra*, Ch. 2. E. Baines, *History of the Cotton Manufacture* (1835), p. 265. (Subsequently cited as *History*.)
45. India Office Lib.: 'Home Misc.' Series, no. 401(3). *Report of the SC of the Court of Directors of the East India Co. upon . . . the Cotton Manufacture of this Country* (1793), p. 5. On mule productivity, see H. Catling, *The Spinning Mule* (Newton Abbot, 1970), p. 54.
46. On O'Brien's occupation, see S. M. Edelstein, *Historical Notes on the Wet-Processing Industry* (New York, 1972), p. 52.

Chapter 1

1. A. K. Longfield, 'History of the Irish Linen and Cotton Printing Industry in the 18th century', *Journ. Royal Soc. Antiquaries Ireland*, LXVII (1937). F. Irwin, 'Scottish Eighteenth Century Chintz and its Design', *BurlingtonMagazine*, Sep.–Oct. 1965.
2. Quoted in F. M. Montgomery, *op. cit.*, p. 24.
3. *MM*, 26 July 1774.
4. W. A. Abram, *A History of Blackburn* (Blackburn, 1877), esp. pp. 210–27.
5. E. Baines, *History*, p. 262.
6. *MM*, 9 Jan 1759.
7. Manchester PL: J. Graham, *History of Printworks in the Manchester District from 1760 to 1846*, Ms., p. 345. (Subsequently cited as *Printworks*).
8. W. A. Abram, *op. cit.*, p. 211. *MM*, 31 Dec. 1765.
9. J. Graham, *Printworks*. *MM*, 14 Oct. 1766. Sun OS, 230B/340011 (1774). Manchester PL: C. 17/2/36/1, Deeds of Chadkirk Print Works.
10. *MM*, 21 Oct. 1783, reports that Ainsworth Print Works have been 'established for many years past'. K. P. Bullock, *The Story of Cockey Moor otherwise Ainsworth* (n.d.) says that John Wilson moved to the locality in 1762.
11. Growing number of references in *MM*. W. Bailey, *Northern Directory* (1784) lists 26 calico printers in the Manchester area, 8 in Blackburn and 4 in Carlisle. Jones's *Glasgow Directory* (1787) lists 27 firms.
12. List compiled from *MM* The bankruptcy rate was also high in the French calico printing industry due to the establishment of numerous small workshops.
13. A. K. Longfield, 'Some Eighteenth Century Advertisements and the English Linen and Cotton Printing Industry', and 'More Eighteenth Century Advertisements and English Calico Printers', *Burlington Magazine*, Mar. 1949, Mar. 1960. See *MM*, 13 Apr. 1779, for Crayford Works.
14. *MM*, 13 May 1783, 28 Mar. 1786. Sun OS: 360/554233 (1789); CS: 8/638574 (1795).
15. S. Parkes, *op. cit.*, p. 219. The London works were insured for £12,500; Sun OS: 235/346532 (1774).
16. A. P. Wadsworth and J. Mann, *Cotton Trade*, pp. 101ff, 304ff.
17. W. A. Abram, *op cit.*, p. 224.
18. PRO: B1/91, pp. 9–10. J. Graham, *Printworks*, p. 407.
19. PRO: B1/92, pp. 107–11; B1/93, pp. 223–4.
20. PRO: B1/79, pp. 258–67; B1/81, pp. 40–9.
21. *MM*, 13 Jan. 1789, 21 Apr. 1789.

22. PRO: B1/78, p. 286.
23. J. Graham, *Printworks*. C. O'Brien, *A Treatise on Calico Printing* (1792), quoted by G. Turnbull, *History of Calico Printing* (Altrincham, 1951), p. 72.
24. Calculation based on 20 workmen and 6 boys printing 640 pieces *per annum MM*, 13 Oct. 1761.
25. E. Baines, *History*, p. 265.
26. *MM*, 31 Jan. 1786.
27. J. Graham, *Printworks*. C. O'Brien, *loc. cit.*
28. [Anon.], *Facts and Observations to prove the impolicy and dangerous tendency of the bill now before Parliament for limiting the number of apprentices and other restrictions in the calico printing business. Together with a concise history of the combination of the journeymen.* (Manchester, n.d. but *c*. 1807) pp. 13–14. (Subsequently cited as [Anon.] *Facts and Observations*.)
29. PRO: E 144/30.
30. J. Graham, *Printworks*. PRO: B3/1845, list of debts of Gibson & Johnson, the London bankers whose failure followed that of Livesey, Hargreaves & Co.
31. Lancashire CRO: DDK/1656, Derby Mss., Steward's letters, 25 May 1788.
32. *Ibid.*, 7 Jun. 1788.
33. [Anon.], *Facts and Observations*, pp. 15–16.

Chapter 2

1. See various nineteenth-century sources summarised in P. Mantoux, *The Industrial Revolution of the Eighteenth Century* (1928), p. 370.
2. Sir Lawrence Peel, *A Sketch of the Life and Character of Sir Robert Peel* (1860), p. 14. (Subsequently cited as *Sketch*.)
3. W. A. Abram, *op. cit.*, for genealogical information on eighteenth and nineteenth-century families in the locality. Sun OS: 134/177744 shows Howarths & Peel established in the Blackburn trade in 1760. The Hargreaves papers at Peel Park Lib., Salford, reprinted in *T H*, I (1968), pp. 120–1, show the firm as employers of local weavers by 1764.
4. A. Rees, *Cyclopaedia*, art. on 'Manufacture of Cotton' (1808); Sir Lawrence Peel, *Sketch*, pp. 15–16. W. A. Abram, *op. cit.*, pp. 405, 621, 758.
5. 'The Peel Family', *Manchester Examiner Supplement*, 12 Oct. 1850.
6. BM: Add. Mss. 40610, Peel Mss. J[ane] H[owarth], 'A Memoir of the Family of Peel from the year 1600' (1836); *DNB*, XLIV, article on Sir Robert Peel I, gives the author's full name.
7. [Matthew Baillie Begbie], *Partnership 'en commandite' or Partnership with Limited Liabilities* (London, 1848), pp. xiv–xvi, quoted in C. Aspin, *James Hargreaves and the Spinning Jenny* (Helmshore, 1964), p. 20.
8. Guildhall Lib., London: Ms. 7252, 5/33356, Royal Exchange registers.
9. Sun OS: 134/177744; *MM*, 6 Oct. 1761.
10. *Blackburn Standard*, Jan. 1841 (Obituary of Roger Walch). H. R. Fox Bourne, *English Merchants* (1866), II, p. 150.
11. Quoted in W. A. Abram, *op. cit.*, p. 218.
12. *Preston Guardian*, 13 Apr. 1878, quoted in A. P. Wadsworth and J. de L. Mann, *Cotton Trade*, p. 322, n 5.
13. C. Aspin, *op. cit.*, p. 20, n 16.
14. Hargreaves papers, *loc. cit.*, quoted in *TH*, I (1968), pp. 120–1.
15. *Report of S. C. on Children in Manufactories*, PP, 1816, III, pp. 134, 141.
16. S. D. Chapman, 'Fixed Capital Formation in the British Cotton Industry 1770–1815', *EcHR*, XXIII (1970). (Subsequently cited as 'Fixed Capital Formation'.)
17. R. S. Fitton and A. P. Wadsworth, *The Strutts and the Arkwrights* (Manchester, 1958), pp. 68–9, 73. Belper Estate Maps, *loc. cit.*

Notes and References   225

18. A. Rémond, *John Holker, Manufacturier et Grand Fonctionnaire en France aue XVIIIe Siècle, 1719–1786* (Paris, 1946), *pp.* 156–7.
19. John Davies, *Pedigree of the Rt. Hon. Sir Robert Peel and the Peels of Lancashire* ... (Salford, 1846). C. Aspin, *op. cit.*, p. 12.
20. Specification of Patent, No. 1,212 (1779).
21. A. Rémond, *op. cit.*
22. A. Rees, *loc. cit.*
23. A. Rémond, *op. cit.* For descriptions of other Arkwright-type mills of the period, see Nottinghamshire CRO: DD4P 79/63, Portland Mss.; and DDBM B & A, William Pearsce's notebook.
24. A. Rees, *loc. cit.*
25. G. J. French, *Life and Times of Samuel Crompton* (1860), pp. 80–1.
26. PRO: BT 6/140, Petitions.
27. E. Butterworth, *A Concise History of Lancashire* (1845), p. 80; G. Unwin, *Samuel Oldknow and the Arkwrights* (Manchester, 1924).
28. J. H. Partington, *History of Halliwell* (1906), pp. 56–63 (Ms. in Chetham's Lib., Manchester). See A. E. Musson and E. Robinson, *Science and Technology in the Industrial Revolution* (Manchester, 1969), Ch. VIII, for a full account of the introduction of chlorine bleaching.
29. R. Campbell, *The London Tradesman* (1747), p. 118. At this period London journeymen printers earned £3.15 a week during the six months season.
30. [Anon], *Facts and Observations*, pp. 13–15. See *supra*, Chapter 1, and *infra*, Chapter 7.
31. Quoted by F. M. Montgomery, *op. cit.*, p. 31.
32. J. Graham, *Printworks*, p. 346.
33. G. Turnbull, *History of Calico Printing* (Altrincham, 1951), p. 97.
34. A. Rees, *loc. cit.*
35. J. G. Dingler, *Journal für Zitz –, Kattun –, und Indiennendruckerei* (Augsburg, 1806), I, p. 65. Thompson's primary interest in quality printing led him to underrate the importance of roller printing while Dingler witnessed its devastating impact on the German producers.
36. E. Baines, *History*, p. 271, for Jas. Burton.
37. E. Potter, *Calico Printing as an Art Manufacture. A Lecture* (1852), p. 21.

Chapter 3

1. J[ane] H[owarth], *op. cit.*, p. 17.
2. BRL: report entitled '7 January 1811. Robert Peel and Thomas Yates'. Lowndes *London Directory* (1789) and *Universal British Directory*, I (1790).
3. *Universal British Directory*, II, p. 409.
4. A. P. Wadsworth and J. de L. Mann, *Cotton Trade*, pp. 496–503.
5. For Smith's London background see [Anon.], *Facts and Observations*, p. 13. The Haworths bought a bankrupt business from another family of the same name, possibly relations; see *MM* 2 Oct. 1781, 23 Jul. 1782.
6. Sun CS: 4/623908.
7. Sun CS: 18/664746.
8. Staffordshire CRO: C36, 37, Deeds 1749–97, Paget Mss., letters of William Wyatt (agent) to Lord Uxbridge regarding the Trent Navigation lease, 15 Dec. 1762 to 6 Apr. 1763. BRL: Lloyd Mss., Vol. 835, nos. 573046–7. Ind Coope Ltd., Burton: Benjamin Willson Mss. Boulton & Watt to John Peel at Burton, 21 Mar. 1793, regarding a complaint from Mr Dickenson.
9. S. D. Chapman, 'Fixed Capital Formation', pp. 256–66.
10. See Specification of Patent No. 1,212 (1779). Taking out an alternative patent was a common method of evading Arkwright's extortionate licence fees; see S. D.

Chapman, *The Early Factory Masters* (Newton Abbot, 1967), pp. 74–5. (Subsequently cited as *Factory Masters*.)
11. The dating of the Bond End Mill is given in BRL: Lloyd Mss., *loc. cit.*, and its enlargement in 1791 by the purchase of a Watt engine (BRL: Boulton & Watt Mss., 'Engine Book'). The date of the Winshill mill is inferred from its inclusion in Sun OS: 347/535221.
12. W. Radcliffe, *Origins of Power Loom Weaving* (Stockport, 1828), p. 28.
13. Staffs. CRO: Paget Mss., *loc. cit.*, Joseph Wilkes (Burton) to Thomas Harrison (agent to Lord Paget), 12 Mar. 1784.
14. Joseph Wilkes, Dickens & Willson, and Anthony Bradley & Co. were the principal Burton entrepreneurs to enter cotton spinning: see S. D. Chapman, *The Factory Masters*, Ch. 5.
15. See J. Aikin, *A Description of the Country from Thirty to Forty Miles round Manchester* (1795), pp. 163–4 for a dramatic account. A. P. Wadsworth and J. de L. Mann, *Cotton Trade* pp. 178–83, offer a more sober summary.
16. See *supra*, Ch. 3.
17. A. E. Musson and E. Robinson, *op. cit.*, Ch. 9.
18. A. Thackray, 'Natural Knowledge in Cultural Context', *American Historical Review*, LXXIX (1974), p. 705.
19. S. Parkes, *op. cit.*, p. 219.
20. W. Bailey, *Western and Midland Directory* (1784); O. Guttmann, 'The Early Manufacture of Sulphuric and Nitric Acid', *Journal of the Society of the Chemical Industry*, XX (1901), pp. 5–8; *MM*, 20 Sep. 1803.
21. *MM*, 26 Feb. 1788.
22. A. E. Musson and E. Robinson, *op. cit.*, pp. 314–5.
23. See *supra*, Ch. 2.
24. BRL: Robert Peel senior to Boulton & Watt, 22 Feb. 1787. *MM*, 6 Dec. 1791, 11 Feb. 1794.
25. Cf. Thackeray, Stockdale & Co. of Cark-in-Cartmell who in 1786 insured 32 workers' cottages for £15 each, (Sun OS: 341/525630).
26. J. Wheeler, *Manchester: its Political, Social and Commercial History* (1836), p. 521. (Subsequently cited as *Manchester*.) *Universal British Directory*, II (Burnley).
27. Sun OS: 376/582862; CS: 9/644236.
28. Pennsylvania Museum, Harrisburg, USA: Joshua Gilpin's Journals, LII (Manchester, September 1799).
29. W. Bennett, *The History of Burnley* (Burnley, 1948), p. 174. *Blackburn Mail*, 30 Oct. 1811.
30. Lancs. CRO: DDX 223, boxes 1, 9, 10, 11, Robinson & Sons Mss., for Peel property plans and inventories; DDPL (unlisted), 'Peel Papers' (miscellaneous deeds, valuations, etc.), 'Church Building Book, December 1812'.
31. D. Hogg, *A History of Church ... 1760–1860* (Accrington, 1971), p. 23. J. Priestley, *Navigable Rivers, Canals, and Railways of Great Britain*. (1831), pp. 385–97.
32. Sun CS: 56/749337–43 (1803). *MM*, 16 Jul. 1811 (Sawley). *Blackburn Mail*, 2 Mar. 1808 (Burnley); 30 Oct. 1811 (Foxhill Bank); 4 Dec. 1811 (Accrington).
33. *MM*, 1 May 1798.
34. *MM*, 4 Jun. 1822; *Blackburn Mail*, 30 Oct. 1811, 4 Nov. 1835 for attempts to sell the Church Bank works. In 1836 they were finally sold to Frederick Steiner, an Alsatian chemist; see J. Graham, *Printworks*, p. 365.
35. D. Hogg, *op. cit.*, p. 15. See Catherine Jacson, *Formby Reminiscences* (1897) for Jonathan Peel at Peel Park, Accrington.

Chapter 4

1. [Anon.], *Public Characters of 1803–04* (1804), pp. 5–9; Sir Lawrence Peel, *Sketch*, p. 13; J. Wheeler, *Manchester*, p. 519. Some accounting, but no science, was taught

Notes and References 227

    at Blackburn Grammar School in the eighteenth century according to G. F. Eastwood, *Queen Elizabeth's. A New History of the Ancient Grammar School of Blackburn* (1967). R. S. Crossley, *Accrington Captains of Industry* (Accrington, 1930), p. 12.
2. Sir Lawrence Peel, *Sketch*, pp. 34–5; B. T. Barton, *History of Bury* (1967).
3. W. C. Taylor, *Notes of a Tour*, p. 6; [Anon.], 'The Putrid Fever at Robert Peel's Radcliffe Mill', *Notes and Queries*, CCIII (1958), pp. 26–35.
4. E. Potter, *op. cit.*, p. 10.
5. Sir Lawrence Peel, *Sketch*. 'Veritas', *Walks around Bury* (Bury, 1842) [John Ainsworth], pp. 52, 55, 86. (Subsequently cited as 'Veritas'.) PRO: 30/8/165, Chatham Mss., pp. 183–6.
6. J[ane] H[owarth], 'A Memoir of the Family of Peel', Ms., 1836, BM: Add. Mss. 40610. *Manchester Examiner and Times*, 26 Oct. 1850.
7. John Wesley's *Diary*, sub 27 Jul. 1787. *MM*, 13 Jun. 1780. *Manchester Examiner and Times*, 26 Oct. 1850.
8. E.g. the younger Robert Peel's negotiations for a steam engine for his father's Warrington cotton mill in 1787 (BRL: *loc. cit.*, Robert Peel senior to Boulton & Watt, 22 Feb. 1787); 'Parsley' Peel's use of the Bury Print Works, cited above.
9. J. Aitken, *op. cit.*, p. 268.
10. J. Wheeler, *Manchester*, p. 519; W. Bailey's *Directory*. Sun OS: 359/555026 (1789).
11. J. Graham, *Printworks*, p. 416. John Key was also a partner up to c. 1798, but his background is not recorded.
12. W. H. Elliott, *The Cheeryble Brothers* (Selkirk, 1893), pp. 121–2, 128.
13. A. Rees, *loc. cit.*
14. BRL: *loc. cit.*, J. Wilkes to Boulton & Watt, 19 Oct. 1783; James Watt to J. Wilkes, 20 Oct. 1783.
15. BRL: *loc. cit.*, Boulton & Watt 'Engine Book'; Thomas Ainsworth to Boulton & Watt, 7 Jul. 1787. *MM*, 11 Feb, 1794 (sale of Warrington mill).
16. BRL: *loc. cit.*, Peter Atherton to Boulton & Watt, 4 Jul. 1791, 1 Sep. 1791; Boulton & Watt 'Engine Book'.
17. For dimensions and experience of other Atherton mills, see S. D. Chapman, *Factory Masters*, pp. 84, 133–4; *Nottingham Journal*, 8 Nov. 1800. PRO: C 12/665/23, C 12/2167/19, E 112/1531/256.
18. E.g. William Douglas of Pendleton and Holywell mills. 13 letters from Douglas to Boulton & Watt, 1791–8 (BRL: *loc. cit.*).
19. BRL: *loc. cit.*, Boulton & Watt 'Engine Book'; A. E. Musson and E. Robinson, 'The Early Growth of Steam Power', *EcHR*,XI (1959), p. 431; G. J. French, *op. cit.*, p. 100.
20. S. D. Chapman, 'The Cost of Power in the Industrial Revolution in Britain', *Midland History*, I (1971).
21. See surviving buildings at Fazeley and Bonehill, near Tamworth.
22. S. D. Chapman, 'Capital Formation in the British Cotton Industry', in J. P. P. Higgins and S. Pollard (eds.), *Aspects of Capital Formation in Great Britain* (1971).
23. Notably McConnel & Kennedy and A. & G. Murray. For size of mills at this period, see G. W. Daniels, 'Valuation of Manchester Cotton Factories in the early nineteenth century', *Economic Journal*, XXV (1915), p. 626.
24. J. Graham, *Printworks*, p. 360.
25. Sun CS: 56/749342 (1803). The 15 agencies were located at Croston (stock valued at £300), Spurspout (£400), Cross (£100), Foxholes (£700), Chapel-en-le-Frith, Derbys. (£350), Darwen (£180), Round Barn (£170), Houghton and Walton (£500), Blackburn (£900), Colne (£220), Carlton, Gisburne and Cowling (£240), and Haslingden (£300).
26. Pennsylvania Mus., Harrisburg, USA: Joshua Gilpin's Journals, LII (1799). *Cotton and Woollen Mills and Factories in the U.K. ... 1803–18*, PP, 1819, p. 48.
27. Sun CS: 56/749342–3.

228 European Textile Printers in the Eighteenth Century

28. Sun CS: 56/749337–9. M. Gray, *The History of Bury 1660–1876* (Bury, 1970), pp. 86–7. The canal was projected in 1791.
29. E.g. by N. Gash, *Mr. Secretary Peel* (1961).
30. J. Wheeler, *Manchester*, p. 521.
31. *Journal of the House of Commons*, XL, 1785, p. 642ff.
32. *Gentlemen's Magazine*, LV (1), 1785, pp. 448–9.
33. *MM*, 14 Nov. 1786.
34. N. Gash, *op. cit.*
35. A. P. Wadsworth and J. de L. Mann, *Cotton Trade*, p. 308. If the wages rated cited by J. Graham, *Printworks*, p. 345, and *MM*, 20 Jul. 1790, are to be believed, block printers' incomes were increasing up to this date.
36. *MM*, 20 Jul. 1790.
37. See *supra*, Ch. 7 for a fuller treatment of labour policy.
38. J. Graham, *Printworks*, pp. 346, 365; J. Wheeler, *Manchester*, pp. 521–2.
39. J. Graham, *Printworks*, p. 422.
40. A. Young, *Tours in England and Wales* (L.S.E. reprint, 1932), p. 272.
41. Deeds of Marquis of Bath at Longleat, cited in D. G. Stuart, *The Parliamentary History of the Borough of Tamworth* (M.A. thesis, University of London, 1958), pp. 117–8.
42. Arkwright bought the manors of Cromford and Willersley for £41,000 in 1789 (BM: Add. Mss., no. 6689, ff. 112, 378).
43. J. Graham, *Printworks*, pp. 360, 463.
44. Sun OS: 376/582847.
45. Sun CS: 7/640036 (1795), 18/666957 (1797).
46. C. Hulbert, *Memoirs of Seventy Years of an Eventful Life* (Shrewsbury, 1852), p. 195.
47. G. Unwin, *op. cit.*, pp. 149 ff.
48. Sir Lawrence Peel, *Sketch*, p. 35.
49. J. Wheeler, *Manchester*, p. 522.
50. *MM*, 7 Mar. 1797; L. S. Pressnell, *Country Banking in the Industrial Revolution* (1956), p. 111. D. Hardcastle, *Banks and Bankers* (1843 edn) pp. 438–9.

Chapter 5

1. Sir Lawrence Peel, *Sketch*, p. 35. John Wesley's *Diary*, *loc. cit.*, records that Robert Peel II had gained £50,000 by 1787.
2. For leaseholding developments, see, for example, *MM*, 13 Jun. 1780 (74 acres at Elton); M. Gray, *op. cit.*, p. 81; D. Hogg, *op. cit.*, p. 14. Lancs. CRO: DDX 223/1, 9, 11, Robinson & Sons Mss.
3. 'Veritas', p. 52. J. Wheeler, *Manchester*, p. 229. B. T. Barton, *op. cit.*, p. 80.
4. *ME*, 9 Nov. 1850. 'Veritas', pp. 50–1, 101, 108. PRO: E 112/1758/5286.
5. 'Veritas', pp. 50, 82.
6. Quoted in E. P. Thompson, *Making of the English Working Class* (1963), p. 335.
7. PRO: E 112/Mich. 39/289; E 112/1765/5477.
8. [A. G. E. Jones], 'The Putrid Fever at Robert Peel's Radcliffe Mill', *Notes and Queries*, CCIII (1958), p. 34.
9. Sun OS: 374/580715 (1791); CS: 3/627272 (1794), 7/640034 (1795). Sir Robert Peel's interests in his father's concerns were relinquished after his death in 1795.
10. Report entitled '7 January 1811. Robert Peel and Thomas Yates' (BRL: Boulton & Watt Mss.) and numerous Sun insurance policies.
11. BRL: *loc. cit.*, John Peel to Boulton & Watt, 27 Sep. 1791.
12. W. Barrett, *Old Merchants of New York* (New York, 1899), II, p. 34.
13. J. Wheeler, *Manchester*, p. 529; W. Bailey, *Western and Midland Directory* (1783).
14. L. H. Grindon, *Manchester Banks and Bankers* (Manchester, 1877) pp. 113, 124–125.

15. J. Graham, *Printworks*, pp. 360, 463; Sun CS: 4/623911.
16. See *infra*, Ch. 8.
17. Other partners who worked their way up through the firm were Richard Yates (see J. Wheeler, *Manchester*), John Harding (J. Graham, *Printworks*), and probably John Key, junior partner in the Ramsbottom works.
18. BRL: *loc. cit.*, Robert Peel II to Boulton & Watt, 20 Jul. 1792; Sun CS: 9/644231, 19/667616.
19. S. D. Chapman, *Factory Masters*, p. 91. Other managers remained with the Peels to the end of their lives, e.g. William Grimshaw of Church Bridge and John Lankford of Ratcliffe Bridge: see their obituaries in *MM*, 16 Jul. 1805, 22 Aug. 1809.
20. S. D. Chapman, 'Fixed Capital Formation', pp. 256–66.
21. Sun CS: 11/648489, for Tipping's own firm.
22. Table *supra*; J. H. Partington, *op. cit.*, pp. 56–63. Ainsworth went bankrupt in 1819 and again in 1828.
23. J. Farey, *Agriculture of Derbyshire* (1811–17), II, pp. 361–2, 474, 492, etc. W. Pitt, *Agriculture of Leicestershire* (1809), pp. 185–6, 201–3, 322, etc. Lancs. CRO: Earl of Derby Mss., DDX 223/1, DE 41/1/73. Leics. CRO: Crane & Walton Mss., DE 358/4030, and Wileman deposit. Warwicks. CRO: Phoenix Fire Office, Atherstone Agent's Registers, CR 1039.
24. D. G. Stuart, M.A. thesis, *loc. cit.*; N. Gash, *op. cit.*, pp. 16–18. Wilkes had previously raised £180,000 for the Ashby Canal and £30,000 for the Measham colliery railroad; see J. Farey, *op. cit.*, III, pp. 301–4. In spite of this experience, Peel was able to withstand the financial strain of the Tamworth purchase better than Wilkes. In 1794 Wilkes had to mortgage a large portion of his Measham estate for £42,000: £20,000 to Sir Robert Peel and William Yates, and £22,000 to Isaac Hawkins, the senior partner in the Trent Navigation (abstract of Measham deeds in Parish records: transcript kindly supplied by Donald Wright).
25. W. F. Crick and J. E. Wadsworth, *A Hundred Years of Joint-Stock Banking* (1936), pp. 244–51.
26. Sun OS: 376/582847 (1791); CS: 7/640036 (1795), 18/666957 (1797).
27. Staffs. CRO: B(M)12, 13, Paget Mss., 22 Jul. 1763. S. Sketchley, *Birmingham Directory* (1777), and subsequent local directories.
28. BRL: *loc. cit.*, Boulton & Watt to John Peel, 21 Mar. 1793.
29. Memo. in Tamworth Baptismal Register, 1790.
30. L. S. Pressnell, *op. cit.* Leicestershire CRO: Wileman deposit, notes on Joseph Wilkes by a descendant, J. Simmonds, *c*. 1902.
31. W. F. Crick and J. E. Wadsworth, *op. cit.* Wilkes's unproven will is deposited in Leics. CRO. D. Hardcastle, *loc. cit.*
32. J. Graham, *Printworks*, p. 463.
33. *MM*, 14 Jan. 1806, 26 Aug. 1806.

Chapter 6

1. Quoted by E. Potter, *op. cit.*, pp. 10–11.
2. *MM*, 14 Nov. 1786.
3. B. T. Barton, *op. cit.*, pp. 64–5, 77.
4. J. Graham, *Printworks*, p. 463.
5. *Journal of the House of Commons*, 1787, pp 584–5, 663. *ME*, 19 Oct. 1850. C. O'Brien, *The British Manufacturer's Companion and Callico Printer's Assistant* (1790), long unnumbered footnote on the Peels. O'Brien described himself as 'late Designer to Mr. Kilburn', presumably William Kilburn, the Wallington calico printer who launched the campaign against the Peels resulting in the 1787

Copyright Act: see A. K. Longfield, 'William Kilburn and the Earliest Copyright Acts for Cotton Printing Designs', *Burlington Mag.*, XCV (1953), pp. 230–3. Nat. Lib. Scotland: Melville Mss. 1064, fo. 102.
6. A. Brown, *History of Glasgow* (1795), II, p. 212. Louis Bergeron, *Banquiers, Négociants et Manufacturiers Parisiens* (thesis, Paris, IV, 1975), II, p. 768.
7. [Anon.] *Old Time Memories and Reminiscences of Bury, 3 May 1873* (Bury PL, 1873). PRO: C 12/2165/30, John Field v. W. Barrett.
8. Winterthur Museum, Delaware, USA: Wister Papers, Order Book 1785–1789, and invoices addressed to Andrew Clow & Co., 1790. (Thanks are due to Museum Assistant Mrs Beatrice Taylor for extracting the Peel invoices.) P. L. White (ed.), *The Beekman Mercantile Papers* (New York, 1956), III, p. 1053: Alex Keith (Nantes) to Beekmans (Philadelphia), 10 Feb. 1785 – 'I am given to understand that the low priced common sort [of prints] meet with a readier sale with you than the fine high price ones.' *Report from SC on Duties Payable on Printed Cotton Goods &c.*, PP, 1818, esp. pp. 16, 41–2.
9. *Mercury Dictionary of Textile Terms. Oxford English Dictionary*.
10. J. Graham, *Printworks*, p. 346.
11. J. Aston, *A Picture of Manchester* (1816), pp. 221–2.
12. J. T. Slugg, *Reminiscences of Manchester* (1881), pp. 32–3.
13. B. T. Barton, *op. cit.*, p. 64. *MM*, 18 May 1784.
14. Cf. S. Bamford, *Early Days* (1849), pp. 276–80, for the daily routine at another Peel St. warehouse. W. H. Elliott, *op. cit.* p. 125.
15. F. Montgomery, *op cit.*, p. 40
16. B. T. Barton, *op. cit.* S. D. Chapman, 'British Marketing Enterprise ... 1700–1860', *BHR*, LIII (1979).
17. Wister Papers, *loc. cit.*, and PRO, C 12/685/30 (1799). New York Historical Society: letter book of F. & P. Rheinlander (1789–93), files of Andrew Cock & Sons (1794–8), and Isaac Cooke letter book, 1791–6.
18. W. Barrett, *op. cit.*, II, p. 34.
19. New York Hist. Soc.: Bolton, Ogden & Co.'s Mss., letters of Peel, Yates & Co. to Ferguson, 16 Oct. 1799, 30 Jun. 1800. (I am indebted to John Killick for these references.)
20. Contract in New York Genealogical Society archives. See J. Killick, 'Bolton, Ogden & Co. A Case Study in Anglo-American Trade', *BHR*, XLVIII (1974), p. 506.
21. New York Hist. Soc.: *loc. cit.*, letters of Peel, Yates & Co. to Ferguson, 27 Jul. 1797, 14 Aug. 1799, 16 Oct. 1799.
22. New York Hist. Soc.: *loc. cit.*, Peel Yates & Co. to Ferguson, 12 May 1798, 24 Feb. 1798; John Day to Ferguson, 12 Oct. 1801.
23. D. Dollfus-Ausset, *Materiaux.*, p. 5. Bibliothèque de l'Assemblée Nationale, Paris, F. de Rochefoucauld, *La Traversée des Provinces d' Angleterre* (1785), II, p. 80. Fred. Aug. Wenderborn, *A View of England towards the End of the Eighteenth Century* (1791), I, pp. 229–230. T. Cooper, *A Practical Treatise on ... Callicoe Printing* (Philadelphia, 1815) p. 335 refers to the sale of patterns at 5s. dozen in London. AN: F 12/2295, Alexandre Andelle's report on Manchester, 1819. PRO: BT 6/113, ev. of R. Peel, J. Smith, S. Salte.
24. By 1795 the Peels were exporting some middle-quality prints to Germany, but the volume is not stated. *Report from SC on Manufactures, Commerce and Shipping*, PP, 1833, p. 238.
25. PRO: FO 33/1, 23 Oct. 1781.
26. Wadsworth and Mann, *Cotton Trade*, p. 239; and PRO: E 112/1530/224 for later development. *MM*, 18 May 1784, for Peels' employment of travellers.
27. PRO: C 12/1739/6, E 112/1541/589.
28. [Anon.], *Observations on the means of extending the Consumption of British Callicoes ....* (1788) [Anon], *A Representation of Facts relative to the Rise .... of the Cotton Manufacture* (1789). Baron F. de Rothschild, 'Reminiscences' (ms.,

1897). S. D. Chapman, 'Rothschilds'. A. Dreyer, *Les toiles peintes en pays Neuchâtelois* (Paris, 1923), pp. 52–3.
29. IOR; Charter series, A/2/10. Report of E. India Co. SC on the Export Trade from G.B. to the East Indies (Ms., *c.* 1792, unpaginated).
30. IOR: A/2/11. Nat. Lib. Scotland: Melville Mss. 1064, fos. 60, 102.
31. IOR: A/1/85a.
32. IOR: A/2/11. 280,750 pieces, reckoned at 30 yards each.
33. *Report from the SC on Manufactures, Commerce and Shipping*, PP, 1833, p. 242. A. Tripathi, *Trade and Finance in the Bengal Presidency 1793–1833* (Bombay, 1956), p. 165.

Chapter 7

1. C. O'Brien, *The British Manufacturer's Companion and Callico Printer's Assistant (1790)*, unpaginated.
2. Series of anonymous articles entitled 'The Peel Family: Its Rise and Fortunes. Bury Eighty Years Ago', *ME*, 5 Oct.–9 Nov. 1850. H. R. Fox Bourne, *op. cit.*, II (1866), p. 159 n., says the articles were compiled from traditions in the memory of various people of Bury.
3. E. P. Thompson, 'Time, Work-Discipline, and Industrial Capitalism', *Past and Present*, No. 38 (1967).
4. *ME*, 19 Oct. 1850. W. Radcliffe, *Origins of Power Loom Weaving* (1828), p. 66, notes that handloom weaving families could earn £2–£5 weekly at this period.
5. R. Campbell, *The London Tradesman* (1747), pp. 116–7.
6. J. Graham, *Printworks*, p. 345.
7. *ME*, 12 Oct. 1850.
8. [Anon.], *Facts and Observations*, pp. 8, 16.
9. *Ibid.*, p. 13.
10. *ME*, 19 Oct. 1850.
11. *ME*, 12 Oct. 1850. *SC on Children Employed in Manufactories*, PP, 1816, pp. 132–3. B. T. Barton, *op. cit.*, p. 61. Assay Office Lib., Birmingham: letter from M. Boulton to S. Whitbread 12 Nov. 1792. 'Veritas', p. 56. Anon., *Old Time Memories and Reminiscences of Bury, 3 May 1837* (pamphlet, Bury PL).
12. *ME*, 12 Oct. 1850.
13. House of Lords Mss: *ev. of R. Peel on Irish Commercial Propositions, 1785*.
14. D. Bythell, *The Handloom Weavers* (Cambridge, 1969), is the most complete study of this subject.
15. [Anon.], *Facts and Observations*, pp. 14, 18.
16. *MM*, 20 July 1790.
17. [Anon.], *Facts and Observations*, pp. 17–18.
18. Calculated from evidence of R. Peel on Irish Propositions, 1785.
19. [Anon.] *Facts and Observations*, p. 18.
20. *Ibid.*, p. 10.
21. H. R. Fox Bourne, *op. cit.*, p. 165.
22. *SC on Children Employed in Manufactories*, PP, 1816, pp. 139–40. Lancs. CRO: DDK/1741/10, Earl of Derby Mss., Lieutenancy Letter Books, pp. 197–210.

Chapter 8

1. H. Chobaut, 'L'industrie des indiennes à Marseille avant 1680', *mem. Inst. hist. de Provence*, 1939.
2. Import of cotton *toiles* (*guinées* and *taffetas*) by the English and Dutch East India companies reached 60,000 pieces before the middle of the century; see K. Glamann, *Dutch Asiatic Trade* (Copenhagen and The Hague, 1958), pp. 135–8.

For the 'Indian craze' and its consequences in Britain, see A. P. Wadsworth and J. de L. Mann, *Cotton Trade*, Ch. VI.
3. On the foundation of this Company, see the older works by H. Weber, *La compagnie française des Indes 1604–1875* (Paris, 1904); P. Kaeppelin, *La compagnie des Indes Orientales*... (Paris, 1908); and D. Dessert and J. L. Journet, 'Le lobby Colbert', *Annales E.S.C.*, 1975.
4. S. Chassagne, *Tournemine*, pp. 38–45.
5. *Ibid.*
6. At the end of the seventeenth century Huguenot calico printers were living in Berlin, Bremen, Frankfurt, Geneva, Lausanne and Neuchâtel, but it is not clear whether they started the industry in these places; see S. Chassagne, *Tournemine*, pp. 45–6.
7. At Nantes in 1721, 1,510 inhabitants confessed to the authorities that they possessed some kind of *indiennes*, including 3,192 bed covers, 504 curtains, 338 armchair covers, 315 wall coverings and 142 valances. Half of those giving this information lived in two of the five parishes of the town; see S. Chassagne, *Tournemine*, p. 50.
8. In Britanny the tax officials discovered 200 contraventions for 'wearing and using' the unlawful fabrics between 1725 and 1738, divided as follows:

	Cases	Prosecutions	Convicted		%
Merchants	69	54	39	=	71
Nobility	11	2	2	=	18
Officers	18	7	3	=	17
Various occupations	82	62	56	=	68
Unknown	20	—	—		
Total	200	125	100		50

SOURCE: S. Chassagne, *Tournemine*, p. 60.

9. P. Dardel, *Les manufactures de toiles peintes et de serges imprimées à Rouen et à Bolbec aux XVIIe et XVIIIe siècles* (Rouen, 1940), p. 21. (Subsequently cited as *Les manufactures*.)
10. AN: F 12, 96/334–350, 96/427/440. S. Chassagne, *Tournemine*, p. 65.
11. One of four *intendants* for commerce, appointed in 1744 and died in 1782. His son succeeded him in office from 1758. Vincent de Gournay, who came of a large family settled at Cadix, became *intendant* for commerce in 1751 and resigned in 1758.
12. See, for example, the 1753 report addressed to Mignot de Montigny (Mazarine Lib.: Ms. 2840, fo. 167).
13. The uncertainty also existed because of the narrow outlook of the Chamber of Commerce, but the secret discussions did not begin to leak out as some members deliberately controlled it.
14. According to P. Dardel, *Les manufactures*, p. 14, the earliest *toiles* with designs in blue appeared at Rouen towards 1709, but they were produced by a process difficult to control, based on potassium and lime. The so-called 'cold' process (*cuve à froid*) extended pencilling to Normandy in the 1730s.
15. The 'liberties' of the port allowed it to evade the prohibition. In 1733 Marseilles counted 24 printing workshops, according to V. L. Bourilly, 'La contrebande des toiles peintes en Provence an XVIIIe siècle', *Annales du Midi*, XXVI (1914), p. 56. H. Lüthy, *La banque protestante en France* (Paris, 1961), II, p. 90n., cites two Genevan manufacturers at Marseilles in 1723 who were recruiting workers of their town by offering employment contracts. The Protestant parish registers of Marseilles record several printers and merchants of printed fabrics from Geneva

Notes and References 233

or Berne. J. R. Wetter established himself at Aubagne after 1753, and then at Orange in 1758.
16. On these different pressures, see AN: F 12/91–6.
17. After a journey in England with their partner Daviais in spring 1751; see S. Chassagne, *Tournemine*, p. 92.
18. *Reflexions sur differents objets de commerce* ... (Geneva, 1759), p. 39.
19. On Cottin, see H. Lüthy, *op. cit.*, II, p. 312, and the summary in S. Chassagne, 'Un atelier de toiles à la réserve à Angers 1763–1807', *Annales de Bretagne et des Pays de l'Ouest*, LXXXIII (1976), p. 176. Cabannes, often recorded as an Englishman, was in fact the descendant of a calico printer from Languedoc who sought refuge in England at the end of the seventeenth century.
20. All this according to AN: Zim/28–30. The earliest Swiss workers engaged were the Genevan printers Isaac Fréchet (previously at Mulhouse), Jacob Pernon and his wife, pencillers from Milan, P. Morlet, colourist, Sandoz and F. Landry, engravers from Neuchâtel, Frantz Leper, Mathias Hindierich, and Rudolph Haller, engravers, from Zurich, and Friederick Bauerschmitt from Basle, and previously of Greng, near Morat.
21. On the earliest factories at Nantes, see S. Chassagne, *Tournemine*, pp. 118–20.
22. Ittier & Reboul bought their first *siamoises façon d'indiennes* from a merchant house at Rouen in Jul. 1755, and their first *indiennes* (*calancas* and *limenas*) from Genevan merchants, André Picot and Plantamour, Rivier and Rillet in December 1758. (On Rillet, see H. Lüthy, *op. cit.*, II, p. 106.) These *toiles* were sent by road from Geneva to Nice, to the address of the Consul-General of the Empire, to be re-exported by sea to Marseilles or Montpellier.

Chapter 9

1. AN: Z I M 28–30.
2. *Ibid.* Morlet then went into partnership with his master, and in 1761 they moved their factory to Corbeil. In 1766 he was found in Troyes, where his factory lasted until the Empire.
3. AN: Z I M 28. The judgement is in the Rondonneau collection, AD XI/52.
4. AN: 41 AQ 2, letter from Aarau, 17 Aug. 1759.
5. 'For three-quarters of the year, the Jouy valley had no other resources, in 1759, for its poor and under-employed inhabitants but the hay harvest and some wood sales,' according to a declaration made to the king in a 1783 petition to be a royal factory (AN: 41 AQ 1).
6. 'My father's life in printing', May 1809 (AN: 41 AQ 1).
7. P. R. Schwartz, 'Contribution à l'histoire de l'application de bleu d'indigo dans l'indiennage européen', *Bull. Soc. Ind. Mulhouse*, 1953, pp. 63–79. Ryhiner's works, the first built in Basle (in 1716), split into two enterprises in 1738 when the two brothers went their different ways. Oberkampf's father worked for Emmanuel Ryhiner at a place called Little Basle on the River Teich.
8. AN: 41 AQ 1. P.-J. Oberkampf was registered as a *schutzburger* (refugee) on 7 Nov. 1750 having provided evidence of his wedding and children's baptisms. He was signed out 27 Jan. 1752.
9. On Kupfer, see A. Jean-Richard, *Kattundrucke der Schweiz im 18. Jahrhundert* (Basle, 1968), II, p. 78. See P. R. Schwartz's Ms. notes at Mulhouse Museum of Printed Textiles.
10. Aarauisches Staatarchiv, Aarau, quoted by P. R. Schwartz, *loc. cit.*
11. P. R. Schwartz, 'Les débuts de l'indiennage mulhousien', *Bull. Soc. Ind. Mulhouse*, 1950–2.
12. Lease of 31 Jan. 1760, Jouy notary. The rent was 300 *l.* a year.
13. From Aarau, 22 Mar. 1760 (AN: 41 AQ 2).
14. Cf. A. Labouchère, *Oberkampf* (Paris, 1966), p. 58. Oberkampf's eldest daughter

Nanine (1775–7) died from smallpox. The second daughter, Julie (1777–1843), married Louis Feray, the son of an outfitter at Le Havre. He later succeeded to the management of the Chantemerle factory at Essonnes.
15. To his nephew Reifft, 22 May 1802 (AN: 41 AQ 2.).
16. AN: Min. Cent., LXXXII, 568, and LXXXVI, 837, marriage settlements, 4 Jul. 1774, 29 Jan. 1785.
17. Jouy parish register. But Oberkampf was never a witness at a marriage ceremony or a godfather at a christening, as his brother Frédéric was at Corbeil. His partner Maraise, or his wife, represented the partnership at official functions.
18. AN: 41 AQ 4. Spelling modernised.
19. From Jouy, 11 Aug. 1776 (AN: 41 AQ 2).
20. An estate in the township of Suhr. In 1799 Oberkampf sold it for 22,000 gold florins (AN: 41 AQ 2).
21. His father acquired citizenship in Rued, which cost him 600 gold florins, the cheapest in the country. Aarau cost 2,000. Mother died 24 Mar. 1779 and was buried at Suhr.
22. Oberkampf's mother warned her son against his brother-in-law.
23. The younger Pétineau brother-in-law was also sent to school there; it cost 600 *l.* p.a.
24. 29 Nov. 1782 (AN: 41 AQ 2).
25. Oberkampf took charge of the five remaining nephews after their mother's death.
26. AN: 41 AQ 1.
27. Philipp 1785–8, Victor 1786–8, with a Vevey master at a cost of 360 *l.* a year each.
28. In 1763 Oberkampf's father had bought, jointly with his son-in-law, Widmer's family property at Othmarsingen and set up a printing works there. It took many years to repay the debts, which gave much trouble.
29. AN: 41 AQ 1, statement on Tavannes.
30. According to Levasseur's letters, AN: F 12/876, AN: 41 AQ 1.
31. *Ibid.*
32. Linguet, *Mémoires et plaidoyers* (Liège, 1776), IV, p. 8.
33. AN: Z IM/29, printed copy in Z IM/32. Cottin took Oberkampf to court for breaking his contract, deserting without leave, stealing drawings and spoiling goods. The fine was 1,500 *l.* (15 times that prescribed by the 1749 decree) plus 3,000 damages for the value of spoiled *toiles*. Maraise obtained leave to appeal to the Paris *Parlement* which suspended execution of the previous verdict and final judgement was never made.
34. There is no record of these actions in AN: Z IE/307–8.
35. Marriage settlement, 3 Nov. 1767, at Rouen. The bride's dowry was fixed at 30,000 *l.*
36. Correspondence in AN: 41 AQ 3.
37. Simon-André (1728–97), author of *Advertisement to the People on Health* (Lausanne, 1761) which made his name. He lived in Lausanne but was often in Paris.
38. See *supra*, n 16.
39. From London, Jun. 1783, (AN: 41 AQ 1).
40. Feb. 1785, (AN: 41 AQ 2).
41. Cf. A. Choisy, *Notice généalogique de la famille Mallet* (Geneva, 1935). On the foundation of the Bank of France, see L. Bergeron, *Banquiers, negociants et manufacturiers parisiens* ... (Paris, 1978), p. 121. (Subsequently cited as *Banquiers.*)
42. Patents of nobility in AN: Z IA/632; AN: Min. Cent. LXXXVI, 850, marriage settlement of Maraise's daughter. The next year, when the girl was still only 16, she became a widow.
43. AN: 41 AQ 3.

44. Jouy commune (town hall) records.
45. AN: 41 AQ 1.
46. H. Chobaut, 'L'industrie des Indiennes à Avignon et à Orange, 1677–1884', *Mem. de l'Acad. de Vaucluse*, 1938. M. Bovet, 'Les toiles peintes ...', *Revue Neuchâteloise*, XX (1976–7), p. 26.
47. AN: F12/676. AD, Rhone: C11.
48. Bibliothèque de St. Gall (Switzerland); handbill dated Jouy 17 Mar. 1792. Copy kindly sent by M. Bovet, who quotes the whole document in *Revue Neuchâteloise*, XX (1976–7), pp. 24–5).
49. AN: 41 AQ 8.
50. Letter from Houel of Caen, 25 May 1797, published by E. G. Leonard, *B.S.H.P.F.*, XCIX (1940), p. 306.
51. AN: 41 AQ 128.

Chapter 10

1. AN: 41 AQ2, letter of 22 Mar. 1760.
2. The tanners and towers of Paris were the legal authorities for the river. There were respectively 29 and 14 of them in 1762 out of the 77 artisans and manufacturers who used the Bièvre (AN: ZIE/307). The other group with an important interest in the river were the millers, of whom there were 22, 17 of them up at Gentilly.
3. AN: 41 AQ1.
4. *Supra*, Ch. 9.
5. AN: 41 AQ5.
6. AN: 41 AQ2, letter of 22 Jul. 1764.
7. AN: 41 AQ5. As early as 1764 he had obtained the mill rental but, on the insistence of the Marquess of Beuvron, he had deferred to the miller, who in 1773 became a tenant in his own right for a higher rent.
8. Averaging 72,000 *l*. (AN: LII, 484).
9. AN: 41 AQ5. In 1790 the company possessed around 21 ha at Jouy, of which 12 had been acquired from the Duke of Beuvron.
10. On this journey, see *infra*, Ch. 11.
11. AN: 41 AQ2.
12. On materials, see *infra*, Ch. 11; and on workers he sent, see *infra*, Ch. 13.
13. On it, cf. P. Caspard, *op. cit.*
14. Established in late 1763 at the chateau of Sèvres with the support of Trudaine, the *manufacture d'indiennes anglaises* engaged a London printer, Louis Beauford; see S. Chassagne, *Tournemine*, p. 250. It went bankrupt in 1767 but was still in existence in 1777. According to Maraise, the launching of the enterprise cost 'nearly 1,500,000 *l*. to eliminate all the competitors and secure exclusive control of this branch of commerce' (AN: 41 AQI, p. 206). For Orange, see H. Chobaut, *op. cit.*
15. See *infra* Ch. 13.
16. No doubt the largest factories of the locality: cf. H. Deonna, 'Une industrie genevoise de jadis: les indiennes', *Geneva*, VII (1930), pp. 185–240.
17. A factory established in 1768 and transferred to the suburbs of the town in 1772; cf. J. Ballofet, *Historique de l'indienne à Beligny, Chervinges et Villefranche* (Villefranche, 1912). Several Neuchâtel workers were employed in this factory. On the supply of *siamoises* (printed fabrics reputed to be in the Siamese fashion), see *infra*, Ch. 11.
18. On the origins of this factory, in which he was associated with P. Morlet, a former colour maker at the Arsenal works, cf. S. Chassagne, 'La formation de la

19. AN: Min. Cent., XXVIII, 422.
20. In July 1774 Christoff virtually ceded the ownership to his younger brother (AN: Min. Cent., LII, 510). But in September 1796 he bought back the whole concern both fixed capital and stock. Frédéric died in December 1798 at Corbeil and his heirs received the balance of what Christoff had paid him: 312,348 *f.* (AN: 41 AQ2).
21. *Supra* Ch. 9.
22. Oberkampf was godfather of Maraise's eldest daughter; Maraise and his wife were godfather and godmother of their partner's second daughter and first son.
23. The actual presentation of the summaries was as follows (example of 1773):

Liabilities	*l.*
Credits on current account	203,197
Bills of exchange due	199,051
Money invested by various people	14,836
Total debts	**417,084**
Capital of the old company	923,751
Total liabilities	**1,340,835**
Assets	
(*Working capital*)	
Bills of exchange and cash in hand	509,605
Debtors, presumed good	835,143
Merchandise, drugs, materials	1,148,167
(*Fixed capital*)	
Buildings, houses, vineyards, meadows, madder growing	127,278
Furniture, horses and carriages	14,958
Utensils	22,770
Total	**2,657,921**
deduct liabilities	−1,340,835
and doubtful debtors	−21,077
Present capital	1,306,009
Capital this time last year	966,589
Improvement this year	**339,420**

24. According to the thesis of Claude Pris, *La manufacture royale des glaces de Saint-Gobain, 1685–1830* (Lille-Paris, 1975), p. 881. See also R. G. Geiger, *The Anzin Coal Company* (Delaware, 1971).
25. *Infra* Ch. 12.
26. The same conclusion is reached by P. Caspard, *op. cit.*, for whom the critical development was the purchase of a roller printing machine (18,000 *f.* in 1802 for building the machine, and 1,700 *f.* for every roller).
27. *Infra*, Ch. 11.
28. The Orange factory had used coal since 1760: S. Chassagne, *Tournemine*, p. 214. The factory of Garnier, Danse & Cie burned turf and the Tournemine factory at Angers used wood as fuel.
29. For the Periers' mining interests, cf. G. Thuillier, *Georges Dufaud et les débuts du grand capitalisme dans la métallurgie en Nivernais* (Paris, 1959), pp. 119–48.
30. Experiments recorded in AN: 41 AQI, pp. 81–3. J. G. Smith, *The Origins and Early Development of the Heavy Chemical Industry in France* (Oxford, 1979), pp. 10, 133.

31. Cf. J. Payen, *Capital et machine à vapeur au XVIIIe siècle* (Paris, 1969).
32. At Falaise and Argentan at the end of 1788; at Rouen and its suburbs in summer 1789.
33. Ebingre patented in July 1800 a machine for putting spots on *toiles*. Then Perrenod, a manufacturer at Melun, complained to Chaptal in November 1801 that one of his workers had 'stolen' his invention of a machine for printing on *toiles* (AN: F12/1002).
34. AN: 41 AQ 84/498 to Rougemont & Behrends.
35. In return, one of the Haussmanns came to Jouy on the 23 floréal VII (1796) and gave Oberkampf several formulae for preparing colours (AN: 41 AQ 1, p. 122).
36. To Bury (AN: 41 AQ 84/624).
37. AN: F12/2353. He was rewarded by a prize in 1810.
38. In 1815, at Oberkampf's death, the Jouy factory had 122 tables and there were a few others at Essones, (AN: 41 AQ 14). The Logelbach factory was awarded a 1st class silver medal at the Paris National Exhibition in 1806.
39. To his uncle from Mulhouse, 12 Jul. 1809, (AN: 41 AQ 4). The Munster factory was founded in 1776 by André Hartmann (1746–1834) and Jean-Henri Riege of Augsburg, with Pourtalès of Neuchâtel as sleeping partners.
40. Aime-Philippe Roman (Geneva 1774 – Wesserling 1867), joint director of the factory with François Gros, another Genevan. Roman introduced the roller printing machine to Wesserling, and also the flying shuttle. He was mayor of Husseren from 1808 to his death: see Sitzmann, *Biographies alsaciennes*, II, p. 603.
41. A new term used by the Jouy workers who turned the cylinder because they were given wine when they worked, much as dancers were.
42. Built in 1802 and managed by Auguste Wetzel. On 1 January 1806 it contained 20 mules (4,320 spindles) and 16 roller spinning machines (2,888 spindles) and employed 185 workers, three-quarters of them children under 15. The weaving shed, also established in 1802, contained 250 power looms employing 392 weavers and producing 12,000 pieces a year (AN: F12/1564).
43. A clear reference to Robert, Bovet & Cie, who moved from Boudry (Neuchâtel) to Thann in 1805 where they printed 13,000 pieces a year with 375 workers, and to Risler, Koechlin & Cie, established in 1808: *Histoire documentaire de l'industrie de Mulhouse* (Mulhouse, 1902), pp. 457–9.
44. Founded in 1808 by the pharmacist Mathieu Risler and Phillipe Kestner, Samuel Widmer noticed that the partners adopted 'the processes and theory of M. M. Clement and Desormes, on the system using nitrogen gas to fix oxygen in the acid'. At this date there were eight other sulphuric acid plants in France: three at Rouen, one at Dieppe, one at Langres, one near Honfleur, and two in Paris that supplied the Jouy works. (AN: F12/937).
45. A continuation of the earliest cotton printing factory in Mulhouse, established in 1746, it now operated under the name of Nicholas Koechlin (1800–76): *Histoire documentaire*, pp. 405–6. In 1806 Koechlin, in partnership with the Merians of Basle and Duport, the Lyons merchant house, established a spinning and weaving mill at Massevaux (AN: F12/2426).
46. Heilmann & Son, a company formed in 1804 by the brothers Jean and Godefroi, and the latter's sons, previously connected with Luc Kohler: *Histoire documentaire*, pp. 454, 456.
47. A factory fitted up at Dornach after 1800, with 800 workers and 34,000 pieces printed in 1804–5 (AN: F12/1564). In 1806–7 this factory produced one-quarter of the total output of Mulhouse (AN: F12/1596). Daniel Dollfus (1769–1818) won a silver medal (1st. class) at the 1806 Exhibition.
48. Undoubtedly introduced on the advice of the Scottish colour maker Robert Hendry, who worked at Jouy from 1803 to 1806 as a prisoner of war confided to Oberkampf's care. In 1805 the Periers of Chaillot built a small steam engine for Oberkampf: J. Payen, *op. cit.*, p. 192. Then, in 1812, he obtained a licence from Napoleon to import two Watt engines of 8 hp (AN: 41 AQ 4). In June 1809

Samuel arranged a demonstration of heating by steam boilers for several members of the *Institut* (leading scientists).
49. Cf. M. Crosland, *The Society of Arcueil* (1967).
50. AN: F12/985, list of awards. Three gold medals were awarded in 1798, 12 in 1801, and 12 in 1802.
51. On this organisation, see S. Chassagne, 'L'enquête de Champagny', *Revue d'histoire economique et sociale*, LIV (1976).
52. See *infra*, Ch. 13.
53. AN: 41 AQ 4, Hendry letters. One of the Hartmanns of Munster visited England in summer 1810 and talked to Samuel on his return, awakening his desire to tour the country. Émile made the journey in September 1816.
54. A. and N. Clow, *The Chemical Revolution* (1952), Ch. 4 for this concern.
55. Paisley was the centre of the Scots cotton industry by this date, so the particular factory cannot be identified.
56. Samuel constructed a similar one at Chantemerle in 1812, the first in France according to his brother Gottlieb.
57. Report to the Minister of the Interior on his return (AN: F12/2312). Oberkampf ordered a 6 hp Boulton & Watt engine in 1811–12, but when news of the order leaked out the export was prevented. (AN: 41 AQ 106, *passim*).
58. AN: 41 AQ 931430, cited by L. Bergeron, *Banquiers*, p. 699.
59. AN: 41 AQ 93/696.

Chapter 11

1. AN: 41 AQ 1, private act for the foundation of the company.
2. *Toiles d'Orange* were the prints made by Wetter at Orange; see *supra*, Ch. 8, n. 15.
3. See, for example, the catalogue of the 1970 exhibition at the Musée de l'Impression sur Étoffes at Mulhouse, *La toile de Jouy, dessins et cartons de J.-B. Huet*.
4. Commission printing was widespread in the industry at the time; see S. Chassagne, *Tournemine*, pp. 300–1, for a more detailed description of the practice. After 1815 the Jouy factory renewed its connections with distinguished patrons such as the Duchess de Berry.
5. AN: 41 AQ 3, letter from Maraise to Oberkampf, 29 Nov. 1776.
6. Cf. Norbert Elias, *Die Hofische Gesellschaft* (Berlin, 1969).
7. AN: 41 AQ 1, Oberkampf's recommendation to his nephews.
8. On Huet, see the catalogue referred to *supra*, n. 3. It seems that he never worked at Jouy, preferring to design on a commission basis paid by the piece. Other men of the same name worked in the factory between 1765 and 1815 as printers and one at Essonnes as an engraver.
9. New designs were registered as follows: 1783 (389); 1784 (488); 1785 (368); 1786 (280); 1787 (324); 1788 (234); 1789 (299) (Bibl. Arts Decoratifs, AA19).
10. All ledgers conserved by Mme de Maraise at the time of the break-up of the partnership in 1789.
11. Cf. L. Bergeron, 'Paris dans l'organisation des échanges francais à la fin du XVIIIe siècle', in P. Léon (ed.), *Aires et Structures du commerce français au XVIIIe siècle* (Lyon, 1975), pp. 237–64.
12. Jacquemart had a shop in the *hôtel Jabach* in rue Neuve-Saint-Méry, occupied by the Parisian office of the factory from 1769 until Jacquemart purchased the premises in 1782. The Maraise family settled then in rue Meslé near Boulevard Saint Martin.
13. On this factory, see M. Garden, *Lyon et les Lyonnais au XVIIIe siècle* (Paris, 1970), pp. 167, 317.
14. Cf. P. Léon, *La naissance de la grande industrie en Dauphiné* (Gap, 1954).
15. On the Cambon factory, see A. Chante, *L'indiennage à Montpellier au XVIIIe*

siècle, unpublished dissertation (Montpellier, 1972). At the Beaucaire fair of 1777 this merchant house alone sold goods to the value of 500,000 *l.*, one-quarter of the whole sales of printed calicoes. AD, Herault: C 2326. On the royal factory at Bourges, see the unpublished thesis by Mlle Girardin (Paris, 1963).
16. AN: 41 AQ 3, letter from Maraise to Oberkampf, 16 Jan. 1774.
17. AN: 41 AQ 82/289.
18. The Parisian office of the factory (*supra*, n. 12) was dealing with correspondence and accounts, not orders or advertising. Orders received there were, nonetheless, passed on to Jouy.
19. AN: 41 AQ 82/94.
20. E.g. Henry Sykes, in partnership with a Genevan merchant called Defernex at the Palais-Royal in Paris from 1786; or J. B. Adeline, a Rouen merchant, both soon to enter mechanised cotton spinning.
21. In 1773, according to letters from Maraise, Oberkampf had plans to export to Spain, Italy and Sicily, but it is not known if he realised them.
22. The Wesserling factory (Alsace) is said to have regularly sold 'more than two million [*l*,] of *toiles peintes*' at the Frankfurt and Leipzig fairs before the French Wars (AN: F12/1564).
23. L. Bergeron, *Banquiers*, II, p. 660 f.
24. AN: 41 AQ 83/21.
25. AN: 41 AQ 83/716 and 858. 79 of the 81 pieces were finally returned by a Hamburg merchant in September 1797 (AN: 41 AQ 84/391).
26. AN: 41 AQ 85/77 and 231, to Sylling & Moll.
27. AN: 41 AQ 3, to Benech brothers of Berlin.
28. AN: 41 AQ 94/410. In 1819 and 1821 the Jouy company thanked two merchants, one from Frankfurt and the other from Leipzig, for their offer of goods sent on consignment.
29. AN: 41 AQ 83/763, to Van der Linden.
30. In 1805 the nine *départements* of Belgium annexed to France included 55 calico printing factories employing 3,386 workers and produced 354,989 pieces (AN: F12/1562-4). The principal factories were situated in two *départments*, Dyle (Anderlecht, Louvain) and Escaut (Ghent), which together accounted for 80 per cent of the Belgian output.
31. AN: 41 AQ 92/903, to G. Choisy & Cie., quoted by L. Bergeron, *Banquiers*, II, p. 678.
32. AN: 41 AQ 4, 4 Nov. 1812. On this depot, see L. Bergeron, *Banquiers*, II, pp. 679–80.
33. AN: 41 AQ 94/277 and 94/296.
34. AN: 41 AQ 95-6, *passim*.
35. AN: 41 AQ 83/300, to Bassolino of Brescia.
36. AN: 41 AQ 94/721. On this depot, see L. Bergeron, *Banquiers*, II, p. 673. At Oberkampf's death the Aubert brothers retained 789 unsold pieces worth 53,539 *f*. (AN: 41 AQ 13).
37. AN: 51 AQ 91/666, to Joly & fils of St. Quentin, 14 Aug. 1810, quoted by L. Bergeron, *Banquiers*, II, p. 247.
38. L. Bergeron, *Banquiers*, II, p. 247.
39. See *infra*, Ch. 12.
40. AN: 41 AQ 13.
41. AN: 41 AQ 90/853 to J. Dewelz.
42. Cf. L. Bergeron, 'Pourtalès & Cie: apogée et declin d'un capitalisme', *Annales E.S.C.*, 1970, no. 2, pp. 498–517.
43. The weaving of linen and cotton fabrics in Beaujolais began in the reign of Louis XIV and developed after 1735 through the initiative of the *intendant* of Lyons, H.-L. Bertin, who became *contrôleur général* in 1760. In 1811, 20 merchant houses of Villefranche marketed the production of 45,000 persons in the *arrondissement* (115,000 inhabitants) employed in spinning and weaving (AN: F12/1551).

44. AN: 41 AQ 1.
45. AN: 41 AQ 3, letter of 28 Nov. 1773.
46. On the London calico printers, see *supra*, Introduction.
47. The Rombergs came from Westphalia and set up in Brussels in 1766. Another branch of the family settled in Bordeaux.
48. Purchases at Bordeaux, Marseilles and Le Havre and carried by water from Rouen to Jouy.
49. Difference with H. Lüthy, *op. cit.*, II, pp. 104–5.
50. AN: 41 AQ 82/7, to Morgan & Massey.
51. AN: 41 AQ 9.
52. Tests of fabrics from Morgan & Massey of Amiens (Dec. 1789), from Vatinelle and from Brown, both of Paris (Jan. 1792), and from Adeline of Rouen (Aug. 1793).
53. AN: 41 AQ 82/685, to Aubertin.
54. *Ibid.*: 82/612, to Pétineau.
55. *Ibid.*: 82/480, to Agniel.
56. *Ibid.*: 82/569 and 641, to Dufresne.
57. AN: 41 AQ 83/55, 195.
58. As can be seen from the visit to Jouy by Couthon in May 1794.
59. AN: 41 AQ 83/791–2.
60. *Ibid.*: 83/741–6.
61. A Genevan family, members of the ruling oligarchy until overturned in 1782, then restored at the French occupation: H. Lüthy, *op. cit.*, II, *passim*. The Hamburg branch had connections with the Manchester textile trade through N. M. Rothschild: see the Rothschild letters at the London bank.

Chapter 12

1. AN: 41 AQ 85/182, to Pierre Aubertin of London, 14 Nov. 1799.
2. *Ibid.*: 85/111, to Rougemont & Fesquet of London, 20 Sep. 1799.
3. L. Bergeron, *Banquiers*. Oberkampf wrote to his London agent, James Cazenove, that 'imports of Indian callicoes are still allowed without a pedigree, but caution is necessary' (AN: 41 AQ 85/594, Jul. 1800).
4. AN: 41 AQ 86/113, to Ripley & Rivier of London. In February 1803 Philippe Rivier retired and the firm became Ripley, Weiss & Co.
5. *Ibid.*: 86/334, 531, 914, to Ch. F. Brandt of Manchester.
6. See R. Dufraisse, 'La politique douanière de Napoléon', *Revue de l'Institut Napoléon*, 130 (1974), pp. 3–25.
7. AN: 41 AQ 87/119, to Schumacher-Overmann of Brussels, 24 messidor XI (Jun. 1803); *ibid.*: 87/147, to Blanquart of Gent, 13 thermidor XI.
8. *Ibid.*: 87/287, to Schumacher, 27 vendémiaire XII.
9. AN: 41 AQ 82–4, *passim*, to Adeline of Rouen, 31 Aug. 1792; to Morgan of Amiens, 27 messidor IX; to Bauwens of Paris, 5 messidor XI; to Bardel of Paris, 11 fructidor XI.
10. AN: 41 AQ 87/521, to Petit-Senn of Geneva, 23 ventôse XII.
11. In prairial XI, Oberkampf encouraged Samuel Joly, a trader of St. Quentin, to begin calico weaving: 'I can assure you their sale is certain, and that for a long time it will be a seller's market, even though many firms may enter the industry' (AN: 41 AQ 87/694).
12. AN: 41 AQ 88/731, to Duhéron, his agent at Bordeaux, 22 frimaire XIV.
13. Deed by the Corbeil notary.
14. William Aitkins (or Aitken), was born at Haddington (East Lothian) in 1774 and lived in France from 1802 and may have been employed by Henry Sykes of Saint Rémy-sur-Avre (Eure-et-Loire) to build his spinning wheels. In ventose XI Aitken sent Molard, warden of the *Conservatoire des Arts et Métiers* in Paris, 'a list of

machines I can make' (Arch. C. N. A. M. A359). He subsequently worked at various mills: Richard-Lenoir's in Paris, Lebrun's at Dourdan, Lehoult's at Versailles, Joly's at St. Quentin. He established his own machine building workshops, to build spinning machines, at Senonches (Eure-et-Loire) in March 1810. He was naturalised by decree 1 May 1812 (AN: BB 114).

15. AD, Yvelines: S, Essonne 40. Feray was made Oberkampf's attorney for Essones in March 1805.
16. See his letter to Fesquet of Marseilles quoted by L. Bergeron, *Banquiers*, p. 628.
17. S. Chassagne, 'L'enquête, dite de Champagny, sur la situation cotonnière au début de l'Empire', *R.H.E.S.*, LIV (1976).
18. AN: 41 AQ 88/819. As early as summer 1805 Oberkampf said that the fabrics of Picardy weavers controlled by Joly had reached 'a high degree of perfection', but were still irregular in quality and width and also too expensive (*ibid.*: 88/567).
19. Correspondence with J. Dollfus and Pluvinage of St. Quentin, Houel of Bohéries, Lansel of Valenciennes and Soyer of Noyon.
20. AN: 41 AQ 88/942–9, to L. D. Féret of Cormeilles, 20 May 1806; to Dufrayer of Vaucelles, 26 Jun. 1806.
21. AN: 41 AQ 88/976, to J. Ratton & Sons, to Pilaer-Vanwinghen of Lisbon, 16 Jun. 1806; *ibid.*: 88/979, to Chapeaurouge of Hamburg.
22. For this speculation see L. Bergeron, *Banquiers*, pp. 239–41. The figure for the loss is from AN: 41 AQ 1.
23. AN: 41 AQ 4, to Oberkampf, 1 Mar. 1810. In July Feray applied for a licence to import 3,000 bales of American cotton (AN: F12/509).
24. The earliest purchases of Naples cotton, from F. Degan, took place in July 1809. Other suppliers were Joseph de Weltz of Milan, de Weltz & Violier of Naples, and L. Audra & Co. of Naples. Levant cotton was imported through Humann Bros. of Strasburg, or Haussner & Co. of Salonica. The value of raw cotton purchased was 2,025,781 $f.$ (1810), 1,974,656 $f.$ (1811), 1,081,690 $f.$ (1812) and 315,100 $f.$ (1813). (AN: 41 AQ 129/36–9.)
25. In 1809 Oberkampf valued the initial cost of Chantemerle buildings at 448,000 $f.$ (AN: 41 AQ 5), and at 851,857 $f.$ in the 1810 balance sheet (AN: 41 AQ 129/1).
26. Under John Bland's supervision, the machine building works at Chantemerle assembled cards, rollers, throstles and mules for Joly's mill at St. Quentin (AN: 41 AQ 111/46). In 1810 the works balance was 630,660 $f.$
27. AN: 41 AQ 111/145, L. Feray to the Mayor of Essonnes, 15 Oct. 1812.
28. The overlooker of these workshops was at first a woman, Mme Collin, to whom Feray gave 0.50 $f.$ for every kg. of cotton picked, allowing four per cent waste (AN: 41 AQ 111/7). In July 1812 he sent her the factory rules, to be placarded in every workshop. From the beginning of 1812 a 'cleaning and picking machine' was working at Chantemerle, (AN: 41 AQ 112/38). Next year the system of picking was 'amended to produce a greater perfection in the work, special supervision of the workshops by a *commis*', personal liability of the overlooker to prevent pilfering of cotton, a 0.30 $f.$ bonus for every kg. picked. 'Cutting our rates [of pay] caused some trouble in our outside [domestic] workshops', Feray told Oberkampf in November 1813, and 'a great many workers rejected them, but they will think again. At Chantemerle there are very few discontented' (AN: 41 AQ 4). Jouy employed 90 females cleaning cotton in the period 1810–16.
29. AN: 41 AQ 111/52, Feray to Joly, 5 Nov. 1811.
30. *Ibid.*: 111/352, Feray to Oberkampf, 29 Sep. 1814. On Rolland's mill, see S. Chassagne, 'La formation de la population de Corbeil – Essonnes', *MS*, 97 (1976), p. 91.
31. AN: 41 AQ 113/235, to Hersfeld of Paris, 17 Feb. 1819. There were a few sales to Chatoney of Tarare, La Rochefoucauld of Liancourt, and Ladrière of St. Quentin in 1812–13 (AN: 41 AQ 111/78, 174, 295).
32. *Ibid.*, *passim*.

33. *Ibid.*: 111/16, to F. Morris of Gisors, 12 Aug. 1811.
34. *Ibid.*: 111/363, to Oberkampf at Jouy. Some months earlier, Feray did not believe it possible 'to find cheaper labour nor better weaving than here' (*ibid.*: 111/332).
35. The first such mortgage was sealed 24 October 1806, signed by a merchant of Verly near Guise (Oise) called Longuet. It was cancelled in April 1823 (AN: Min. Cent., LXXXVI, 943, 1021).
36. An early spinning work contract was made with John Dean at Le Houlme and at Bondeville near Rouen. In 1811 he was prosecuted by Oberkampf.
37. AN: 41 AQ 111, *passim*.
38. *Ibid.*: 111/206, to Benoit Legrand of Avon.
39. AN: 41 AQ 94/313, to Féret of Cormeilles, 30 Sep. 1815.
40. AN: 41 AQ 112/22, to Oberkampf, 11 Sep. 1815.
41. On Richard-Lenoir, see C. Ballot, *L'introduction du machinisme dans l'industrie française* (Paris, 1923), pp. 103–12; N. Moniot and Cl. Lazerges, *L'entreprise Richard-Lenoir*, unpublished dissertation (Paris, 1969), 229ff.

Chapter 13

1. This chapter summarises a long article in *MS*, 97 (1976), pp. 39–88.
2. Anzin had 4,000 workers in 1791; see M. Gillet, *Les charbonnages du Nord de la France au XIXe siècle* (Paris, 1973), p. 28. The Royal Glass Factory at Saint-Gobain, near Chauny (Aisne), employed 1,200 workers in 1764, nearly 2,000 in 1787, 1,100 in 1811 and 1,356 in 1820: C. Pris, *The Royal Glass Factory at St. Gobain, 1664–1830*, thesis (Lille, 1975).
3. The next largest works at the end of the *ancien régime'* were the tanneries, dyeworks and flour mills situated on the Bièvre between Gentilly and Paris. The next after that was the Sèvres porcelain factory.
4. Studied by P. Caspard, *La Fabrique-Neuve de Cortaillod ... 1700–1850* (Paris, 1979); for a summary, see *TH*, VIII (1977).
5. Roller printing was started at Jouy in 1787, but the Revolution delayed its application until the Consulat period. Oberkampf accused Lefebre, a Parisian mechanic, of having copied a model of the machine which was put into operation by Oberkampf's nephew, Samuel Widmer, at the Perier brothers' workshops at Chaillot. Lefebre made similar ones for competitors' works at Saint-Denis, Wesserling and Cortaillod (AN: 41 AQ 1).
6. AN: 41 AQ 5.
7. AN: 41 AQ 8.
8. At Cortaillod, according to P. Caspard, *op. cit.*, the proportion of skilled workers fluctuated between 28 and 53 per cent in the century 1754–1854.
9. 'Consigne pour le portier', signed by Oberkampf, a note of October 1812. The janitor stopped any worker who was late and prevented him going in (AN: 41 AQ 1).
10. Examples of dispersed factories: the linens and cambrics of St. Quentin, the *rouenneries* of the *Pays de Caux*; of nebulous factories: the weavers' workshops of the Paris area at the beginning of the nineteenth century (cf. L. Bergeron, *Banquiers*). Similarly, at the important Van Robais cloth factory at Abbeville, which employed 1,692 people in 1716 and 1,529 in 1759, only the preparation of the wool, weaving and cloth finishing were concentrated in the fine building constructed at the beginning of the eighteenth century. All the spinning was done in the homes of the *contremaîtres* for some miles around the town, according to M. Harel, *La manufacture de drap fins Van Robais d'Abbeville*, unpublished thesis (Paris II, 1971).
11. It has only been possible to trace records of the deaths of four child workers

between 1793 and 1822, and these were between 10 and 14 years old: four per cent of workers' deaths in the period. The deaths all occured between 1795 and 1801, just at the moment when war increased the scarcity of adult male labour. At Wesserling between 1800 and 1860 the deaths of two *tireurs* aged 11 were recorded.
12. 82 apprenticeship contracts were recorded by the Jouy notary between 1768 and 1774.
13. About 1800, 50 of the 80 boys of Jouy aged 5 to 12 years (62 per cent) 'were employed in industry' and 25 out of 70 girls of the same age (35 per cent) (AN: 41 AQ 1).
14. About a quarter of the workers who died between 1760 and 1815 were 65 or over, and three per cent over 80. A few were called *rentiers* at their deaths, but not before 1815–20. Before this time it was normal to remain in employment up to death.
15. In nineteenth-century Wesserling no women were recorded as engravers or designers, but some appeared as printers.
16. Pierre-François Pétineau (1760–1830), the elder of Oberkampf's two brothers-in-law, was appointed in charge of a pencillers' workshop in 1792, where it was said that a glance from him terrified the female workers.
17. 28 per cent of the women workers married by the notary recorded an occupation on marriage, but nearly all subsequently worked at the factory.
18. Ulrich Bossert (Aarau 1739 – Jouy 1794) accompanied Oberkampf on his first journey to London in 1773 and was replaced at the head of the factory management two years later by Ludwig Rordorff (Zurich 1742 – Jouy 1810). Bossert supervised the engravers' workshops and Johannes Schramm (Basle 1738 – Jouy 1809) the printers' workshops, with Rordorff taking overall responsibility. Schramm's salary and status did not reach the level of the other two.
19. Guillaume-Vincent Champs (Bièvres 1756 – Jouy 1837), in charge of the engravers from 1792, was listed as *rentier* after 1815, while his brother Louis (Bièvres 1749 – 1827), in charge of the engravers from 1798, appeared as *cultivateur* at his death. Two generations of the Champ family totalled 11 workers at the factory.
20. A similar guard was also found at Wesserling at the beginning of the nineteenth century, created from former soldiers of the Revolution and Empire armies. Oberkampf recruited them at Jouy from among the King's Swiss guards.
21. Following thefts in autumn 1783, Oberkampf advertised a reward of 1,000 *l.* (more than twice the annual income of his printers) 'to anyone who could bring to justice the thieves taking pieces of *toiles* from the fields or from the factory'.
22. Several thieves were arrested on information from other workers of the enterprise. Oberkampf, who preferred to catch the thief red-handed, did not hesitate to search any suspected worker himself, or organise a trap with his nephew Samuel.
23. In 1806 the Wesserling partners petitioned the Emperor 'for a police regulation to prevent the seduction of workers by jealous competitors'. (AN: F12/1564).
24. 'Outsiders' (*horsains*) indicates those who were strangers to the local 'culture', but there were very few of them. This group was quite distinct from the foreigners (*étrangers*) who generally came of the same German-speaking and Protestant culture as Oberkampf.
25. The population of Jouy and of five neighbouring parishes in the Bièvre valley increased by 8.4 per cent in the period 1740–60 (Jouy alone more than 11 per cent), and 89 per cent between 1760 and 1790 (Jouy 204 per cent), and then remained stable up to the middle of the nineteenth century.
26. Launched in spring 1799 by the Parisian manufacturers Gremont & Barré and at first limited to making-up, they were succeeded by the Dollfus family of Mulhouse in 1803, until their failure in 1840.
27. During Oberkampf's lifetime the notary arranged only one worker's employment contract: in 1770, when the entrepreneur decided to introduce copper plate

244 European Textile Printers in the Eighteenth Century

printing. He aimed to secure the secrecy of three of his printers to whom he confided the new method. After his death his successors engaged four technicians on long contracts of between six and 10 years.

28. AN: 41 AQ 5, memo. from Sarrasin, 12 Oct. 1780.
29. Not the same as the Perriers of Saclay, a family of royal pond keepers, one of whom (Étienne-Denis, 1761–1845) became a *commis* at the time of the Revolution. Two sons followed him into the factory.
30. In 1806 François-Marc the elder borrowed 2,000 *f*. from his master to build a house, contracting to repay at 90 *f*. a month. In 1812 the members of the Perrier family were no longer in possession of any property outside the village; the ancestral plot had been sold to enable them to settle in the village.
31. The occupations of the fathers of 296 male wage earners known for the period 1760–1815 (149 printers, 67 labourers, 34 engravers, 30 *commis*, 14 designers and two others). In 41 per cent of the cases, the social origin was rural and agricultural, and it was greater only for labourers (70 per cent), with printers, designers, *commis* and engravers together 37 per cent. Moreover, more than one-third of the workers included in the sample changed their socio-professional status during their period at the Jouy works with the probability of promotion as much as to a higher level than a lower. There was a further channel of social mobility, leaving paid employment for small trade (e.g. shop keeping). Between 1760 and 1820, 19 workers became independent in this way, four returning to their ancestral land.
32. 37.8 per cent of all workers were sons of factory wage earners; labourers of the second generation were 26 per cent, engravers 32 per cent and designers 35.7 per cent, while the *commis* grade were 40 per cent and printers 43.6 per cent sons of Jouy workers.
33. Homogamy (bridegroom and father-in-law both workers at the factory) was 45 per cent before 1792, 60 per cent afterwards. But half of the *commis* grade and of the engravers found a wife outside factory employment.
34. The only claims for wage increases that have been traced refer to printers in 1792 and in 1797; see *supra*, Ch. 9.
35. '20 sols for the short days, 24 for the others' in 1770; 35 sols a day in winter and 45 in summer in 1787; 50 sols in winter and 60 in summer in 1799.
36. See Table 24. The average salary at Jouy rose from 190 *l*. in 1780 to 400 *f*. in the years 1804–6.
37. The savings bank at the Wesserling factory was opened in 1821, that of Mulhouse in 1827. The pioneer Paris savings bank, started by Delessert, the banker, and a group of Protestant and liberal anglophiles in 1818, was imitated at Bourdeaux and Metz (1819), Rouen (1820), Nantes and Marseilles (1821), and Le Havre and Lyons (1822).
38. According to his inventory his personal estate amounted to only 2,500 *f*., along with 1,000 *f*. cash.

Conclusion

The principal sources for this summary are contained in the preceding biographical essays. The following references are limited to materials not listed there, or which are not easily identified.

1. J. J. Waitzfelder, *Der Augsburger Johann Heinrich von Schuele* (Leipzig, 1929). H. Hallwich, *Firma Franz Leitenberg, 1793–1893. Eine Denkschrift* (Prague, 1893), esp. Chs. 3, 4.
2. S. D. Chapman, 'The Textile Factory before Arkwright: A Typology of Factory Development', *BHR*, XLVIII (1974).

3. H. J. Habakkuk, *American and British Technology* (Cambridge, 1967), p. 112.
   Cf. Ryhiner of Basle, cited in the Introduction, *supra*.
4. Cf. D. Landes, 'Religion and Enterprise: the Case of the French Textile Industry', in E. C. Carter, R. Forster and J. N. Moody (eds.), *Enterprise and Entrepreneurs in ... France* (Baltimore, 1976).
5. See especially Selma Stern, *The Court Jew. A Contribution to the History of the Period of Absolutism in Central Europe* (Philadelphia, 1950).
6. *Cum Privilegio Sacrae Caesareae Majestatis*. Johann Henrich Edler von Schuele; see F. E. von Seida, *J. H. E. von Schuele* ... (Leipzig, 1805), Appendix, p. 42. H. Hallwich, *op. cit.*, p. 59.
7. H. J. Habakkuk, *op. cit.*, p. 133.
8. The case for science as an independent variable in eighteenth-century industrialisation is pressed by A. E. Musson and E. Robinson, *Science and Technology in the Industrial Revolution* (Manchester, 1969). They do not, however, deal with calico printing, on which the historians of technology are much more sceptical: e.g. F. Brunello, *The Art of Dyeing in the History of Mankind* (Vicenza, 1973), p. 236. A. Thackray, 'Natural Knowledge in Cultural Context', *American Historical Review*, LXXIX (1974), p. 705.
9. S. M. Edelstein, *Historical Notes on the Wet-Processing Industry* (New York, 1972), pp. 83–7.
10. M. Lévy-Leboyer, *Les banques*, pp. 49, 65–6, 169–71, 288–92.
11. F. F. Mendels, 'Proto-Industrialisation: the first phase of the industrial process', *Journal of Economic History*, XXXII (1972).
12. S. D. Chapman, *Factory Masters*, p. 71. John Butt (ed.), *Robert Owen, Prince of Cotton Spinners* (1971), esp. pp. 170–3.
13. *SC on Children in Manufactories*, PP, 1816, III, p. 136.
14. P. Caspard, 'L'accumulation du capital dans l'Indiennage au XVIIIème siècle', *Revue du Nord*, LXI (1979).
15. P. Caspard, *op. cit.*, p. 119. Cf. C. O'Brien, *The British Manufacturer's Companion* (1790), quoted by S. M. Edelstein, *op. cit.*, pp. 53–4.
16. Prices of Jouy prints per ell (1.20 m. or 1.3 yds.) in
    1790 print of 'The Flemish Feast' = 3 *l*. 5 sols = 2s. 7d.
    1791 prints on muslins 26–28 inches wide = 50–60 sols = 2s. 4d.–2s. 8d.
    1791 prints on muslins 34–50 inches 60–80 sols = 2s. 8d.–3s. 4d.
    1811 monochrome copper prints (new designs) = 7 *f*. = 2s. 9d.
        machine printed – 1.60 *f*. = 7d.
    (Source: AN: 57 AQ.)
17. Musée des Arts Decoratifs, Nantes, *Toiles de Nantes des XVIIIe et XIXe siècles* (1978).
18. J. G. Dingler, *Journal für Zitz-, Kattun-, und Indiennendruckerei* (Augsburg, 1806), I, p. 63.
19. A. K. Longfield, 'Earliest Copyright Acts for Cotton Printing Designs', *Burlington Magazine*, XCV (1958).
20. AN: T1128/3, observations by Daguet, owner of a printing works at Coye (Oise) to his partners, 20 Nov. 1772.
21. Sample books in Forney Lib., Paris; Res. 677.064 G2. See also designs collected by H. Clouzot, *loc. cit.*, e.g. 'Branches Montantes de fleurettes' (*c*. 1775) and 'Fleurettes à la planche' (1780).
22. See also W. Kurrer, *Geschichte der Zeugdruckerei* (Nuremburg, 1840), for Schuele's prints.
23. *ME*, 16 Nov. 1850.
24. J. J. Waitzfelder, *op. cit.*, passim.
25. P. O'Brien and C. Keyder, *Economic Growth in Britain and France 1780–1914* (1978), esp. pp. 91, 158.
26. For a different type of product, see e.g. S. Chassagne, *Tournemine*, p. 239, for Danton Frères output of *mouchoirs*.

27. D. Dollfus-Ausset, *Materiaux*, II, p. 16. For the Nuremburg roller printing machine of 1699, see *supra*, Introduction, n. 21.
28. AN: F12/2295, 21 Mar. 1819.
29. K. N. Chaudhuri, *The Trading World of Asia and the English East India Company 1660–1760* (Cambridge, 1978), p. 273.
30. C. P. Kindleberger, 'Commercial Expansion and the Industrial Revolution', *JEEcH*, IV (1975), p. 632.

Index of Subjects

Agents abroad, 86, 15ff
Alsatian calico printing, 8, 11, 92, 130–31, 151
American market, 18, 86–7, 205, 215
American War of Independence, 28, 86, 157
Apprenticeship, 43, 52, 97–8, 173–5; *see also* Artisan training
Arkwright mills, 16, 37–8, 48, 60, 127, 201, 202
Artisan training, 7, 39, 43, 65, 67, 94ff, 186–7, 194–5; *see also* Apprenticeship

Bankruptcy, 26–8, 30, 68, 77, 86, 109, 167, 200
Banks, 28, 33, 70, 73, 76, 203
Bleaching, 25, 49–50, 140f, 196
Book printing, influence on calico printing, 11
Brewing industry, 36, 76

Canals, 52, 62, 66
Capital formation, 70–71, 119, 121, 127, 134–8, 201ff
'China Blue' prints, 16, 26, 45, 113
Colonial trade, 5, 6, 86
Commission printing, 147, 151
Consumption of printed textiles, 3, 58, 91
Continental market, 88–92, 207, 208
Copper plate printing, 13, 18–19, 28, 96, 113, 131–3, 218–9
Copyright of designs, 79, 205
Costs, analysis of, 139, 198, 216–17
Cotton mills *see* Arkwright mills; Crompton; Hargreaves
Cotton
  spinning, 3, 36–42, 163–6, 197
  weaving, 3, 50, 52, 62, 165–6, 168–170

wool, import of 71, 155, 164–5
Credit, 29, 33, 68, 70–71, 138, 149, 203
Customs duties, 65, 108, 162–4

Derby silk mill, 16
Design, 5, 18, 36, 78–84, 88, 130, 132, 205, 208
Designers, 13, 58, 79, 95, 127, 132, 148, 178, 205, 208
Division of labour, 15–16, 40, 95ff, 172ff
Domestic system, *see* Cotton weaving
'Drugs', *see* Dyestuffs
Dyestuffs, 71, 88, 143, 158, 196
Dynasties, 4, 73, 68–9, 114, 178–9, 200, 207

East India companies, 92, 103, 156–157, 161, 207
Entrepreneurs
  numbers in calico printing, 7–11
  personalities, 55–6, 68, 78, 94, 111ff, 109f, 186ff
Exhibitions of industry, 142
Exports, *see* various markets: American market, Continental market, India (exports to) etc.

Factory discipline, 40, 56, 98, 123, 127, 172, 174, 177, 209
Factory system, origins of, 6, 59–60, 125ff
Fairs, 8–9, 89, 92, 207
Farming, and textile industry, 36, 178, 194
Fashion, 3, 18, 119, 200, 204–5, 208
Fixed capital, 14, 16, 17, 19, 51, 53, 75–6, 108–9, 134–8, 201–2
Friendly societies, 56, 122, 209

Fustian weaving, 13

German émigres
 artisans, 6–7, 111ff, 119, 176
 merchants, 5, 89, 91, 159, 203
German market, 89ff, 150–51
Government controls, 6, 9, 45, 65, 104ff, 162f, 190f, 211
Guild restrictions, 7, 191, 210

Handloom weaving, 50, 62, 98
Horse gins, 20, 201
Housing, of workers, 52, 59, 218
Huguenots
 craftsmen, 10
 merchants, 5, 10, 162

India
 exports to, 89, 92–3
 imports from, 18, 79, 92, 103, 156–157, 159, 195, 198, 214
Indigo, 12, 19, 26, 106–7
Inflation, 123, 160, 162
Insurance valuations, xv, 45–6, 51, 53, 58–9, 217–19
Inventors
 cotton spinning, 37–40
 calico printing, 12–13, 16–20, 44, 82, 138ff
 muslin weaving, 41f
Italian market 151–2

Jewish merchants, 5, 7, 90–91, 189

Labour costs, 28, 194
 recruitment, 67, 95, 177ff, 124; *see also* Apprenticeship
 relations, 31–2, 65, 94ff, 122–3; *see also* Riots
 scarcity, 67, 96, 177, 192, 194–5
Labour force, size of, *see* Workforce
Legislation
 cotton factories, 100
 calico printing, 9, 45, 65, 104–5, 190
Location of calico printing
 Blackburn, 25, 43
 Bolton, 49
 Burton, 47
 Bury, 57
 Europe, 6–11
 France, 103ff
 Lancs., 26, 63
 London, 28
 Tamworth, 65–6
 comparative advantages, 207f

cotton spinning, 29, 38, 41, 42, 47, 49, 60–63, 75, 163, 170, 174

Machine building, 39, 50, 67
Management, 71–4, 76, 97, 168, 174, 176–7, 180, 200–201, 214
Marketing, 18, 78ff, 132–3, 147ff, 199, 204ff
Medical supervision, 97, 182
Mercantilism, 104ff
Merchants, 4, 5, 28, 47, 70–71, 74–5
Methodism, 56, 72
Migration
 calico printing industry, 9–10
 apprentices, 97
 calico printers, 6–10, 26, Ch. 8
Mordants, 12, 197
Muslin manufacture, 50

Output
 Peel, 58, 79, 99, 213
 Oberkampf, 126ff, 145, 148
 other printers, 213
Outriders, *see* Travellers

Patent litigation, 63
Pattern books, 83–4
Pencilling, 12, 65, 96, 99, 195, 218–19
Picotage, 19, 80, 82, 96, 99, 195
Plagiarism, of designs, 80–81, 197, 205
Political ideology, 189–91
Prices
 printed calicoes, 79, 82, 84, 87, 90, 153–4, 159, 204, 207
 yarns and fabrics, 84
Productivity, 20, 21, 44, 198, 211–15
Profits, 35, 67, 70, 126, 136–7, 144, 203
Proto-industrialisation, 4, 194, 199
Proto-factory, 16–17, 194, 199

Raw material supplies, 71, 207
Religion, 56, 68–9, 72, 116–17, 121, 189, 195–6
Resist printing, 12, 105–6, 195
Revolution, French, and industry, 121, 132–3, 138, 151, 160–61, 211
Riots, 17, 37, 46, 210
Roller printing, 11, 20, 30, 32, 43–4, 65, 140, 143, 212
Royal factories and patronage, 7, 114–15, 174, 191–2
Rural labour force, 94

Scale of industry, 14–15, 29–30, 175, 202
Science, influence on industrial development, 74, 138, 140ff, 195ff
Scottish calico printing, 8–10, 81, 146
Silk industry, 6, 28, 119
Social mobility, upward, 7, 58, 73–4, 177, 179–181, 186–7, 191
State control, *see* Government controls
Steam power, 20, 48, 60–61, 143, 202
Sulphuric acid manufacture, 28, 49, 140, 143
Swiss calico printing, 8–9, 11, 81, 89, 130–31, 133
Swiss emigrés, 111, 131–2, 156, 177, 179

Technology of calico printing, 10ff, 42ff, 130ff, 192ff
Trade marks, 147, 150

Trade unions in calico printing, 31–32, 65, 98–9, 210–11
Travellers, 85, 89

Verlegers, 25, 34, 36, 70, 185
Verlagssystem, *see* Cotton weaving, *Verlegers*

Wages, 32–3, 66–7, 96–9, 166, 170, 172, 180–81, 198
Warehouse sector (Manchester), 85
Water power, 19–20, 28, 47, 59, 61, 70, 125, 126, 163
Wood block printing, 11, 17, 19, 26, 28, 34–5, 42, 44, 45, 58, 80, 82, 96, 132, 217
Woollen industry, 16, 28, 34, 47, 66, 67
Workforce, size of, 15, 28–9, 57, 172–6, 213
Working capital, 17, 71, 134–8, 149, 203

Index of People and Places

Aarau, 130, 141
Aberdeen, 79
Accrington, 52, 53, 210
Agen, 8
Aikin, Dr J., 57, 58
Ainsworth, 26, 27, 45
Ainsworth, Peter, 42, 50
Ainsworth, Richard, 42, 50
Ainsworth, Thomas, 41, 42, 50, 61, 75, 195
Aisne, 166
Aitkins, William, 163
Albert, Rene, 109
Alencon, 169
Allen & Co., 28
Altham, 46, 52
Altona, 161
Amiens, 11, 159
Amsterdam, 4–7, 13, 103, 130, 185, 197, 199, 207
Amyard, George, 18
Anderlecht, 175
Anderton, 41
Angers, 109, 111, 135, 155, 159, 175, 179
Anglesey, 49
Anjou, 8, 106
Annécy, 175
Anstie, John, 28, 30
Antwerp, 7, 14, 15, 153, 158, 185, 213
Appenzell, 14
Arbuthnot, John, 156
Argentan, 169
Arkwright, Sir Richard (& Co.), 3, 16, 33, 37–41, 48, 52, 56, 63, 65, 67, 74, 187, 190, 200, 202, 209
Arsenal (Paris), 111
Ashby-de-la-Zouch, 75, 76
Ashton, 41
Ashworth brothers, 202
Asterleys, 20

Atherton, Peter, 47, 61, 74
Athis, 169
Aubert brothers, 153
Audra, 154
Augsburg, 7, 11, 17, 18, 20, 60, 187, 188, 192, 194, 197, 201, 202, 207, 208, 210, 214
Aunay, 169
Avignon, 100

Bacup, 62
Baden-Durlach, Margrave of, 114
Baines, Edward, 20, 25, 30
Bakewell, 38
Bamber Bridge, 25
Bancroft, Edward, 142
Banks, Sir Joseph 146
Bannister Hall, 29
Barbet, 154
Barcelona, 7, 8, 14
Baron, Jacques, 16, 17, 109, 133, 213
Baron, Saue & Cie, 15, 17
Baroud & Cie, 175
Barrau brothers, 154
Basle, 7, 9, 13, 14, 130, 142, 150, 187
Battersea, 28
Beaucaire, 207
Beauford, Louis, 131
Beauvais, 15, 109, 122, 135, 175, 213
Belfast, 10
Bell, Thomas, 20, 30, 31, 140
Belper, 38, 39, 50, 202
Bergeron, Louis, 5
Berlin, 6
Berne, 9, 14, 130, 187
Berthollet, 49, 143, 146, 196
Besançon, 150
Bethmann, 203
Beuvron, Duke of, 126
Bienne, 175
Bièvres, 179

Index of People and Places   251

Bickerdike, Gideon, 47
Birmingham, 76, 92
Bland, John, 165
Blackburn, 8, 13, 25, 29, 30, 34–6, 42, 43, 45, 46, 52, 53, 97, 207
Bolton, 26, 40–43, 46, 49, 50–52, 60, 73, 203
Bolza, Count, 7
Bond End, 48
Bonehill, 67
Booth, William, 165
Bordeaux, 8, 151, 154, 160
Borgogne, 151
Bossert, 130, 177
Bouchard & Cie, 148
Boulton & Watt, 73, 76, 146
Bourges, 131, 149, 175, 213
Bourgoin, 18
Boussard, 177
Brandt, Charles-Friederich, 146, 159, 162
Bremen, 6, 13, 89, 113
Breng, 131
Brenier & Cie, 109
Bridgewater Canal, 49
Brookside, 36, 37
Brussels, 153, 157, 162
Brütel brothers, 115
Bulwell (Notts), 38
Burch, 43
Burnley, 46, 50–52, 53, 62
Burton, James, 44
Burton-on-Trent, 38, 46–8, 73–6, 194
Bury, 34, 38, 40, 43, 46, 52, 53, 57, 59, 63, 70–74, 95–7, 99, 187, 188, 194, 203, 213

Cabannes, 107
Caen, 104, 169
Cambon, 149
Campbell, 19
Canals, Esteban, 14
Cark-in-Cartmel, 38, 47
Carlisle, 10, 20, 79
Carolina, 10
Caspard, Pierre, 203
Cennini, 11
Chadkirk, 26
Chaillot, 138, 140
Chalmassy, Mallet de, 121
Chamber Hall, 57
Chamberlain & Cuzzins, 7
Champs brothers, 177
Chantemerle, 136, 163, 167
Chapeaurouge, 161, 162, 164

Chapel, 62
Chaptal, 146, 196
Chaudhuri, Dr K. N., 214
Cheapside (London), 45, 47, 76
Choisy, George & Cie, 153
Chorley, 50, 51
Church, 45, 46, 52, 53, 60, 63, 73
Clayton
   Edward, 25, 26, 96
   family, 25, 34, 35
Clitheroe, 29, 30, 52, 74
Colbert, 103, 104
Colmar, 18, 142
Colne, 50, 62
Copenhagen, 7
Corbeil, 17, 18, 131, 133, 134, 155, 169, 201
Cormeilles, 164
Coromandel, 156
Cortaillod, 171, 175, 178, 208
Cottin, Jacques-Daniel, 107, 115, 120, 125
Coye, 109
Crayford, 28, 156
Cromford, 38, 39, 67, 202
Crompton, Samuel, 40, 41, 50, 188
Cunliffe, Dr Ellis, 97

Dagnet & Moll, 109
Dailly, 119, 140
Daintry, Ryle & Co., 62
Dale, David, 200
Dambrugge, 175
Danton brothers, 106, 159
Danton-Moreau & Cie, 109, 135, 175
Darcel, Mary-Katherin, 120
Darwen, 62
Davais, Pierre, 107
Davison & Hawksley, 100
De Broen, Jan, 7
Deneufville family, 6, 185
Denize, Nicholas, 109
Derby, 16
Derby, Lord, 33
Devizes (Wilts), 28
De Vos, 175
De Waldner, 15
Dewelz & Cie, 154
De Wisser, 15, 213
Dickenson, Edward, 76
Dickenson, William, 76
Dickenson & Goodall, 76
Dietrick, 158
Dijonval factory, 202
Dingier, 44, 205

Dollfus & Cie, 15
Dollfus, Meiz & Cie, 143, 175
Dosthill, 76
Douglas, Atherton & Co., 38
Douglas, William, 47, 75
Drayton Manor, 67
Drinkwater, Peter, 61, 85
Dubais-Moreau, 162
Dublin, 8–10, 14, 18, 25, 131
Duck, Robert, 74
Dufay, 5, 105
Dufrayer, 164
Duheron, 154
Dunkerque, 151
Dupasquier, 17, 203, 208
Dupasquier & Cie, 175, 213
Dupont & Cie, 175
Durham, 47

East India Co., 20, 156, 157, 161, 198
Ebingre, 140
Eccles, 49
Ecouché, 169
Edinburgh, 10, 25
Elton, 57
Emmedingen, 114
Empaytaz, Friederich, 151
Erlangen, 7
Essonnes, 17, 20, 109, 163, 167, 172, 174, 178, 213
Eure, 168

Fazeley (Tamworth), 66, 67
Feray, J. B., 161, 167–8
Feray, Louis, 114, 123, 144, 163
Feret, Louis-David, 164
Ferguson, Samuel, 87
Fevez-Ghesquier, 153
Fisher, Samuel Rowland, 43
Floud, Peter, 16, 18
Forberger, Rudolf, 10
Forbonnais, Veron de, 105
Fourcray, 196
Foxlow & Bazin, 175
Franche-Comté, 151
Frankfurt, 5, 6, 89, 90, 91, 115, 187, 199, 207
Fresnay, 169
Friederich, Mme, 205, 208

Garnier, Danse, Thévard & Cie, 109, 135, 175
Gay-Lussac, 143, 196
Geiselbronn, 142
Geneva, 6, 8, 9, 14, 107, 133, 150, 175

Genoa, 154
Ghent, 10, 11, 153, 175
Gibson & Johnson, 28
Gillet, Montaut, Seimandy & Liquier, 135
Gisburn, 52
Glasgow, 8–10, 34, 92, 144, 146
Goldschmidt, 203
Gontard, 5
Gontaud, Duke of, 147
Gorgerat, 205
Gosset, 126
Gournay, Vincent de, 106, 108
Grant brothers, 60, 85
Grant, Samuel, 14
Greaves, James, 73
Greenfield, 47
Gregg, Samuel (& Co.), 62
Grenoble, 119
Gros, Roman & Davilliers, 175
Guerbette, 208
Guillaume, Imhoff, 135

Haffner, Henri, 120, 125, 130, 172
Harguenau, 131, 142
Haigh, John, 47
Hall, William, 28, 30
Hollwell, James, 58, 73
Hamburg, 5–7, 11, 13, 89, 151, 161, 162, 164, 197, 199
Hamer, 71, 72
Harcourt, 169
Hardman, Mr, 72
Harewood, 52
Hargreaves
  Mary, 37
  James, 20, 30, 37, 39, 40, 46, 188
Harrison, William, 74
Hartmann family, 142
Hartmann-Riege, 213
Haslingden, 52
Haussmann, 142, 213
Heilbronn, 113
Heilmann, 117, 143
Hellot, 106
Hendry, Robert, 144, 146, 196
Henry, Dr, 49
Herison, 156
Heywood, 59
Hinds, 38, 59
Hindus, 12
Hodgson, J. & T., 74
Hoghton Tower, 29
Holker, Jean, 13, 25, 38, 39, 140
Holt, David & Co., 42
Holywell (Flint), 38, 47, 75

Index of People and Places 253

Horgen, 41
Horrocks, Samuel, 42
Houldsworth, Henry, 42
Howarth family, 30, 34, 46, 68
  Edmund junior, 36
  Edmund senior, 36
  Giles, 36
  Jane, 35
  John, 46
  Jonathan, 35, 36, 45
Howarths & Peel, 36, 37
Howarth, Peel & Yates, 35, 45
Howarth & Yates, 34
Humblot, 133
Huet, Jean-Baptiste, 132, 148, 204–206, 208
Hulbert, Charles, 67

Imhoff, 109
Ingram, Archibald & Co., 81
Ittier & Reboul, 108, 109

Jacquemart & Bichebois, 148
Jollieu, 149, 177
Jones, Robert, 18, 28, 156
Joseph II, Emperor, 7, 188, 191, 192
Josserand *frères*, 109, 135
Jouy, 18, 60, 95, 109, 113, 115, 116, 118–26, 129, 130, 135, 137, 138, 140, 143, 144, 145, 147, 150, 154–6, 161, 162, 167, 168, 171–174, 176–9, 187, 188, 194, 196, 203, 207, 210, 211, 213
Julien, Claude, 106

Karlsruhe, 115
Keittinger *père*, 109, 135
Kennedy, James, 42, 75
Keyder, Caglar, 211, 212
Kindleberger, 215
Kinsky, Count, 4
Koechlin, 4, 143, 169, 209

Laigle, 169
Lambeth, 28
Latchford, 51
Lausanne, 6
Lawrence, Sir Thomas, 55
Leeds, 89, 146
Lefebvre, Benjamin, 140, 143
Legrand & Hermel, 111
Lehault, 175
Le Havre, 148, 161
Leipzig, 7, 89, 151, 207
Leitenberg, Johann Joseph, 7, 185–187, 189, 192, 199, 203, 204
Lesage, 149
Lesage & Cie, 175, 213
Lesourd de Lisle, 109, 135
Legrelle, 175
Levasseur & Cie, 126
Levin, 194, 199
Lévy-Leboyer, Prof, M., 5, 9, 198
Lille, 153
Linby (Notts), 38
Lisbon, 102, 103
Liverpool, 50, 52, 62, 63, 71
Livesey family, 28
  John Thomas, 30
  Robert James Richard, 28, 30
Livesey, Hargreaves & Co., 3, 20, 29–33, 42, 43, 46, 57, 58, 63, 71, 78, 89, 95, 98, 99, 187, 194
Lloyd, Sampson, 47
Logalbach, 142, 213
London, 4–6, 10, 11, 13, 14, 16, 17, 20, 26, 28–32, 34, 35, 42, 43, 46, 58, 65, 79, 96, 103, 130, 131, 136, 151, 156, 157, 159–62, 185, 197, 198, 207, 212, 215
Lorient, 4, 136, 148, 159, 160, 207
Lörrach, 114, 115
Louis XVI, 188
Louvais, 104
Lüthy, Prof. H., 4
Lyons, 8, 10, 133, 147, 149, 151–3, 168
Lyon-Vaise, 135

Macclesfield, 62
Mainville, J., 175
Mamers, 169
Manchester, 5, 8–10, 25–31, 38, 39, 41–3, 47, 49, 50–52, 53, 58, 60, 63, 64, 66, 67, 70–74, 89, 92, 146, 162, 205, 207, 212
Maraise, Joseph-Alexandre Sarassin de, 119–21, 126, 133, 134, 136, 138, 147, 188, 190, 196, 203
Maraise, Mme de, 118, 134, 138
Maria Theresa, Empress, 7, 188
Marsden, 47
Marseilles, 6–8, 103, 106, 133, 149, 151, 153, 177
Marshall, 209
Marsland, Peter, 42
Massieu, Anna Michelle, 121
McConnel, 75
McConnel & Kennedy, 42
Measham, 75, 76
Melun, 109, 135

Mendels, Prof. F., 199
Mennacy, 138
Merle, 168
Merton (Surrey), 18
Meynier, 148
Middleton, 50, 51
Midol, G., 167
Milford, 38
Mill Hill (Bolton), 49, 50
Mitcham, 156
Mollieu, J. J., 109
Montalivet, 154
Montaran, Michan de, 105
Montpellier, 8, 109, 135, 149, 151, 153
Morat, 131
Morellet, Abbé, 108
Morlet, 108, 111, 133
Mortagne, 169
Moscow, 7
Mosney, 29–31, 43
Mottet, Roche & Cie, 154
Mulheim, 114
Mulhouse, 8, 17, 18, 115, 130, 148, 151, 175, 208, 213
Mulsant, Sebastian, 168
Munich, 7
Munn, John, 26, 156
Munster, 142, 175, 185, 199, 213
Murray, A. and G., 42
Musée de l'Impression sur Etoffes (Mulhouse), 13

Nantes, 8, 10, 17, 18, 107, 109, 179, 199
Naples, 154, 165
Napoleon, 172, 188, 191
Nash, Thomas, 28, 185
Navier, 165
Need, Samuel, 74
Neuchâtel, 6, 8, 9, 17, 18, 107, 130, 140, 150, 185, 213
Neuhofer, 7
Neumeister, 7
Neuville, 175
Newcastle-under-Lyme, 74
New Lanark, 202
New York, 86
Nicholson, W., 142
Nixon, Francis, 18
Norris, Mr, 72
Nottingham, 38, 47, 100, 122
Nuremberg, 187

Oakenshaw printworks, 52

Oberkampf
 family pedigree, 114
 Christoff-Philipp
  family and background, 111ff, 113ff, 114–18, 120, 121, 130, 187, 189, 195, 196
  personal career, 18, 112, 114–116, 121, 122, 131, 143, 154, 172, 185, 187, 188, 190–92, 199, 215
  capital, 126, 134–6, 138ff, 148–150, 153, 168, 170, 198
  partnerships, 17, 119–21, 125, 126, 133, 134, 151, 156, 167, 188, 203ff
  marketing, 127, 130, 147–51, 153ff, 156, 158–61, 163, 165, 168ff, 197, 202, 204, 205ff, 207ff, 208
  industrial relations, 122–4, 140, 146, 171, 174ff, 176, 177ff, 180–182, 201ff, 209–11
  production methods, 130–33, 136, 138, 140ff, 147, 151, 155–157, 159, 162, 163, 195ff, 196, 208, 214
 Emile, 114, 121, 152, 153
 Emilie, 114, 121
 Friederich (Frédéric), 17, 113, 115, 121, 126, 130, 131, 133, 157, 172
 Laura, 114, 121
 Matheus 113, 114
 Philip-Jakob, 113–16
 Sophia-Dorothea, 113–17
Oberkampf & Cie, 135, 136, 138; see also Sarassin, Oberkampf & Cie
O'Brien, Charles, 21, 26, 31, 32, 80, 208, 211, 212
O'Brien, Patrick, 211–12
Old Ford (London), 18, 28
Orange, 15, 17, 18, 122, 131, 155, 159, 175, 213
Orléans, 8, 175
Osnabruck, 185
Oswaldtwistle, 36
Othmarsingen, 130
Owen, Robert, 202

Padiham (Lancs), 52, 62
Paisley, 50, 51, 146
Paris, 4, 5, 8, 10, 106, 109, 115, 121, 143, 149–51, 157, 159, 166, 167, 170, 175, 177, 190, 199, 207, 212
Paris & Chalard, 109
Parsons, 18, 131
Passavant family, 5

Index of People and Places   255

Peel
  family pedigree, 68
  Arthur (First Lord), 68–9
  John, 61, 68, 76
  Jonathan, 45, 48, 68, 73
  Joseph, 68, 73, 76, 77, 80
  Laurence, 45, 68, 70
  Robert ('Parsley'), 34–6, 45–50, 52, 57, 60, 63–5, 68, 71, 98, 186, 197, 200
  (Sir) Robert I (first bart., 1750–1830)
    family and background, 36, 38, 40, 54ff, 69, 186, 187, 195, 200
    personal career, 53, 54, 56ff, 62, 63ff, 65, 68, 69, 70, 72, 73, 77, 187, 188, 190, 191, 209
    capital, 57, 62, 66–8, 70–72, 76, 202–3
    partnerships, 40, 45, 48, 57, 58, 72, 74, 76ff, 203
    marketing, 78ff, 84, 85, 87, 92ff, 204, 205, 207, 208
    industrial relations, 72ff, 94, 97–9, 100ff, 209ff
    production methods, 61, 78, 82, 84, 195–7, 202–3, 212, 214
  (Sir) Robert II (prime minister), 62, 68
  William, 45, 65, 68
Peel, Ainsworth & Co., 42, 50
Peel, Greaves & Co., 73, 76
Peel, Joseph & Co., 80
Peel, Wilkes & Co., 68, 75–7
Peel, Yates & Co., 40, 45, 46, 48, 58, 59, 65, 73, 81, 86, 96
Peel 'Cut' (canal), 48
Pelloutier, 199
Percival, Dr Thomas, 190, 196
Perkin, 196
Perier brothers, 138, 140, 144, 209
Perrenod, 109, 130–32
Perrenod & Cie, 135
Perrier family, 179–80
Pétineau family, 114, 144, 159
Petit & Senn, 175
Petitpierre, 205
Petre, Lord, 46
Philadelphia, 80
Philips & Lee, 39, 61
Picot-Fazy, 149
Pitt, William, 65, 92
Plauen, 7
Pont, Gaillard & Cie, 154
Pont, Rainaldi & Cie, 148
Potts, Charles, 74

Pourtalès & Cie, 154, 156, 185, 199
Pouyer-Quertier, 202
Prague, 7, 199
Preston, 10, 20, 25, 29, 30, 33, 42, 100, 140
Preston, Thomas, 156
Preval, 168
Pyner & Woodward, 156

Radcliffe (Lancs), 38, 39
Ramsbottom, 58, 59, 73, 74
Rees, Abraham, 202
Rennie, John, 20, 26
Rheims, 150
Ribchester, 52
Richard-Lenoir, 169, 170, 175, 209
Ripley & Riviers, 162
Risler, 151
Rivier, M. Théodore, 161
Roanne, 162
Roberts, Christopher, 43
Roberts, John, 73
Robin of Versailles, 157
Robinson (cotton spinners), 38, 42
Rocester (Staffs.), 38
Rochdale, 59
Rochefoucauld, Francois de, 88
Rohdorff, 130, 156, 181
Rolland, F. A., 167
Roman, 142
Romberg, F., 157
Rother & Koechlin, 109
Rothschild, Mayer Amschel, 90
Rothschild, N. M., 5, 91
Rotterdam, 158
Rouen, 103, 109, 140, 148, 149, 154, 157–61, 168, 169, 202
Ryhiner
  Samuel, 7, 13, 18, 19, 214
  family, 14, 15, 113

Saint-Denis, 109, 140, 148, 175
Saint-Marcel, 116
Salford, 61
Salt, (Sir) Titus, 202
Sandfords, 75
Sandoz, 107
San Sebastian, 164
Sarassin, Oberkampf & Cie, 109, 135
Sawley (Lancs), 52, 53, 65
Sayer, 162
Schafisheim, 115
Schavye & Sons, 175
Schillinger, Ruth, 10
Schramm, 130, 177

Schuele, Johann Heinrich von, 7, 15, 18, 20, 60, 185–92, 195–7, 200–205, 207–11, 214
Sedan, 202
Sées, 169
Seimandy & Liquier, 109, 135
Senebier, 196
Senegal Company, 136
Senn-Bidermann, 185, 199, 213
Sèvres, 18, 20, 131, 155, 172
Sheffield, 146
Sherwin, William, 6
Shrewsbury, 67
Simon, Francois, 109
Smalley family, 30
  John, 75
Smith, Adam, 104
Smith, Josephus, 28, 30, 42, 46, 65
Soehnée & Cie, 175
Soleure, 130
Stafa, 41
Standish, 29, 30
Stanley, Edward Smith, M. P., 100
Stevens & Parker, 16
St Gall, 41, 115
Stockholm, 7
Stockport, 41, 42, 49, 60, 62
St Petersburg, 7
St Quentin, 169
St Symphorien-de-Lay, 155, 168
Strasburg, 158
Stratford (London), 156
Strutt family, 33, 39, 100
  Jedediah, 3, 38, 52, 74, 202
Summerseat, 59, 62, 64

Tamworth, 48, 61, 62, 65–8, 72, 73, 76, 77, 95, 99, 188, 191, 194, 203, 210
Tavannes, Abraham Guerne, 119, 125, 126
Taylor, Charles, 31, 49, 89
Tennant, Charles, 146
Thackeray, Joseph (& Co.), 38, 47
Thann, 15, 142
Thuzy, 160, 168
Thomson, James, 39, 40, 43, 44, 74
Thomson, Richard, 74
Tiberghien (& Bardel), 153, 175
Tillen, 175
Tipping, Thomas, 70, 71, 74
Toggenbourg, 14
Topper, James, 46
Toulouse, 154
Tours, 100
Troyes, 8, 122, 178
Turcase, 153
Turin, 153
Turton (Lancs), 51, 202

Uhde (Ulde), 89

Vaihingen-an-der-Enz, 113
Valence, 149
Van Robais factory, 202
Vancelles Abbey, 164
Vaughn, Fenning & Halfhide, 156
Verdan, 175
Vernaison, 109, 122, 135
Verneuil, 169
Versailles, 10, 113, 119, 148–50, 154, 175, 190
Verville, Claude-Francois Levasseur, 119, 120, 126, 133, 134, 147, 155
Victoria & Albert Museum, 13
Vienna, 7, 188
Villefranche-en-Beaujolais, 133, 154
Vizille, 149, 178
Von Fries, Reichsgraf Johann, 203
Voortman, 35

Wadenswil, 41
Waldner, 213
Walker & Singleton, 28
Walton & Sons, 71
Wandsworth, 20
Wareing, 33
Ware family, 26
Warren, Henry, 58, 74
Warrington, 42, 50, 51, 61
Waterhouse, Nicholas (& Co.), 71
Watson, John & Son, 33
Watt, James, 60
Weber, Max, 188
Wedgwood, Josiah, 209
Wesserling, 142, 175, 177, 178, 185, 199, 213
Wetter, Jean-Rodolphe (& Cie), 15, 106, 131, 159, 175, 216
Widmer family, 114, 175
  Gottlieb, 114, 142, 146, 152
  Johann-Christoff, 114, 142
  Johann-Philipp, 114, 119, 144, 163
  Samuel, 114, 118, 122, 124, 140–146, 196
  Victor, 114, 119, 144
Wigan, 50, 51
Wiesenbach, 113
Willer, 169

Wilkes, Joseph (& Co.), 47, 60, 66, 67, 75, 76, 203
Wilson, John, 49
Wilson, William, 26, 27, 45
Wilson & Dickinson, 47
Wirksworth, 38
Wiss, 162
Wisser, De, 185

Wurtemburg, 188
Wyatt & Paul, 16

Yates, Edmund, 58, 73
Yates, Ralph, 81
Yates, William, 35, 45, 48, 73, 200

Zurich, 14, 30, 41, 156, 185